Carlson, Marvin A.

French Stage In The Nineteenth Century

The French Stage in the Nineteenth Century

by

MARVIN CARLSON

The Scarecrow Press, Inc.,
Metuchen, N.J. 1972

Library of Congress Cataloging in Publication Data

Carlson, Marvin A 1935-
The French stage in the ninteenth century.

1. Theater--France--History. I. Title.
PN2634.C35 792'.0944 72-3981
ISBN 0-8108-0516-2

To Pat

CONTENTS

INTRODUCTION

When the nineteenth century began, France had been the dominant nation in Europe for a century and a half. The Continent had long become accustomed to looking to her for models in dress, architecture, art, court fashion, even in revolutions. The French hegemony reached its climax with Napoleon, who set the French flag flying over much of Europe, briefly achieving politically what France had already achieved culturally and artistically. Napoleon's Empire was brief, but its effects were long-lasting, and few of them in harmony with his own desires. He stirred nationalist ambitions throughout Europe, most notably in Germany where he began the unification that Bismarck would complete. He shattered irrevocably the eighteenth century political systems, though several generations of statesmen after his defeat tried to undo what he had done. He also ended the long period of French dominance by setting himself against the great powers that were to replace her as the nineteenth century passed--Germany and England.

The orientation of more than 150 years was not quickly broken, however, and though France steadily declined in political and economic power during the century, Paris remained the center of much of Europe's cultural, intellectual, and artistic life. French was still the language of diplomats and the cultured aristocracy, French styles in clothing and deportment the models for others, recognition in the salons of Paris the ultimate goal of aspiring artists. The great expositions grew out of the French festivals of the Revolution and Empire, and even the European-wide revolutionary movements of 1830 and 1848 received their major impetus from uprisings in Paris.

The theatre shared with other arts this French focus, and an understanding of the European theatre of the nineteenth century must also certainly begin with Paris. Many of the major movements of the century originated here; others came from elsewhere and were spread to Europe by their acceptance in Paris. The Parisian stage produced not only great innovators such as Hugo, Antoine, and Lugné-Poe, but many of those dramatists ignored by literary historians yet beloved by the public and produced far more frequently throughout Europe than the literary giants--dramatists such as Pixérécourt, Scribe, and Sardou. The nineteenth century was an age of great actors, and many of the greatest were French--Talma, Rachel, Frédérick Lemaitre, Réjane, Sarah Bernhardt. It was a theatre as diverse as it was influential, from Corneille to the crudest farce, from the poetic dramas of the symbolists to spectacle plays featuring erupting volcanoes, from the neoclassic operas of Spontini to Offenbach's merry destruction of Olympus, from the ethereal fantasies of the romantic ballet to the harsh realism of Zola and of Antoine's Théatre-Libre. The development of this rich tradition, from Napoleon to the dawning of the twentieth century, is the subject of this book.

The three major artistic movements of the century--classicism, romanticism, and realism (with a whole cluster of anti-realistic "isms" appearing as the century ended)--each naturally had a distinct effect on the theatre, and each had its period of predominance. Yet the theatre world, like the cultural and political world of the century, was full of odd combinations and cross-currents. This is clear from the very beginning of the century, though Napoleon's desire to regularize the theatre made the theatrical situation in this period simpler than it ever has been since.

When Napoleon came to power, the theatre reflected the confusion and rootlessness of most of French society after a decade of revolution. Outside of France, Napoleon tends to be remembered primarily as a soldier, but the French rightly emphasize his more lasting contributions as a statesman creating internal order and stability. Few aspects of public life escaped his attention. He reformed taxation, established a national bank, improved the means of transportation, centralized and regularized the government, completed the educational and agricultural reforms of the Revolution, and established a major new legal system, the Code Napoléon, which influenced others throughout Europe. A similar order and regularity was imposed on the theatre. During the Revolution theatres had sprung up freely, subject to no checks other than open competition and an erratic censorship. Napoleon restricted their number, assigned specific genres to each theatre, and divided them clearly into major "literary" theatres and minor "popular" ones, a division which remained essentially in effect for the first half of the century.

The two major theatrical currents of Napoleon's time were clearly reflected in the contrasting offerings of his major and minor theatres. The neoclassicism which swept most of Europe at the end of the 18th century was given extra support in France by Napoleon's desire to model his Empire after Rome. Roman motifs and design affected hair and clothing styles of the period, Empire furniture and decoration, and the subjects of the popular painter David. In the major theatres, subsidized and frequently attended by Napoleon and his court, a similar neoclassicism prevailed, producing a cold and sterile theatre that resisted all the Emperor's attempts to bring it to life. The minor theatres, on the other hand, were scorned by the court and the rhetorically oriented critics of the time, but were enormously popular with the general public. Their major contribution was the melodrama, unquestionably the dominant dramatic genre of the century.

The prolific Pixérécourt combined many elements which were already present in popular theatrical fare to produce the melodrama form which swept Europe: stock characters such as the dark villain, virtuous heroine, and comic servant; thrilling episodic plots; a strong moral tone; and all the attractive extra elements the theatre could provide in the way of elaborate scenery and machinery, dances, and musical accompaniment. The Revolution had caused a sharp break with the old tradition, and Napoleonic audiences came to the theatre generally with few pre-Revolutionary assumptions about it. The major theatre had to rely for the first time on critics as middlemen between their offerings and their audiences, but the minor theatres developed fare which could be enjoyed, as mass entertainment has always been, without special background or explanation. These boulevard houses, as they were collectively called, spoke to that broad public which in our own century turned for entertainment from the theatre first to the films and then to television.

Napoleon's departure in 1815 removed many of the restrictions he had placed on the theatres and allowed the minor houses in particular to grow in number and importance. The dominant European artistic movement at this time was romanticism, already in full flower in England and Germany. In France, however, it encountered strong opposition for a variety of reasons: politically, the movement grew up in nations with which France had been twenty years at war; historically, France could oppose romanticism, Europe's strongest modern classic tradition; and emotionally; France was accustomed to leading the artistic world and reluctant to acknowledge a major movement developed outside her borders (even though such Frenchmen as Rousseau had provided much of its inspiration). The success of Hugo's Hernani at the Comédie in 1830 secured the movement a place in the French theatre, but Hernani was in many ways an end rather than a beginning. Hugo built his triumph on groundwork that had been laid all during the first third of the century by the minor theatres of Paris. His theatricalism, his mixing of genres, his disregard of the unities, all came from the melodramas, as did the interest in local color, picturesque scenery, and spectacle which was so important a part of both romantic opera and romantic drama. It is scarcely an exaggeration to call the French romantic drama melodrama elevated to the status of literature. Its interest in display brought new prominence to designers and even to machinists. Ciceri, who designed for all the major theatres of Paris and many of the minor ones, established the first independent scenic studio in Paris in 1822 and trained most of the generation of designers that would dominate the French stage after 1850.

If a single development can be consistently traced throughout the nineteenth century, it is probably a steadily growing interest in illusionistic detail in playwriting, acting, design, and of course in directing, concerned with unifying the other elements. We commonly think of realism, as this development came to be called, as being opposed to romanticism, an idea which is perhaps not as useful in the theatre as outside it. Certainly, philosophers of realism such as Comte renounced the transcendental concerns so critical to romantic idealists like Kant. Socially and politically, romanticism, with its focus on the past, on the states of the soul or the emotions, or on other worldly ideals, seemed increasingly irrelevant to a society grappling with very real and present tangible problems. Romanticism became gradually equated in the public mind with conservatism or escapism (and indeed late romantic works did little to dispel this idea), as opposed to realism, a modern, engaged movement.

In fact realism in the theatre developed more as a variety of romanticism than as a reaction to it. It was the romantics who first became concerned with such questions as historical authenticity of settings and costumes, the effects of physical environment on human action, and the presentation on stage of realistic emotions. However exaggerated melodrama acting may have been, its audiences invariably described it as closer to life than the statuesque classicism of the traditional theatre. No dramatist before Pixérécourt was so careful of physical detail and so concerned with its accuracy, and after him Hugo and Dumas supervised every aspect of their productions as Pixérécourt had done, preparing the way for the modern director.

The great actors of the romantic period, Bocage, Marie Dorval, and Frédérick Lemaître, all showed the movement's liberating influence. They brought to the French stage a new range of emotions and an equally new concern for the details of everyday life, though like their dramatists and designers, they preferred the novel and effective to the typical, encouraging a new set of mannerisms which seemed as artificial to reformers later in the century as the old classic style seemed in the 1830s. This sort of experimentation in all aspects of theatre production was never particularly welcomed by the conservative company and audience of the Comédie, and even Hugo, after his success with Hernani, left for the more congenial boulevard theatres.

The breakdown of Napoleon's system removed the centuries-old dominance of the state-supported theatres, and one of the most striking characteristics of the nineteenth century was that significant artists might be found at any theatre in the capital. The greatest actor of the romantic period, Frédérick Lemaître, never appeared at the Comédie at all. After the 1830s the Comédie still produced new works, but it became more exclusively the repository of the great works of the past. Hugo was the last important dramatist of the century to create his major works here.

The rise and ebb of the romantic movement occupied the French theatre for the entire first half of the century, producing that period's major dramas in the works of Hugo, Dumas, Vigny, and Musset, its major operas in the works of Meyerbeer, and its greatest ballet with Marie Taglioni. In truth, however, the full flowering of romanticism in the French theatre was extremely brief, lasting from the triumph of Hernani in 1830 to the failure of Hugo's Burgraves in 1843. By the 1840s, new forces were gathering strength in the theatres. The école de bon sens sought without notable success, to rescue the stage from romantic excesses while retaining a distinct poetic elevation. The dormant classic tradition was given new life at the Comédie through the genius of Rachel. But for the good bourgeois audiences who supported much Parisian theatre after 1830, and for their counterparts across Europe, the theatre was ruled by Scribe and his school. Some 300 operas, comedies, vaudevilles, and dramas were produced by htis most popular author of this generation, and while the "well-made play," as his formula-drama came to be known, possessed little artistic or philosophic depth, it provided a structure for the works of more significant dramatists, in France and elsewhere, for the rest of the century.

The first to turn the Scribean formulas to more serious ends were Augier and Dumas _fils_, the major dramatists of the Second Empire, lasting from 1852 to 1870. Their plays depicted the salons and drawing rooms of that glittering period, their characters the inhabitants of these drawing rooms (and the audiences of their plays), and their subjects--the social concerns most important to well-to-do bourgeoisie: financial speculation and the threats to the family posed by adultery or the ubiquitous courtesan. The plays were rich in melodramatic turns and in the artifices of Scribean construction, but they attempted nonetheless to provide their audiences with an acceptable mirror of their own society in customs, dress, language, and surroundings. With Augier and Dumas _fils_ the French theatre unquestionably entered the realistic period.

The new style of drama naturally demanded a new style of interpretation. Acting became subtler, less declamatory, and filled with realistic business such as lighting cigarettes or rolling newspapers. The box set depicting a realistic interior became the standard theatrical setting and the influential director Montigny at the Gymnase encouraged actors to move about in it in patterns more suggestive of those of everyday life.

The other major theatrical form of the Second Empire was the operetta, carried to its peak by Offenbach. These gay works form a striking complement to the grim castigations of the early realists. Here is glittering gaslit Paris at its most charming and seductive, but even in Offenbach there is a sharp edge, which may remind us from time to time that these light works were created under one of the most repressive dictatorships France had ever suffered. The social drama which turned to the salon and the operetta which turned to burlesque mythology were both to a degree escapes from the grim political system of Louis Napoleon. For all the spirit of Offenbach and the reforming zeal of Augier, a distinct odor of corruption permeated the entire society, as well as its theatre. The veneration for the classic past could never survive Offenbach's burlesque Olympus, but burlesque, however ingenious, is the product of the end of a tradition, and the almost universal feeling in the French theatre by the end of the Second Empire was that the century's experiments had been exhausted, that the theatre desperately needed some fresh impetus.

While this was unquestionably true of the literary drama, despite the honest efforts of such novelists as Flaubert and Daudet, no such crisis afflicted the popular genres, and the Parisian public flocked to new operettas by Offenbach's successors, to the light comedies of Meilhac and Halévy, to the farces of Labiche, to the melodramas of Dennery, and to spectacle plays of all sorts. These were headed by magic and fairy plays which consisted of little more than a series of dazzling and mysterious stage effects. The old boulevard, center of such theatre for over a century, came to an end during the Second Empire. Napoleon III's vast project for the rebuilding of Paris required demolition of this area and of others throughout the city to open spaces for the grand boulevards and squares that still give Paris much of its unique character. The ultimate effect of the demolition was a dispersal of secondary theatres rather than a decrease in their number. The more prosperous relocated elsewhere, and new ventures soon sprang up to replace those which were permanently closed. Several major new theatres were specifically included in Napoleon III's plans, most notably the present Opéra, the outstanding expression of the neo-baroque Second Empire style.

Permits had to be obtained for the opening of new theatres, but the government was much more concerned with controlling the material presented in these houses than with limiting their number. The first Napoleon's vision of a few minor houses, each with a defined genre, was totally forgotten. Certain of the better-established theatres tended to favor particular types of plays--social drama at the Gymnase, comedy at the Palais-Royal, spectacle at the Porte-Saint-Martin--and therefore appealed to certain segments of the public, but this situation was extremely fluid during the entire last quarter of the century. The repertoire of a theatre could change rapidly with changes in public taste, in the scripts available, or in the interests of actors or directors. Even the most insignificant theatres could, by the discovery of a popular play or actor, assume at least for a time a major importance.

It was in these secondary theatres that a new pattern of presentation grew to dominance. Traditionally, all French theatres followed to a greater or lesser extent the pattern of the Comédie, with a permanent company, each member playing a certain type of role in a great number of plays given in repertory. However, as productions became more complex and elaborate and as improved transportation greatly increased the potential audience for any offering, theatres found it more profitable to present a play for as long as it continued to attract a public. The traditional repertory system eventually gave way to the modern practice of the long run at almost every theatre but the Comédie. A run of 100 consecutive performances was achieved by Le Gamin de Paris, a minor comedy, as early as 1835, though runs of this length were not common before the 1870s. By 1890, no play was considered a proven success until it had achieved a run of at least 100 performances, and runs of 200 and 300 were not uncommon. Cyrano de Bergerac ran continuously at the Porte-Saint-Martin from its opening in 1897 until the middle of 1899.

This pattern of production had serious effects on the French theatre. The classics, which did not suit the long-run pattern, were generally left to the Comédie, and emphasis was placed on new works. This did not encourage the development of young dramatists, however--quite the contrary occurred. As runs increased in length, fewer new plays were given, and as the theatres became financially organized on the expectation of long runs, theatre managers grew increasingly wary of risking unknown playwrights or fresh techniques. The commercial theatre sought proven authors and encouraged repetition of already proven formulas, however stultifying to the art, as it has tended to do ever since. The effect on the actors was that the old repertory companies with actors playing traditional "types"--the soubrette, the romantic lead, the noble father--disappeared. A large versatile company made no sense when a play running a year or more might use only part of them, and actors were increasingly hired, according to modern practice, for a single production.

The disappearance of more or less established companies led to an ever-greater emphasis on the leading players, contributing significantly to the development of the modern star system. The Comédie was fortunate enough to possess several excellent actors during this period who were as faithful as they were talented, led by Mounet-Sully in tragedy and Réjane in comedy; but more commonly such major figures as Sarah Bernhardt and Constant Coquelin pursued careers largely free of obligations to any theatre, director, or company. Their greatest successes were often in vehicle plays, designed primarily to demonstrate their particular talents. Occasionally, as with Cyrano de Bergerac, such plays reached a high artistic level as well, but more often, as in the long series created for Bernhardt by Sardou, only the presence of the star imbued the play with any power. National and international touring was an important part of the careers of most of these popular figures, and this of course further increased the instability of theatre in Paris. Though the capital is our major concern here, it should perhaps be noted that the effect on provincial theatres was more serious still. Well-established regional theatres developed throughout France during the century, but when major actors began to tour regularly from Paris, local companies were pushed aside and in many cases disbanded. Today the provincial theatre is still attempting to regain the impetus it lost during this period.

Clearly there was much to complain of in the French theatre of the 1870s and 1880s, since the uneasiness of those critics who realized that the generation after Augier and Dumas fils had produced no important dramatist was reinforced by a concern over the effect on the art of such interrelated phenomena as the long run, the star system, and the breaking up of traditional ensembles. The most influential of the theatre's critics was Zola, though he concerned himself more specifically with revivifying French playwriting than with curing the more general ills of the stage. Strongly influenced by the scientific spirit of the time and by such positivist thinkers as Comte and Taine, he sought to create a "naturalist" theatre to parallel reforms he had already introduced in the novel. Though Zola had little tolerance for Augier or Dumas fils, the theatre he advocated was in many respects the logical step beyond their advance in realism. They had made the clear break with traditional poetic forms in serious drama, and had treated the social concerns at least of the upper classes with considerable honesty. Zola and his followers turned to the neglected lower strata of society and to a more uncompromising expression which seemed crude and vulgar beside such authors as Augier. Physical surroundings had been important ever since the romantics, but the naturalists introduced the idea that their characters were in large part a product of these surroundings. The setting no longer provided only atmosphere, but exposition. The stated goal of naturalist writing was scientific objectivity, but in fact there was a strong tendency toward pessimism in the movement. The tragedies were cruel, the comedies bitter and ironic. Doubtless the defeat of the French by the Germans in 1870 contributed to this spirit, since that defeat hung like a cloud over French life for the rest of the century, but a more immediate source intellectually was the philosophic determinism upon which the naturalists' theory was based.

Zola's success in the theatre was slight, but his ideas and those of his followers strongly influenced the Théâtre-Libre of Antoine, itself the most influential theatre organization of the latter part of the century. Antoine's striking success resulted from a fortunate combination of man and time. He arrived when concern over the future of the French theatre was more widespread and predictions more pessimistic than at any time in the century, and put together the scattered experiments of others to form what was in effect an alternative theatre. The Théâtre-Libre developed the assumption that the traditional system was too encrusted and compromised to be reformed from within, and challenged that entire system with a generation of actors, directors, and playwrights developed outside it. This was in fact similar to the development of romantic ideas outside the Comédie and Opéra in the boulevard theatres before 1830, but the attitude of the general public and of influential critics was very different at the end of the century. Antoine demanded to be considered, and was considered, not as a second-rate or minor producer in the boulevard tradition but specifically as the innovator of the theatre of the future. He, more than anyone else, set the pattern for the avant-garde, the experimental, the off-Broadway theatres of our own century. Even before 1900, independent theatres had sprung up in many parts of Europe, inspired by Antoine to seek new artists and new approaches to the art outside the traditional system.

Perhaps the idea of the independent, experimental theatre was itself Antoine's major contribution, but his Théâtre-Libre made more tangible contributions to the French stage. It gave a hearing to most of a generation of French playwrights who had been deprived of one by the commercial system of long runs and reliance on established reputations. The plays presented were of many types, but the majority were naturalistic and this, with the simplicity of settings required by Antoine's finances and the lack of traditional training in his amateur company, encouraged him to develop a style of production more effectively and simply realistic than any seen before in Paris.

The influence of Antoine on the rest of the French theatre, while distinct, was of course not overwhelming, especially before 1900. Théâtre-Libre authors and actors entered many other theatres, even the Comédie, during the 1890s, but the traditional genres remained as popular as ever; spectacular fairy plays and historical pageants, melodramas, vaudevilles, operettas, and farces, the last of which achieved particular brilliance in the works of Feydeau. Dumas _fils_ and Augier were gone, but Sardou remained as popular as ever, and his great interpretress Bernhardt was at the peak of her power. The long run and star system remained intact, though many of the major theatres attempted to provide more varied fare by the introduction of special matinees of classics or experimental modern works.

Ultimately much more important than these measures, however, were other independent theatres that grew up in imitation of or in reaction to Antoine. As the century drew toward its close, new literary schools succeeded each other with increasing rapidity, and as our own century has witnessed, the continuing avant-garde followed Antoine's example in founding new experimental theatres to reflect its changing concerns. Hard on the heels of the Théâtre-Libre came a major rival, Lugné-Poe's Théâtre de l'Oeuvre, which focused its attention on the new symbolist school. Here a whole new vision of the theatre was introduced, a mystic, evocative, evanescent theatre far removed from Antoine's bold and spare realism. Here also the international interest shown by Antoine in bringing Ibsen, Strindberg, and Hauptmann to the Parisian stage was carried much further, with a repertoire ranging from contemporary European dramatists to Ford and Otway, to classic Indian and Chinese works. It is typical of Lugné-Poe's eclecticism that among his productions was Jarry's _Ubu Roi_, now considered a major precursor of the theatre of the absurd. Throughout the century the French stage had generally presented only French works, even during the romantic period when England and Germany contributed greatly to the basic stock of themes and images. Antoine and Lugné-Poe were the first major artists of the century to turn the Parisian theatre outward, thus opening it to that major productive period which affected theatres across the continent at the turn of the century and to which they themselves each made a significant contribution.

I. NEOCLASSICISM AND MELODRAMA 1800-1830

When Bonaparte came to power in 1799, the theatre of Paris was scattered and disoriented by ten years of revolution. The old companies were broken up, traditions lost, much of the aristocratic public which had supported the major houses dead or in exile. The most typical drama of the Revolution had been fulsome propaganda, reflecting closely the rapidly shifting interests of the parties in power. In the theatre, as elsewhere, the new ruler set to work at once restoring system and order. Between 1800 and 1807 he established a system of theatres quite similar to that of the *ancien régime:* a few large subsidized houses, their artists on regular call for the entertainment of the sovereign and his court, and a few smaller houses for popular entertainment, rigidly restricted in the type of presentation offered, and never overlapping the prerogatives of the national theatres.

Within a month of coming to power, Bonaparte showed his interest in breaking with the theatrical fare of the Revolution. His arrival in Paris had been marked by the usual occasional plays such as the Troubadour's *Le Retour à l'espérance ou l'Arrivée du général Bonaparte,* and the *coup d'état* at Saint-Cloud on November 9 which put the government under his control, stimulated plays in half a dozen theatres. His predecessors had either ignored or actively encouraged such public manifestations of support, but Bonaparte clearly considered them dangerous encouragement to the spirit of factionalism he wished to destroy. On November 16, all propaganda plays were banned, whether their messages were directed for or against the new regime.

This ban left the way open for the development of the two types of drama which most distinctly marked this period --neoclassic plays and melodramas. Napoleon's major theatres, the Odéon, Comédie, and Opéra, were dominated by the former, while melodrama flourished in his minor houses, particularly at the Ambigu and Gaîté. Details of the development of these two approaches may be postponed until we consider their respective homes, but we might note here that neither was an invention of the Napoleonic period. Napoleon's classic theatre was one of the last manifestations of the neoclassic movement which swept Europe in the late eighteenth century, though under the French Emperor it was given particular encouragement by the Roman orientation of his government, his society, even the styles of furniture and clothing. Dramatists and painters were encouraged by the new court to select classic themes and to develop them in classic ways, which in the theatre resulted generally in sterile imitations of Racine and Molière, whose works were the most immediate classically-oriented ones at hand. Acting styles, staging, even criticism of the plays showed the same influence.

The melodrama, a form scorned by Napoleon and beloved by the populace, was in many ways the opposite of neoclassicism. Its authors sought effect at any price, regardless of the classic rules. Movement and spectacle took precedence over elegant language, and emotional excesses were encouraged. The exaggerated fantasies of the Revolutionary stage clearly contributed to the melodrama, but its roots spread outside France, to the German _Sturm und Drang_ and and the English Gothic revival. In France, and particularly in the works of Pixérécourt, many disparate experiments around the turn of the century were woven into the form which would become the most popular of the next century. Despite the many minor developments, the story of the French theatre from 1800 to 1830 is more than anything else the story of the defeat of the neoclassic vision of Napoleon and the triumph of the melodrama.

1. The Theatres Reorganized

In his restructuring of Parisian theatres, the Comédie first occupied Bonaparte's attention, and his ties to this theatre remained personal and strong throughout his career. The Comédie had already begun its slow return from near-oblivion when Bonaparte came to power. The actors, authors, and directors of French theatre had naturally shared the agonies of their nation during the past decade. In the early days of the Revolution, the company of the Comédie, like most of society, divided into liberal and conservative camps. Eventually the theatre itself split along these lines, into the liberal Théâtre de la République and the conservative Théâtre de la Nation. The latter fell under official suspicion, was finally closed and its actors imprisoned and threatened with death. The end of the Terror brought their release but did little to soothe old animosities. If anything, political differences were more bitterly expressed now that a certain freedom of speech was possible. The best actors in Paris, who traditionally would have worked as an ensemble, were thus scattered, apparently irrevocably, among three and sometimes four major theatres, with certain individuals appearing in still other places. Administrative and financial instability worsened this already disheartening situation. The République closed in January of 1799. In March the Odéon burned, and interest in restoring it was slight. The closing of the Feydeau in May left homeless the last substantial body of actors once associated with the Comédie and seemed to mark the end of that century-old enterprise.

Yet at this moment, with the Directory close to anarchy, the public indifferent, the actors physically scattered and emotionally divided by professional rivalries and political hatred, two men undertook the seemingly impossible task of reconstituting the Comédie-Française, and miraculously succeeded. Citizen Mahérault, a government commissioner, led this undertaking, with the encouragement and advice of François de Neufchâteau, Minister of the Interior. Their efforts were opposed by many of Paris' best-established dramatists, led by Beaumarchais, who argued that re-establishment of the Comédie would stifle creative competition. In the midst of the struggle, however, Beaumarchais died, and with its leader gone, the opposition faded away. On May 30, 1799, the former République re-opened as the Théâtre-Français with *Le Cid* and *L'Ecole des maris.* The company included all surviving members of the original Comédie, 23 in number, plus five which had worked with Talma's company at the République, and four coming from other theatres in Paris and the provinces; this made 32 *sociétaires,* to which were added seven lesser *pensionnaires.* The major figures among the men were Molé, the dean; Talma, and Dugazon; and among the women, Raucourt, Petit-Vanhove, Louise and Emilie Contat, and finally Mlle Mars, the outstanding new member of the company.

This was the Comédie as Bonaparte found it when he returned to Paris in 1799--an excellent company uncertain of its future, racked still by the divided loyalties of the past, its relationship to the recently formed and unstable Directory anything but clear, yet undertaking, however hesitantly, to resume its interrupted tradition. The First Consul moved quickly to increase the stability of the theatre.

As early as 1800 he guaranteed the Comédie permanent possession of its lodging, and although the Comédiens had to pay rent on the building for another fifty years, an annual subsidy of 100,000 francs was accorded them towards this expense beginning in 1802. State funds were set aside for pensions and indemnity for artists of the Comédie in 1801, and the artists reciprocated by reserving a permanent box for the First Consul. A decree of 1803 established rules for the society, covering such matters as debuts, retirements, pensions, division of profits, and selection of new plays. When the Consulate gave way to the Empire in 1804, confirming Napoleon's one-man rule, the Comédie was rechristened the Théâtre de l'Empereur and the former *Comédiens ordinaires du roi* became the *Comédiens ordinaires de l'empereur.* Legislation was passed this same year which became the theatre's commercial constitution, as the later and more famous Moscow Decree became its administrative constitution.

We must remember, however, that while the Comédie enjoyed Bonaparte's particular attention, all theatres in the capital were in some measure affected by the re-structuring which he brought about. In October of 1801, Jean-Antoine Chaptal, who had succeeded Neufchâteau as Minister of the Interior, granted the Théâtre Favart a government subsidy, took it officially under the protection of the Consulate, and rechristened it the Théâtre National de l'Opéra-Comique. In 1803 the Opéra joined these two as a recognized and subsidized national theatre.

Two further theatres were accorded "official" recognition under the Consulate--the Opéra Buffa and the Louvois. In the former, Bonaparte attempted to resuscitate the dead Comédie Italienne--the traditional third state-subsidized theatre (with the Comédie-Française and the Opéra)--but it closed in 1806 after several years of a marginal existence.

The Louvois was much more successful. The troupe at this theatre when Bonaparte came to power was a remnant of the original Comédie company, but far removed from its source. An abortive attempt at a reconstituted Comédie in 1796 at the Odéon, the troupe's original home, had actually produced only another branch of the already divided company. The relatively minor Odéon group had subsequently taken refuge in the Louvois when their theatre burned in 1799, and had been passed over in Neufchâteau's general reunion later that year. Even so, this company was considerably more distinguished than those of the capital's other minor theatres, and Bonaparte clearly saw its potential for a "second Comédie," which dramatists of the time were demanding to protect themselves from the monopolistic control of a single national theatre. Thus a second group of _comédiens ordinaires de l'empereur_ was established at the rebuilt Odéon, now renamed the Théâtre de l'Impératrice. The foundering Italians were joined to this venture, and the whole placed under the leadership of the popular dramatist Louis-Henri Picard. A decree of 1806 reaffirmed that the "major theatres" of Paris were to be the Opéra, the Empereur, and the Impératrice plus the Opéra-Comique. Each had its own carefully defined repertoire, echoing the monopolies of the pre-Revolutionary state houses: the Théâtre de l'Empereur had exclusive rights to the old Comédie repertoire and part of the repertoire of the Comédie Italienne; the Théâtre de l'Impératrice had the rights to the rest of the Italienne repertoire plus those of any new play premiered at this theatre; the Opéra and Opéra-Comique had exclusive right to their respective genres.

There remained now only the regulation of the minor theatres. The Revolution had destroyed almost all restrictions on such ventures, stimulating a flood of new houses in chaotic competition for companies and repertoires. Only seventeen minor theatres survived this brutal rivalry until 1807, when Napoléon reduced their number to four, to balance the four major houses. The Gaîté and Ambigu-Comique were restricted to melodramas, farces, and pantomimes; while the Variétés and Vaudeville were to be dedicated to parodies, peasant plays, and simple musical entertainments. Though this specific and rigid system could not even be maintained for the few years remaining to the Empire, it provided a basis for theatre activity in the capital the influence of which can be seen for the entire nineteenth century. In tracing the history of the pre-Romantic theatre, it is possible to follow Napoleon's divisions fairly closely. We shall therefore begin with the theatre which inspired his greatest interest, the Comédie; next consider the other major houses, the Odéon and the lyric theatres; and finally turn to the four minor official houses, and the unofficial rivals which soon joined them.

2. The Comédie, 1800-1825

The Comédie-Français (or Théâtre de l'Empereur,

as it was officially called from 1804 until 1815) desperately needed the guidance and support of the new government in the first decade of the century. The Revolutionary years had accustomed actors to constantly shifting conditions and now many of them found it difficult to adjust to a regular program with steady commitments and the give-and-take of a permanent repertory organization. Mahérault, the new director, was often unable to control either the pernicious rivalries which divided his troupe or the growing abuse of leaves of absence. Tours to the provinces, pleas of indisposition, even totally unexplained disappearances from the theatre were common. In the spring of 1800 the part of Panope in Phèdre had to be played by a man simply because no actress was available. Fortunately Mahérault's assistant Bernard proved a strong support for his authority, and when Bonaparte returned from Egypt he added another stabilizing agent in Rémusat, a lawyer selected as financial adviser.

The Emperor's financial support of the Comédie and his development of its organizational structure were both unquestionably of great benefit to the theatre. Unfortunately, however, his involvement with the national theatre did not stop there, and his command performances and attempted development of the repertoire must be admitted to have brought far more harm than good to the Comédie. Some of Napoleon's financial support of the theatre has already been mentioned. In addition, he required all members of his family and court dignitaries to maintain boxes there, thus guaranteeing the Comédie some 144, 000 francs per year. This meant that many nominally public presentations were actually court presentations, since Napoleon's visits to the Comédie far outnumbered his visits to all other Parisian theatres combined, and when he was in the city it was not uncommon for him to attend the national theatre several times a month. Command performances outside the theatre, however, became, during this period, far more significant in the life of the Comédie, so significant, indeed, that the theatre seemed almost to have returned to its old function of existing largely for the amusement of the sovereign, with its public performances justified only as a series of open rehearsals.

As early as 1802 Napoleon had a small private theatre built in the courtyard of Malmaison. It was a plain wooden structure with a parterre that could seat almost 200 persons, a row of boxes and a gallery, quite unadorned without and decorated within only by painted drapes which covered the ceiling and walls. Here members of the court presented such works as Le Barbier de Séville, with coaching by Talma and Michot, and the leading actors of the Comédie appeared in selected scenes. Many felt that Talma in particular gained in impressiveness in these simple surroundings:

> One day when he gave some scenes from Othello with his wife, he caused us to hold our breath in terror and froze us in fear; the scene was so well played that all felt themselves actually witnesses of the most terrible drama, inspiring the deepest emotion in us. [1]

Official court presentations began in 1803 at Saint-Cloud, which remained the major court theatre for the next four years. Among its productions were the first performance of Athalie since the Revolution and the first uncut presentations of Cinna and Le Cid in more than a century. Other royal residences were more popular after 1807; Fontainebleau, the Tuileries, and Compiègne saw the most productions, though a few were given at Saint-Cloud, Malmaison, the Trianon, and the Elysée Palace. In all, Napoleon requested 45 tragedies and 79 comedies from the actors of his Imperial Theatre.

The scene designer for these royal theatres was J. B. Isabey, who won Napoleon's favor with a series of drawings and models for his projected coronation. His designs for the court theatres were executed by some of the best scene painters of the period--Ciceri, Gigin, Lemaine, Mathis, Desroches, Moench père and fils--and the Emperor paid well for their contributions. One session of only a few days at Saint-Cloud cost him 29,000 francs, while the 1806 festival at Fontainebleau, involving several productions, cost a total of 150,000. It should be noted, however, that by traditional standards, Napoleon was relatively frugal in such entertainments. The Fontainebleau festivals of Louis XVI involved expenditures of almost two million francs.

Even during his frequent absences from the vicinity of Paris, Napoleon was rarely deprived of the services of his national theatre. Before he became Emperor, such demands were modest: in 1802 he summoned to Lyon Mme Raucourt, Talma, and Mme Petit-Vanhove, soon to become Talma's second wife; in 1803 Talma, Monvel, and Mme Raucourt were called to Brussels. After 1804, however, larger and more frequent demands were made. In September and October of that year, for example, the entire company was summoned to Mayence for six performances. The most famous of these command performances was held in 1808 in Erfurt, where Napoleon was in conference with Alexander. A selected company, the men headed by Talma, Saint-Prix, and Lafon, the women by Mmes Raucourt, Talma, and Duchesnois, performed the classics of the French stage for sixteen consecutive evenings before what came to be called the "parterre of kings." In addition to Alexander and Napoleon, the audience included the kings of Bavaria, Saxony, Württemberg, Westphalia, the Prince Primate, Prince William of Prussia, the Prince of Baden, the Prince of Neufchatel, the Grand Duke Constantine of Russia, the Duke of Oldenburg, the Duke of Saxe-Weimar, the Duke of Mecklenburg-Strelitz, and a host of marshals and generals. Nor was the assembly entirely political and military. A number of artists and writers gained admission, most notably Goethe, who came over from Weimar to observe this manifestation of French classic spirit and was apparently quite pleased. The program was a great success, though the responsibility of organizing it and of hastily constructing a theatre worthy of such a gathering was a terrible burden for the aging Dazincourt who directed the venture, and his death the following year was clearly hastened by this expedition. Napoleon was so pleased with the Erfurt productions that he demanded an even more elaborate display in Dresden in the summer of 1813 for his conference with the King of Saxony and other princes. Here a company of twenty-four was required (only fourteen had gone to Erfurt) for a program lasting the better part of two months.

These ambitious expeditions and the frequent calls to imperial dwellings near Paris were impossible for the Comédie artists to refuse, either politically or financially. This effectively cancelled whatever good had been done by a governmental decree of 1804 against abuse of leaves. In 1812 the absences were so serious that not a single new play was presented. Advance planning was almost impossible when _sociétaires_ might be called to Saint-Cloud or to Fontainebleau with only a few hours notice. In an attempt to stimulate audience interest, the Comédie began about 1805 to announce actors' names on its playbills. Such announcements now served only to discourage or irritate the public, who would arrive to find certain promised actors gone from the city and replaced by understudies. Napoleon's particular interest in the Comédie thus proved ultimately pernicious, by separating the theatre from the general public.

The Emperor's interest in the Comédie's repertoire was similarly unfortunate. In an attempt to encourage the creation of drama which would be an ornament to his reign, Napoleon in 1804 established prizes of 10, 000 and 5, 000 francs to be given annually to the best new tragedy and the best new comedy presented at the Comédie. Unfortunately, the Emperor's personal preference for close imitations of classic models tended to discourage dramatists who were truly interested in revitalizing the art. Only the financial support of Napoleon and the superlative acting of Talma kept alive the sterile neo-classic tragedy of the Empire, constructed by faithful followers of the rules. The critic Geoffroy could have spoken for any one of many Empire plays when he characterized Mazoyer's Thésée (1800) as "reasonably dull. One does not laugh at it, but one may doze."[2] Baour-Lormain's Omasis (1806), based on the story of Joseph, was probably the most successful of these plays, and won its author an Imperial prize. Luce de Lancival, a professor of rhetoric, turned his study of style to dramatic ends in six plays presented at the Comédie, the most popular of which was Hector (1809). Lesser contributors to this genre were Le Hoc, with Pyrrhus (1807), Delrieu, with Artaxerce (1808), and Brifaut, with Ninus II (1813).

It is surely significant that the few really successful plays of the period all departed, albeit cautiously, from neo-classic practice. François Raynouard's Les Templiers (1805), the greatest commercial success of the decade, ran for an impressive thirty-five performances and could not be denied the first Imperial prize. The plot, dealing with Philip IV's persecution of the Templars, grudgingly followed classic rules, but purists condemned its emphasis on effects, its melodramatic turns, and the unreality of packing so much incident into the expected twenty-four hours. Similar attempts to press beyond neo-classic bounds could be seen in Gabriel Legouvé's La Mort de Henri IV (1806) and Népomucène Lemercier's Christophe Colomb (1809), which its author claimed was modelled on Shakespeare.

The attempted revival of French classic comedy was even less successful. Napoleon's annual prize for the best comedy was never awarded since, as the judges explained, "these writers were further from Molière, not only in genius, but in genre, than the tragedies from Racine and Voltaire."[3] Certainly, the most popular comic dramatists of the time, Louis-Baptiste Picard, Alexandre Duval, and Charles Etienne, gave little thought to classic formulas, but all were in the main lines of development of French comedy. Though their style and structure were more informal, Picard and Etienne clearly followed the comedy of society as it had been developed in the previous century by such writers as Dancourt, Dufresny, and d'Harleville. Picard was associated primarily with the Odéon, but Etienne contributed to the Comédie a popular verse comedy of contemporary life, Les Deux Gendres (1810). Duval continued the sentimental bourgeois comic tradition of La Chaussée and Mercier in Les Héritiers (1796) and Le Tyran domestique (1805), and, far more reprehensible in Napoleon's eyes, developed and by his own claim invented dramas of modern history, a source of particular irritation to Imperial censors.

Here again we encounter a paradox in Napoleon's desire to support the drama, for stage censorship was rarely so severe in France as during his reign. He established the censoring of plays as early as 1800, and rigorously enforced it thereafter. Leniency was not shown even for the major theatres, so favored by the government in other respects, nor for authors whose political sympathies could hardly have been suspect. Dupaty's L'Antichambre (1802) was banned at the Opéra-Comique when Napoleon saw in it presumed thrusts at the members of the new court. At the Comédie, Talma was forbidden to perform Tibère by Marie-Joseph Chénier, the outstanding tragedian of the Revolutionary period, and even certain classics, such as Mérope and Tancrède, were banished from the repertoire. Etienne, though he had dedicated his comedy Les Deux Mères (1804) to Josephine and shown an unwavering dedication to the new regime, found his L'École des familles (1813) on the proscribed list. Raynouard, the first recipient of the Imperial prize for Les Templiers, was not allowed to present his next work, Les États de Blois (1810).

Works dealing with "modern" historical events were viewed with particular suspicion. Duval achieved a European success with Edouard en Écosse (1802), though it was banned immediately after its opening in Paris, where political reaction to it as a suspected royalist work was so severe that Duval felt obliged to spend most of the next year in Russia. His Guillaume le Conquérant (1803) was also banned, despite favorable comparisons suggested in it between Guillaume and Napoleon. Still Duval persisted, and managed at last in 1806 to keep La Jeunesse de Henri V running by changing its hero to Charles II of England, causing not a few anachronisms. Even this ruse was not always successful. Charles Brifaut was able to get his Philippe II (1813) past the censor by changing his Spaniards to Assyrians and renaming the work Ninus II, but Napoleon, upon returning from Leipzig, heard of the subterfuge and had the play closed anyway.

Thus Napoleon, with his demands for court presentations, his devotion to a sterile classicism, and his support of a rigid and often arbitrary censorship, often worked in opposition to the theatre he so clearly wished to support. A similar paradox can be noted in the company of this period, for though the Comédie rarely possessed a more talented group of actors than those of the Empire, their effectiveness was steadily undermined by a series of the most bitter artistic rivalries of the century.

Much of this conflict grew out of the major changes which took place in the Comédie company between 1800 and 1810. Many important actors left the house during these years--almost all of those whose careers stretched back to pre-Revolutionary days. Molé retired in 1802, Mme Vestris and Vanhove in 1803, Dupont in 1804, Mlles La Chassaigne and Suin in 1805, Naudet in 1806, Monvel, Florence, and Larochelle in 1807, Dazincourt, the first Figaro, in 1808, Louise Contat, Dugazon, and Mlle Fleury in 1809. Since the Revolutionary years had caused a break in the development of young actors, Talma and Mlle Mars were left almost alone as the established talents of the theatre, and a whole group of younger actors had to be integrated rather rapidly into the company without clear guidelines as to what parts would fall to each. Friction was therefore inevitable, and neither Talma nor Mlle Mars were immune from the disputes which followed.

Indeed, the first major conflict involved Talma himself. In 1800 the dramatist Raynouard introduced to the Comédie a young tragedian named Pierre Lafon. Though Talma at first welcomed and encouraged his new colleague, there were those both within and outside the Comédie who felt that Talma's superiority had gone too long unchallenged and who saw in Lafon a talent which could be developed to Talma's discredit. Chief among these opponents of the older actor was Julien-Louis Geoffroy, newly installed as dramatic critic of the influential Journal des Débats. One of the first dramatic critics in the modern sense, he published articles twice weekly from 1800 until his death in 1814. Though his power was not absolute, it was enormous, due in part to the artistic instability of the times. The new society of the Consulate found at the Comédie an equally new organization, similarly cut off from its roots by Revolutionary upheaval. Links with the past were few and rapidly disappearing; the number of debuts at the Comédie under the Consulate was enormous. Young writers and actors found themselves praised beyond their merits by some, condemned beyond their faults by others, and desperately sought some reliable and respected criticism. A similar desperation was felt by their audiences, for few were qualified by memory or training to judge the art, yet society demanded that everyone seem informed and hold intelligent opinions. Under these circumstances, the enormous popularity and influence of almost immediate reviews in the journals is easily understood. Geoffroy, a former professor of rhetoric and poetic and an assiduous spectator at the Comédie before the Revolution, possessed just the background to dominate the field. In his columns there was information for everyone: summaries of the plays, informed comparisons with similar earlier works, critical judgments, anecdotes of author, play, and actors, and regular news of happenings backstage. Unfortunately for Talma, his orientation was distinctly conservative; he upheld the classic and neo-classic style, and viewed Shakespeare, the Germans, and early hints of romanticism with considerable suspicion. Talma's unorthodox interpretations of many classic roles drew particular scorn from Geoffroy, and the critic lost few opportunities to praise Lafon at Talma's expense.

In certain parts there seems to have been justice for this apparently exaggerated claim. Lafon had a youthfulness and dash, what the French call *panache*, which was far removed from Talma's passion and fury and which gave the young actor a distinct advantage in part of the repertoire. This was clearly demonstrated in 1804 when Talma was at last goaded into accepting a series of productions in which he and Lafon could be seen on alternate nights in roles where Lafon's supporters claimed he was superior. The older actor soon had cause to regret allowing his wounded pride to prevail over his prudence. Lafon's best roles, such as Achille and Orosmane, were precisely those which Talma had always found most difficult, both physically and temperamentally. Moreover, Mlle Raucourt and other members of the company who resented Talma's pre-eminence organized a cabal which hissed him throughout each performance. When the dramatic duel was over, Lafon seemed to have carried the day. He began almost contemptuously referring to Talma as "the other."

Talma finally realized the folly of fighting his battle on the enemy's home ground, and turned his abilities to works more suited to them. The first of these was a revival in 1804 of Ducis' version of Hamlet. As in all of Ducis' Shakespearian adaptations, great care had been taken to adjust or weed out English irregularities. Ophelia is made the daughter of Claudius to give Hamlet a Corneillian choice between love and duty. Gertrude deserts the king to aid Hamlet, who is not killed, but crowned at the end. Even so, the work remained sufficiently distinct from traditional French tragedy to encourage Talma to attempt some experiments in production and interpretation. The designer Garnerey was set to work studying lithographs of productions of Hamlet in Denmark and Germany. He found actors playing the role in Hamburg and Copenhagen in the black costume of a sixteenth century Spanish captain, and designed a similar costume for Talma, in the name of historical exactitude. The experiment, though modest, is a significant example of Talma's concern for costume reform in a period when little such reform was occurring. Thanks to Empire interest in all things classic, including dress, plays set in ancient Rome suited costume to period, but tragic heroes of all other periods wore standard costumes such as that of the chevalier--with plumed helmet, velvet-lined tunic, great knotted sash, white tights, and yellow boots. Contemporary critics were less struck by Talma's costume, however, than by the emotional quality of his interpretation. Geoffroy took a predictably dim view of both play and actor:

> What draws audiences to Hamlet? Well developed characters? No, for the play has no character but a lunatic and a visionary. Well-motivated and truly pathetic situations? No, for the only situation in the play, Hamlet with his mother, is both horrible and improbable. Therefore it must be Talma's acting which draws the curious--his distorted features, his wild eyes, his quivering voice, his sombre, lugubrious tone, his taut muscles, his trembling, his convulsions. What noble, natural and refined actor will not appear cold and insipid if the public comes to be pleased only by such bursts of frenzy?[4]

The financial success of the play was dismissed by Talma's

enemies as a result of the decadent taste of the contemporary Parisian public.

The 1806 revival of Antoine de Lafosse's Manlius Capitolinus, on the other hand, drew praise even from the classicists and the cabal of Talma's enemies. The play, a classicized version of Otway's Venice Preserved, focused much more than its English original on the relationship between the two central male characters. The ambiguous feelings experienced by Manlius upon discovering that he has been betrayed by Servilius, his passionately loved friend, allowed Talma to develop a character of such subtlety and power than even Geoffroy was moved to praise. Talma was widely hailed as the greatest actor of the time and a worthy successor to Lekain. After this triumph, he revived Manlius Capitolinus regularly, and even in these generally unprofitable years, it could always bring large crowds to the Comédie. In a single blow, the rivalry with Lafon was over. The defeated challenger made a rather unsuccessful foray into comedy, then returned to serious roles, but remained ever after a respectful second to Talma. It was he who gave the address representing the actors of the Comédie at Talma's funeral in 1826.

The Talma-Lafon controversy was scarcely under way when other rivalries developed, this time among female members of the company. In 1801 appeared two promising young comic actresses, Mlle Marie Bourgoin and Mlle Claudine Volnais, who from the beginning engaged in bitter disputes over roles and prerogatives. This antagonism was in turn quite over-shadowed the following year by the debuts of Catherine-Josephine Duchesnois and Marguerite-Josephine George, whose rivalry sharply divided the theatre world of Paris. Mlle Duchesnois, who appeared first, was not a physically attractive woman, but gained the adulation of many by her lovely voice and her natural and spontaneous delivery. Mlle George, a protegée of Mlle Raucourt, provided an almost perfect contrast. She was as beautiful as Duchesnois was plain, and the classic delivery she had learned from Mlle Raucourt was in direct opposition to Duchesnois' spontaneity. Indeed, a dispute between proponents of classic and of natural acting was to some extent involved in most of the apparently more personal conflicts of the period. Opponents of Talma's realistic innovations rallied behind the classicist Mlle Raucourt in the Lafon controversy, later supported Mlle Volnais against Mlle Bourgoin, and later still gathered behind Mlle George. Geoffroy, of course, lent his support to this party. His first reviews of Mlle Duchesnois were mildly favorable, but when Mlle George appeared, he was enraptured:

> Preceded on the stage by an extraordinary reputation for beauty, Mlle George did not at all fall short of expectation; her features unite the French graces with the nobility and harmony of the Greeks; her figure is that of a sister of Apollo, and when she appears on the banks of the Eurotas in Iphigénie en Aulide surrounded by her nymphs with her head raised above theirs, her entire person would be a perfect model for the brush of Guérin.[5]

This third dispute was the most heated yet, and Rémusat was forced to promote both actresses to sociétaires on the same day, March 17, 1804, to avoid disputes over seniority. Paris was sharply divided between the Georgiens and the Carcassiens, who gained their rather inelegant name for their heroine's leanness, and both sides wore tokens on hats or lapels to indicate their preference. Critics, journalists, cartoonists fanned the flames. Geoffroy's praise of Mlle George in the Journal des Débats was balanced by Le Pan's praise of Mlle Duchesnois in the Courrier des Spectacles. Even the Imperial family became involved; Mlle George was for a time the mistress of Napoleon while Josephine discreetly supported Duchesnois. Each side hired audience members to applaud its favorite and to hiss the other, thus developing the claque, which within a few years became an accepted theatrical institution. The feud continued until 1808 when Mlle George abruptly disappeared from the Comédie after a grand success in Delrieu's Artaxerce. Eventually, word arrived in Paris that she had gone to Austria to escape her creditors. This defection scandalized the capital. The Opinion du Parterre complained: "I have leafed through all the histories of the Théâtre-Français; I swear that I have found nothing to equal this action of Mlle George." Unfortunately, such actions were to become more common in the future. Mlle George merely gave the Comédie a foretaste of the agonies it would suffer with Rachel and Sarah Bernhardt. From Austria the delinquent actress went on to St. Petersburg, tempted, it was said, by a prospect of an aristocratic Russian marriage.

The field of tragedy was thus left open to Duchesnois, but other conflicts kept the Comédie in turmoil. Mlles Dupont and Merson fought over the soubrette roles left by the retirement of Emilie Contat until Mlle Merson's ill health forced her to retire. The public was the ultimate loser in this contest, for Mlle Dupont's talent was slight, but her victory over Mlle Merson left her in a position sufficiently strong to prevent the development of any subsequent rivals. The roles left by the retirement of Louise Contat, Emilie's sister, inspired an even more bitter contest between the well-established Mlle Mars, who had made her debut in 1795, and Jeanne-Emile Levard, who had come to the Comédie in 1808, only a year before Louise Contat's retirement. The stir over division of these parts was so great that in 1812 Napoleon wrote back from Moscow to attempt to resolve it. He instructed Rémusat, now general superintendent of the Comédie, the Feydeau, and the Odéon, that Mlle Mars, already playing leading roles, should not be given any of the "grandes coquettes"--a second major employ. The ruling, however, was never enforced. Rémusat's director of the Comédie, the rather weak Mahérault, was edged out of this position by his assistant Bernard in 1813, but neither Bernard nor Rémusat was a match for Mlle Mars. She was generally acknowledged the superior talent and had moreover the argument of her longer service. Rémusat eventually yielded to her demands, granting her a special dispensation to play "first roles, first loves, and grand coquettes."[6] Poor Mlle Levard spent the rest of her career obscurely understudying these parts. Like Mlle Dupont, Mlle Mars emerged from this struggle determined to brook no more rivals. She refused to train young actresses and held on to her wide range of parts, including young lovers, until her retirement in 1841 at the age of 62.

Fortunately for the Comédie, Napoleon found time while in Moscow to consider matters of much greater importance to the theatre than the dispute between Mlles Mars and Levard. In the comprehensive Moscow Decree, signed on October 15, 1812, he laid down in 101 articles what has since remained the organizational basis of the society. The specific powers and responsibilities of the Emperor's representative at the theatre, the superintendent of spectacles, were established here, as well as the administrative organization of the theatre beneath him. Most financial aspects of the organization were considered: the duties of the cashier, the drawing up of the budget, salaries, pensions, and sharing of profits. A procedure was set for the selection of new plays and the revival of old ones. The rights of authors were outlined, and the duties of actors, with lengthy and detailed statements on such particularly touchy matters as casting procedures and leaves of absence. Finally, rules were set for the running of the Conservatory and the training of young actors. Though certain parts of the document caused great irritation then and later at the Comédie (particularly troublesome was the superintendent's list, which was to assign every part in the repertoire to a specific actor, according to genre and seniority), in the main its clarification of procedures and structure was welcomed, and as the foundation of the Comédie's organization, it proved Napoleon's most important contribution to the theatre.

The entry of the Allies into Paris in 1814 stimulated the presentation of royalist plays on almost every stage. Henry IV, founder of the Bourbon dynasty, was the hero of no less than seven productions, including the previously banned Les États de Blois at the Comédie. The Emperor's sudden return in 1815 called forth no such demonstrations, possibly because the theatres felt the uncertainty of his new bid for power, but more likely simply because his dislike for political drama was still clearly remembered. Only two months later came Waterloo, and the imposition of a new government on France. Napoleon's elaborate organization of Paris' theatres was naturally seriously disrupted by the political shifts of 1814 and 1815. His appointments and monopolies were eliminated in 1814, restored again during the 100 days, and then once more eliminated. The eventual reestablishment of the monarchy in 1815 had a distinctly ironic side for the world of the theatre. The situation of twenty-five years before was in many respects restored. Theatres long prevented from presenting political drama were suddenly allowed to do so, the rigorous monopoly of a handful of theatres was broken and restrictions on new theatres removed, and a flood of new plays resulted, glorifying this enlightened and indulgent new regime. The irony was that in 1791 the force for freedom was the developing Revolution, overturning the strictures of the monarchy, while in 1815 it was the returning monarchy which freed the theatres from the binding regulations of Napoleon.

At the Comédie, most of the regulations of the Moscow Decree remained intact, though the Superintendent of Spectacles was replaced by a royal Commissioner, in turn responsible, as before the Revolution, to the First Gentlemen of the Chamber. François Chéron, the editor of the Journal des Débats, was appointed to this post. Paris, after the 100 days, was divided into bitterly opposed parties as it had not been since the Thermidorian reaction, and audiences were frequently unruly. A major riot shook the Comédie during a production of Antoine-Vincent Arnault's Germanicus in 1817. The drama was itself quite inoffensive, but Arnault, as a close friend of Napoleon, was now in exile and his friends seized this opportunity to demonstrate for his return. To make matters worse, Mlle Mars appeared in the afterpiece wearing the Imperial violet and Mlle Bourgoin the Bourbon lily, encouraging further reaction from both factions in the audience. The following day Germanicus was banned and sticks and canes were forbidden in all theatres.

Talma continued to dominate the Comédie during the Restoration, though he achieved no important success after the ill-fated Germanicus until he portrayed Leycester in Pierre Lebrun's Marie Stuart (1820). The author styled himself a major innovator by going to the sixteenth century instead of to the classic world for a subject, though, as we have seen, a number of Empire dramatists had already attempted this. Talma rightly detected a more authentic originality in the character of Leycester, a distinctly more ambiguous hero than the traditional noble figure of neo-classic tragedy. The great actor was growing increasingly concerned with the problem of reviving audience interest in the genre and welcomed opportunities for experimentation. His addition of new and realistic detail to traditional roles was at this time the subject of much discussion. In the fourth act of Britannicus, for example, during Agrippine's lengthy harangue of Néron, tradition kept the young emperor glum and quiet, but Talma wearily adjusted his robe, toyed with the arm of his chair, followed patterns on his garment. Some critics, such as Charles Nodier, Geoffroy's successor on the Journal des Débates, protested against this spreading of the drame into tragedy, but the general public was delighted. Even more daring were the innovations in Étienne de Jouy's Sylla (1821), probably the best tragedy of the period, and certainly the most popular one. For the first time a classic tragedy made extensive use of crowd scenes; for the first time a tragic hero lay down in a bed on stage. Further scandal was caused by Talma's decision to play the leading role in the likeness of Napoleon, who had just died on St. Helena. Popular acceptance of this interpretation showed not only Talma's hold on the public, but a change which was now taking place in the formerly distinctly royalist Comédie audience. As a result, the Comédie successfully risked a return to Arnault, whose Régulus (1822) praised Napoleon in classic guise and was full of thinly disguised references to the exile, the war with England, and the Battle of Waterloo.

Despite Talma's personal successes, these were not years of great achievement at the Comédie. Upon his coming to power in 1824 Charles X restored freedom of the press, but his censorship of the theatre was extremely rigorous. New authors were few, and these few highly imitative. The hired claque now dominated a dwindling audience. Perhaps most serious, the same sort of bitter and debilitating feuds which had begun during the Empire continued to occupy much of the energy of the company and its administrator, Chéron. Claude-Louis Monrose was accepted in 1817, but stimulated so many disputes with other actors that only the strongest public demand forced his fellows to allow him the significant comic parts his talent deserved. The dazzling debut of Louise Mante in 1822 touched off another bitter fued with the aging Mlle Mars. When Casimir Delavigne submitted a comedy called _L'École des veillards_ in 1823, Talma insisted on the lead, which belonged by rights to the comic actor Damas. Chéron, already embroiled with Talma in a dispute over leaves of absence, supported Damas, but Talma appealed to the public and prevailed, adding greatly to his reputation but little to company harmony. Chéron retired soon after, and his difficult and thankless position was assumed by Baron Isidore Taylor, who was to become one of the Comédie's most revolutionary directors.

Taylor was not primarily a man of the theatre, though he included that among the many accomplishments in his varied and impressive background. He was a military hero from the Spanish campaign of 1823, an archaeologist and preserver of the French cultural heritage, a popular writer, as well as a theatre author, designer, and entrepreneur. He possessed many friends, tremendous energy, a gift for diplomacy, and incorruptible integrity--all of which would be needed to restore the ailing national theatre. Taylor's theatrical background, significantly, was related exclusively to minor boulevard entertainment, and he approached the problem of dwindling audiences with the experience of what had proved successful in attracting at least the boulevard public. Obviously experiments in unadulterated melodrama or spectacle plays were out of the question in the venerable national theatre, yet clear traces of Taylor's boulevard training could be seen in his first offering, and his first success, _Léonidas_, by one of his friends, Michel Pichat.

The work was almost perfectly calculated to prove attractive to the widest possible audience. Its form and subject were classic, but it violated the unity of place and was sufficiently romantic in tone to appeal to those tired of the old tradition. The subject, moreover, capitalized on popular enthusiasm for the 1821 Greek revolt against the Turks, and the publicity-conscious Taylor saw to it that relatives of Greek patriots received free admission to the production.

The settings showed a concern for "local color" and "historic fidelity," which had until this production been considered the province only of the boulevards. These were the work of the outstanding designer of the period, Ciceri, whose career suggested in miniature the changing tastes of the period. He had begun not as a scene designer but as a landscape artist. Whatever romantic leanings this occupation might have encouraged, however, were at least temporarily diverted by the usual classical instruction at the Académie des Beaux-Arts. Upon graduation, he followed his father-in-law Isabey in 1810 to the post of decorator-in-chief for the court theatres, producing at Saint-Cloud and the Tuileries the first of the more than 400 designs which would earn him the title "first designer of the age." Although his work for the Emperor gained him a European reputation and assured him a position at court during the Restoration, these early designs were all in the pompous, neo-classic architectural style which Isabey had developed to please Napoleon. A major change came in the 1820s when Ciceri, in addition to his duties as court painter, began to design for boulevard theatres. When he was called in 1823 to design _Léonidas_ at the Comédie, Ciceri had already proved his skill with all the trappings of romantic design--exotic foreign cities, ruined castles, ragged and desolate mountain passes. None of this, of course, appeared in the thoroughly Greek _Léonidas_, but Ciceri brought from the boulevards a concern for historically exact detail quite new to the Comédie, but acceptable to traditionalists because of the "classic" subject. The costumes, by Auguste Garnerey, were similarly satisfying and exact. In all, the production was the most successful the theatre had seen in some years, and Talma echoed the general sentiment in calling Taylor "the savior of the Comédie-Française."[7]

The approbation of Talma was a great benefit for Taylor, since the powerful actor had been a major obstacle to previous administrators. Taylor began his administration by forming a new governing committee of the Comédie, in which Talma, by virtue of his position, had to be included, but which was otherwise composed of considerably more malleable actors. In the long run, however, such circumspection proved unnecessary, for Talma apparently found the fresh perspective Taylor brought to the theatre quite stimulating. In 1826 Taylor introduced Talma to the young Victor Hugo, who outlined his plans for a drama called Cromwell which would be far more revolutionary than Pichat's Léonidas. "Go finish your play," said Talma, "I am anxious to present it."[8] Unfortunately for the French stage this fascinating promise was never fulfilled, for Talma died four months later. Despite the great actor's interest in the new drama, his tie with neo-classic tragedy, the dominant form during his greatest years, and with the Revolution and Napoleon, caused his death to be widely considered the end of an era in the French theatre. The first productions of Taylor's administration, moreover, gave the indication, for those who wished to read, of an impending change. The time of tradition, the era of classic emphasis, had indeed come to an end. The triumph of romanticism lay just ahead.

3. The Odéon, 1800-1827

For the first quarter of the nineteenth century, the dominant figure of France's second national house was Picard, whose contributions as actor, director, and as his theatre's most popular and productive playwright earned him the title "the little Molière." Yet the works produced by Picard were so thoroughly reflections of and reactions to his own times that none have survived in the more recent repertoire. Picard himself realized this shortcoming in his work, but complained in one of his prefaces that general comic concerns were no longer possible in a period of social upheaval such as his own:

> Not only our habits, but our institutions change from year to year. Manners cannot remain constant. What then should the comic dramatist do? Should he consider the manners of the past? Should he rather select the fleeting manners of the present? I have made the latter choice. I try to paint those of the day in which my play is written.[9]

Even his titles often reflect this concern; the majority no

longer suggest universal types, such as L'Avare, Le Misanthrope, or Le Glorieux, but more ephemeral social groups--Les Collatéraux, Les Provinciaux à Paris.

After the 1799 fire at the Odéon, Picard took his company to the Louvois where they remained until a new theatre was built in 1808. In addition to himself, the leading actors of the company were Vigny, Armand, Thénard jeune, and Mmes Molière, Molé, and Régnier. Picard's own La Petite Ville (1801) was the first major success at the Louvois and remained his most popular work. It was a typical Picard play, loose and informal in structure, written in colloquial prose--a little provincial review framed by the overnight journey of two young Parisians. Duhoutcours, the same year, prefigured a significant portion of the century's serious drama by making the specific dealings of finance a central concern for the first time. So successful was this little didactic piece on the evils of declaring bankruptcy that the orchestra had to be removed to provide additional seating.

Picard's most reflective and philosophic works were Marionnettes (1806) and Ricochets (1807). Their common themes are that small causes produce great effects, that all actions are linked and fate depends on the slightest chance or caprice. This philosophy, it should be noted, is precisely that which informs Eugène Scribe's much better-known Verre d'Eau (1840), a single, striking example of how Picard's influence continued even while his plays did not. The popular dramatist was called in 1807 to direct the Opéra, and chose as his successor Alexandre Duval, another well-known dramatist who had achieved success at the Comédie with Le Tyran domestique (1806) and La Jeunesse de Henri V (1807). Duval's own plays at the Odéon, such as La Femme misanthrope (1811), proved less popular during his administration than further new works by Picard, L'Alcade de Molorido (1810) and La Vieille Tante (1811). Since tragedy was restricted to the Comédie, lesser comic writers provided the remainder of the Odéon offerings during the Empire: Jean Aude, who created topical pieces and one long-running sentimental work, Monval et Sophie (1809); Emmanuel Dupaty, later a vaudeville and comic opera librettist, whose Prison militaire (1803) and other works still showed the influence of his early interest in harlequinades; Planard, whose typical La Paravent (1807) was set in a Spain-like land of fantasy where a plot similar to the proverbs of Musset unfolded. Surely the most interesting work at the Odéon during this period was Népomucène Lemercier's

Christophe Colomb (1809), a "Shakespearian comedy" which unleashed a memorable riot, anticipating the battles of romanticism by twenty years, by its heretical mixing of genres and violations of the unities.

During most of the upheavals which marked the end of the Empire, the Odéon was without a director, for Duval left for Russia in 1813, his successor Gobert went bankrupt, and the political situation made a stable reorganization impossible. When calm returned, the company begged Picard to lead them again, and from 1816 to 1821 he restored the prosperity of the theatre, even despite another major fire in 1818. Though his own plays continued to appear during his second administration--most notably Les Deux Philibert (1816), which inspired sequels by others for some years after--Picard's interest in building up the Odéon could be seen in his regular encouragement of young dramatists and in his obtaining royal permission in 1818 henceforth to present tragedy and drama as well as comedy. Soon after, Picard was empowered to reorganize his company more along the lines of the Comédie. The new "second Théâtre-Français" thus opened in 1819, headed by Joanny, a brilliant young actor who for more than a decade had been building a reputation outside Paris and who was now widely spoken of as the "Talma of the provinces."[10] Other new talents destined for important careers were Samson and Provost.

The theatre was rebuilt on the traditional Odéon site in the heart of the Latin Quarter, a location which explained many of the events there in the immediately succeeding years. The students of the area provided a significant and vocal portion of the Odéon audience and were for the most part determinedly liberal anti-royalists. The year the new Odéon opened, the Quarter was the scene of a series of riots over the suppression of a course by a professor who had questioned the relations between penal and natural law. The opening poem called specifically for the support of the volatile students, and its author, Casimir Delavigne, a great favorite with the liberal party, was the first new dramatist presented. His Les Vêpres siciliennes (1819), with Joanny and Mlle Guérin, was an enormous success, and its author was hailed, at least in the liberal press, as "the new national poet."[11] The following year Delavigne showed his ability in comedy as well with Les Comédiens, a great success for the actor Samson.

Picard apparently possessed a rare gift for administration, since his retirement in 1821 once again meant an end to prosperity for the Odéon. Two short and financially catastrophic administrations followed: those of Adolphe Gentil and Colonel Gimel. The latter ran the Odéon so strictly that it was frequently called the Théâtre Militaire, but discipline could not create success, and his failure was so complete that the theatre became the delight of Paris wits.

The Pandore reported that Gimel was planning on lighting one gas jet for each paying customer, and half a jet for children under seven, despite the considerable danger of playing in total darkness.[12] The few moderately successful works given were by Wafflard and Fulgence, a team trained by Picard. They achieved at least a shadow of his success with Le Voyage à Dieppe (1821) and Le Célibataire et l'Homme marié (1822). Ironically, Gentil's undistinguished administration saw the debuts of two of the most outstanding actors of the coming romantic period: Bocage, and Frédérick Lemaître, the latter so obscure that he did not even earn the customary debut performances.

In 1823 Claude Bernard, an actor from the Comédie, offered to direct the Odéon at his own risk, and the government gratefully accorded him a twelve-year lease. Again prosperity came to the theatre, though many of the actors complained and some left as Bernard placed increased emphasis on musical theatre. Joanny, Perrier, and Samson were accepted by the Comédie, and Bernard replaced them with singers such as Duprez rather than with actors. The major productions of this administration were the Rossini works, Le Barbier de Séville (1824), Otello and La Dame du lac (1825). The nonmusical works are mostly remembered for the student demonstrations which certain of them stimulated. Ledreuille's L'Orphelin de Bethléem (1825), with an inoffensive but conservative religious theme, aroused protest when the claque tried to applaud. The student faction then demanded to see the tickets of all present, since the claques had none, and ruthlessly tried to expel from the theatre all who could not produce them. The resulting mêlée, which became known as the battle of Bethlehem, was quieted only by Bernard's promise to abolish the claque, a reform that was almost as short-lived as the unfortunate play. A less famous but equally bitter conflict erupted over La Mort de César (1825) by Jacques-Corentin Royou, a royalist who committed an error unforgiveable by Odéon audiences in making Caesar a sympathetic victim. Despite such setbacks, Bernard sold a thriving and profitable Odéon to Frédérick du Petit-Méré in 1826. The new director continued the same sort of offerings during his short administration (bad health forced his retirement after only a year), most notably Castil-Blaze's adaptation of Mozart's Mariage de Figaro (1827).

4. Lyric Theatre, 1800-1829

Napoleon's legislation provided three Parisian homes for lyric theatre and dance--the Opéra, Opéra-Comique, and Opéra-Buffa--but as early as 1804 the Opéra-Buffa, which the Emperor visualized as the equivalent of the former Comédie Italienne, had ceased operating as a truly independent venture. Discouraged by their indifferent reception in Paris, the Italian actors whom Napoleon had invited to the Opéra-Buffa departed, and the Emperor gave that theatre little further attention. Its company, sadly depleted, survived by presenting Italian opera three days a week at the Odéon under the direction of the two composers whose works made up the basis of the repertoire: first Spontini, a minor neoclassic follower of Gluck, then, after 1812, Ferdinand Paër.

The venture, never particularly popular during the Empire, continued to decline during the Restoration. Deprived of its base at the Odéon, the Théâtre Italien, as it was now called, took refuge for a time at the Favart, under the leadership of the noted singer Mme Catalani, then settled at the Louvois. New works by Paër proved unattractive, so the theatre sought fresh material in Italy. There Gioacchino Rossini was at the height of his fame and productivity, and the Italians found Paris as receptive to his genius as his native land had been. Il Barbiere di Siviglia (1816), Otello (1816), La Cenerentola (1817), La Gazza ladre (1817), and Semiramide (1823) brought the Italien a popularity which it had never previously known.

When in 1823 the venture was seeking a new director, it is hardly surprising that many persons suggested inviting Rossini from Italy. Berton and other French composers fought the appointment bitterly, Paër vowing to disassociate himself entirely from the theatre if Rossini should come. Fortunately for the Italien, these protests were over-ruled. Rossini directed the theatre for only one year, but thanks to his talents and those of his leading artist, Mme Pasta, the Italien was restored for a time to one of the most brilliant of Paris' theatres. Two more short and undistinguished directorships followed his, but Rossini laid the foundations for the far more prosperous and stable Théâtre-Italien which developed under the direction of Robert and Severini after 1828.

The Opéra-Comique, formed by the union in 1801 of the Favart and Feydeau theatres at the home of the latter, remained at this home until 1829. It was a prosperous, though not distinguished period. The theatre was content to rely largely on the still popular repertoire inherited from the Revolutionary period--Grétry, Gossec, Dalayrac, Méhul, Berton, Nicolo, and Boieldieu. Méhul was represented by several new works after 1800, most importantly Joseph (1807) and La Journée aux aventures (1816), but the favorite composer of the Empire period was Nicolo, who contributed significantly to the popularity of the Opéra-Comique with Les Rendez-vous bourgeois (1807), Cendrillon (1810), and Joconde (1814). After the Restoration, Boieldieu, who was in Russia until 1812, became more popular, with such works as Le Petit Chaperon rouge (1818) and La Dame blanche (1825). The same years saw the first successes of composers whose major contributions were to come during the romantic period: Esprit Auber, with La Bergère Châtelaine (1820) and Le Maçon (1825); Ferdinand Hérold, with La Clochette (1817); and Paër, who, true to his threat when Rossini was engaged, now deserted the Italien to compose for the Opéra-Comique.

The Emperor's own predilection for the Opéra assured that theatre of the dominant position among lyric houses, but here, as at the Comédie, his support of a ponderous classicism drove a wedge between the theatre and its audience. Napoleon's favorite composer was Lesueur, who was invited to the Emperor's own box to witness the premiere of his Les Bardes (1804), the first new production under the Imperial director, Bonnet de Treiches. Doubtless the most noteworthy aspect of this production was the spectacular and original scenery designed for it. Bonnet de Treiches was interested in Italian design for the theatre, observing in a pamphlet published this same year that at close range Italian stage scenery appeared as random blotches of color but from a distance was strikingly true and effective, while the French concentrated on perfect detail which at a distance became vague and confusing. A Lombard painter, Fuentes, was therefore commissioned to introduce the Italian method to the Opéra in Les Bardes. The result was a series of memorable visual effects, and not solely in painting. A dream sequence in the fourth act was particularly praised. Ossian was shown sleeping in his cave, its depths hidden in mist. The mist slowly disappeared--a series of great gauze hangings lifted one by one--to reveal corteges of girls, old men, and warriors. To emphasize the forced perspective, small boys and girls were placed in the furthest depths of the cave. The vision over, the great hangings successively closed back in.

The opera itself was generally condemned by the Paris critics, who considered its solemn music more suitable for the church than for the stage. Still Napoleon supported subsequent productions at the Opéra of Lesueur's Le Triomphe de Trajan (1807) and La Mort d'Adam (1809)--works of significance only in that they provided opportunity for the Opéra's chief designer, Degotti, to develop the ideas introduced in Les Bardes, and because they contained respectable roles for Lainé, Lays, and the great tenor of the Empire, Louis Nourrit. At last, however, neither these talents nor court favor could compensate Lesueur for the public's indifference to his efforts, and he retired to follow the advice of his critics and write music for the church. He was replaced by Spontini, formerly of the Opéra-Buffa, who won admittance to the Opéra only with great difficulty. The singing master Persuis and orchestra leader Rey were hostile to new talents, and refused to accept even Spontini's innocuously classical La Vestale (1807) until he had obtained the backing of Josephine. The victory was in any case a small one, for the general public found Spontini no more interesting than Lesueur. The Journal de Paris found little to praise but the settings, which included the Roman Forum in the opening act and "a moonlight effect represented with an exactness and truth never before seen in the theatre."[13] Spontini's Fernand Cortez (1809) boasted similarly spectacular settings, and even horses borrowed from Franconi's circus, but this scenic display was no longer enough to attract the public to Spontini's sterile offerings.

In ballet, the choreographer Pierre Gardel, who had been with the Opéra since 1777, and his assistant Milon were as rigid and suspicious of innovation as Persuis and Rey, but their mythological ballets precisely suited the classic inclinations of the court: Vénus et Adonis (1808), Persée et Andromède (1810), and L'Enlèvement des Sabines (1811).

The only development in dance during this period was an increased emphasis on technique, especially on the pirouette, which had been discovered around the turn of the century. The great innovator Noverre, who had freed dance from its subservience to opera in the previous generation, wrote bitterly from retirement in 1807:

> Dance formerly involved careful and balanced execution, gained interest by polish and lovely proportions; it offered to the enchanted eye successive tableaux when the graces of the dancer were displayed. Today's dance offers only periods of leaping, staccato steps, and a frantic prancing which dishonors this beautiful art.[14]

Yet within these unpromising circumstances a renaissance in French dance was developing, and the Restoration period, when dance rivalled or surpassed opera in popularity, clearly foreshadowed the great years of romantic ballet. The way was opened for a new generation of dancers when the fall of Napoleon brought the retirement of Milon and the end of the tradition of mythological ballet. Chief among the new generation was Emilie Bigottini, who made her debut in 1801 but who only began to achieve prominence with Milon's *Nina* (1813). She stressed elegance and grace instead of the common spectacular technique, and had moreover an unusual gift for mime, especially in sentimental roles. Her interpretations in *Proserpine* (1818), *Clari* (1820), and *Aladin* (1822) made her the first dancer of Paris, and her retirement in 1823 was considered by many to be the end of a great period in ballet. Her success also encouraged scores for the first time to be composed for the ballet instead of being casually patched together from works previously presented. The pioneer composer of these early works was Jean-Madeleine Schneitzhoeffer, though after Bigottini's retirement he was overshadowed by Hérold, composer of *La Somnambule* (1827) and *Lydie* (1828).

Bigottini's generation was the last to make use of the traditional three "types" of classic ballet. Bigottini herself was considered a *demi-caractère*, a dancer of medium build who assumed the broadest range of roles and who studied the most varieties of technique. Other important dancers in this category were Fanny Bias, Bigottini's understudy, and the male dancer Paul, known as "the aerialist" in tribute to his skill in leaps. Traditionally the most important type was the *noble*, which required tall and imposing dancers and stressed majesty and solemn elegance. The decline of the old ballet meant the end of this type, and Bigottini's contemporaries, Albert and Mme Anatole, were its last significant representatives. The third type was the _comique_, for dancers with slight builds. By the Restoration, early romantic influence had turned this in the direction of interpretation of exotic national dancers--Spanish in Aumer's _Les Pages du Duc de Vendôme_ (1820), Hungarian in the same author's _La Fête hongroise_ (1821). Soon this sort of dance was also absorbed by the _demi-caractère_; Pauline Montessu during the romantic period was considered the last true representative of the _genre comique._

Aumer, the composer of these ballets, had been ballet master at the Porte-Saint-Martin before coming to the Opéra as Milon's successor. Under his direction, setting, subjects, and interpretation of ballet began distinctly to turn toward romanticism. _Alfred le Grand_ (1822) was memorable for its elaborate scenery, but was also significant as the last ballet of the century with a male hero played by a male dancer. Albert, now near retirement, had no successor in the _genre noble_, and the romantic ballet placed all its attention on the ballerina. This change was reinforced by the development of _pointe_ work, first used near the beginning of the Restoration and regularly employed, though still as a _tour de force_, all through the 1820s.

On February 13, 1820, the Opéra was the unfortunate scene of a national tragedy. The Duc de Berry, leaving a performance, was assassinated on the steps of the theatre. Since the last rites had to be administered in the lobby of the building, the Archbishop of Paris demanded that this consecrated area be no longer used for profane entertainment. The government agreed, and the huge building erected during the Revolution by Montansier and used by the Opéra during most of the Revolution and all of the Empire was now permanently closed. The architect Debret was commissioned to design a new home for the theatre in the rue Le Peletier; it opened in 1821. Much of the interior decoration was simply moved from the previous structure, but there was one major difference. Since the beginning of the century, Parisian theatres had been illuminated by Argand lamps, but experiments with gas lighting in London encouraged some Parisian entrepreneurs to build a laboratory for similar experiments in Montmartre. The products developed by this laboratory were tested in the new Opéra, first only as lighting in the house and corridors, but soon on stage as well. The first work to use gas lighting on stage was the somewhat coyly-named Aladin ou la lampe merveilleuse (1822), designed by the two most popular scenic artists of the time, Ciceri and Daguerre, the most noted pupil of the Empire designer Degotti. So great was the success of this work that Ciceri and Daguerre collaborated on two more spectacular productions before the year was over: Florestan and the already-mentioned ballet Alfred le Grand. Elaborate and original scenic effects had long been considered the province of Paris' minor theatres, but the critic Delaforest, writing of Alfred le Grand, observed that the Opéra "now need envy the boulevards nothing."[15]

In music, unfortunately, the picture was not so bright. Aside from the ballet composers Schneitzhoeffer and Hérold, no musician appeared to take the place of Spontini, who retired after the failure of his Olympie in 1819. Boieldieu, Paër, Berton, and Kreutzer, alone and in various combinations, attempted without success to continue traditional lyric tragedy, but a fresh start was needed here as in the ballet. Rossini's enormous success at the Opéra-Comique prepared the way for him to begin a similar revitalization of the Opéra. His first contribution was Le Siège de Corinthe (1826), then Mosès (1827). Adolphe Nourrit, son of the famous Opéra tenor of the Empire, emerged in these two works as a major talent in his own right, and Rossini created for him an operatic version of Scribe's vaudeville, Le Comte Ory (1828). A few nationalist and conservative journals still held out against Rossini, despite his tremendous popular appeal, but Guillaume Tell (1829) won over even the most intransigent. Nourrit again sang the leading role, supported as usual by Mlle Cinti. A whole succession of similar triumphs was anticipated, but to the astonishment of all, Guillaume Tell marked the end of Rossini's career as a composer of opera. At thirty-seven years of age, and already the author of thirty-eight operas, he gave up his successful career in Paris and, for reasons never really understood, returned to Italy. He often came back to Paris in the thirty-nine years remaining to him, but as a brilliant and popular member of the social world, never again as a contributor to the theatre.

5. Minor Theatres, 1800-1829

The enormous success of the minor houses, which drove Napoleon to place strict regulation on their number and repertoire, was due in large part to the appearance just at this time of a new genre of great popularity--the *mélodrame*. The term *mélodrame* was apparently first used in 1766 by Rousseau in a critique on Gluck. His usage suggested two somewhat different meanings: a synonym for opera, and a play where music interrupted the dialogue. By the end of the century, the first meaning had quite disappeared, and critics such as Lepan were applying the term with increasing frequency to a then-developing genre which suited the second. The end-of-the-century *mélodrame* did not, however, grow out of any musical form, but out of the purely dramatic *pantomime dialoguée* of the 1780s and 1790s.

The apparently contradictory title of *pantomime dialoguée* suggests something of the motives for developing this form. Regular dramatic productions were discouraged at minor theatres before the Revolution, but pantomime, like acrobatics, was generally considered acceptable. The *pantomime dialoguée* allowed its interpretors to remain within the bounds of the law, while skirting as close as they dared to conventional drama. With the freedom of the theatres in 1791, such circumspection was no longer necessary, but the visual side of such productions--the scenery as well as the pantomime--was by then so well established that neither audiences nor actors would have tolerated a shift to a more literary drama. Many of the basic characters and plot situations of these *pantomimes* were by the early 1790s well established: the persecuted heroine, her evil guardian, her noble rescuer, and so on. Throughout the last decade of the century, authors sought with increasing desperation for new thrills and more elaborate variations. The German *Sturm und Drang* contributed an interest in rebels and outcasts, and Lamartellière's *Robert chef de brigands*, derived vaguely from Schiller's *Die Räuber*, was one of the great successes of 1792. The same year Loaisel-Tréogate opened new dimensions of the horrible and fantastic with *Le Château du diable*. Obviously the English Gothic movement could provide much such material, and two adaptations, *Le Moine* at the Théâtre de l'Emulation and *Montoni ou le Château d'Udolphe* (both 1797), were widely copied. Not surprisingly, most of the "sublime" trappings of the late eighteenth century found their way into these works. Desandrais' popular *Adèle de Sacy* (1795) had, in addition to the usual persecuted victim and grim tyrant, rugged Alpine scenery--rocks, crags, and caverns, even a ferocious bear. Musical numbers and ballets were often a part of such productions, as an additional decorative element, but by the end of the century these had become common enough so that the *Courrier des Spectacles* began applying the term *mélodrame* to such works as Loaisel-Tréogate's *Forêt Noire* (1797).

By 1799, however, the old formulas were declining in popularity, audiences turning from Gothic horror and exotic fantasy to adaptations of the sentimental bourgeois dramas of Iffland and Kotzebue. The first, and most successful dramatist to combine this new interest in naturalness and sentimentality with the old *mélodrame* form and subject matter was Guilbert de Pixérécourt. His *Victor ou l'Enfant de Forêt* (Ambigu, 1798) was a very successful but traditional offering, while *Rosa ou l'Ermitage du Torrent* (Gaîté, 1800) clearly reflected a new spirit and was warmly praised by the *Courrier des Spectacles* for its "feeling and truth." Pixérécourt's new formula was fully developed in *Coelina ou l'Enfant du Mystère* (Ambigu, 1800), which made his fortune with 387 performances in Paris, over 1000 in the provinces, and translations into English, German, and Dutch. The traditional hero, heroine, and tyrant of *mélodrame* were retained, though distinctly sentimentalized, and a major new element, comic scenes, was added. This also meant the appearance of a fourth standard character, the *niais*, or simpleton, allied with the hero, and a whole new tonality, for Pixérécourt's *niais* generally spoke in a low, vulgar dialect far removed from the artificial but noble expressions of the hero, heroine, and villain. The similarity of the *niais* to the comic servants in Gothic romances is clear, but Pixérécourt's introduction of such a character onto the stage was none the less revolutionary, since it directly challenged the old French abhorrence of mixing genres. Pixérécourt did not consider subtlety a virtue, and all actions were violent, simple, direct, and frequently underscored by appropriate music. The new comic scenes further interrupted plot lines already broken by ballet and musical interludes, though in his *Derniers réflexions sur le mélodrame* Pixérécourt boasted: "With the exception of *Charles le téméraire* and *La Fille de l'exilé*, I have in all my dramas respected the three unities as much as possible."[16] Beginning with *La Femme à deux maris* (1802), Pixérécourt regularly used the term *mélodrame* in referring to his works.

Few, if any, of these plays had original plots, though Pixérécourt added scenes, situations and characters to his originals with fecund imagination. Recent French novelists such as Paul de Kock, George Sand, and Chateaubriand were his favorite sources, the inspiration for most of the works already mentioned. English gothic and romantic novelists inspired such works as Le Château de Lochleven (1822) and La Tête de mort (1827). He reworked earlier French plays, particularly the pantomimes dialoguées, to produce such works as Le Solitaire de la roche noire (1806). Finally, he drew from recent German drama plots for such works as Pizarre (1802) and Guillaume Tell (1828).

We have already noted at the Comédie a growing interest during this period in plays based on historical subjects, an interest to which Pixérécourt also responded. His Tékéli (1803) came from seventeenth century Austrian history and Christophe Colomb (1815) primarily from the writings of the explorer's son, but French history was naturally the dramatist's favorite source, inspiring a whole series of dramas. Nothing in these works is so impressive as their documentation. Charles le téméraire (1814), for example, was prefaced by letters from a general and a historian on the battle of Nancy and a lengthy article on the historical background by Pixérécourt himself, complete with maps and plans. The play was liberally sprinkled with notes affirming, "These details are taken from history," or "The actual words of the Duc de Bourgogne taken from a manuscript of the period." Similar care was taken with physical details, even to changes of name ("now the Porte Notre Dame," "now the rue de l'Opéra"). Rather amusingly, this concern for historical accuracy did not prevent Pixérécourt from employing artistic license or introducing anachronisms, so long as he could clear his conscience in the notes: "All characters are historical except Léontine and Marcelin, which are invented; but it is reasonable to suppose that Cifron was married, and there is nothing to indicate that he was not married to the daughter of Gérard Daviller."

Even the settings, of course, "conform to the plans and descriptions of historians of the time," and Pixérécourt was a major innovator in scenic design, demanding new scenery suited to each production, exact in detail and with more three-dimensional elements, fewer wings and curtains. In all of these concerns, Pixérécourt was laying the groundwork for the later romantic theatre, and we can almost hear the old mélodrame author speaking through Hugo when the latter boasts in the notes to Ruy Blas: "Moreover, and this goes without saying, there is not in Ruy Blas a detail of private or public life, of interiors, of furnishings, of sound, of manners, of biography, of character, or of topography which is not scrupulously exact."[17]

Although Pixérécourt rarely took more than twenty days, often less, to write a play, he spent much of this time in the development of scenic effects particularly suited for the individual production. As early as 1803 he insisted on elaborate subterranean settings for the third act of Les Mines de Pologne and a realistic river for the second act of Tékéli. Complex machinery was his particular delight and some of this he invented himself. Clearly, the contemporary taste for historical accuracy encouraged this, as may be seen in his introduction to Christophe Colomb:

> I was particularly concerned with retaining technical words and portraying what might be called the customs of a ship. In the third act, I took the same care in the customs, dress, and actions of the savages. All conform strictly to truth.[18]

This ideal even led Pixérécourt to write dialogue for the natives with the aid of a dictionary of the language of the Antilles, so that everything they said was incomprehensible to the audience. Scenery demanded equal care, and included a two-story ship accurate in its smallest details. Pixérécourt noted proudly in his collected works that this play had to be retired after 117 performances because the scenery was too elaborate to keep it in the repertory. It was a source of great pride to him that only eight theatres in France were sufficiently equipped to present it at all. Later works were no less ambitious: La Fille de l'exilé in 1819 required a flood scene with the heroine floating off stage on a plank, and La Tête de mort in 1827 featured an eruption of Vesuvius, with lava inundating the stage.

Pixérécourt's major rivals were Caigniez and Victor Ducange. A popular saying of the time called Pixérécourt the Corneille of the boulevards and Caigniez the Racine.[19] Caigniez did in fact draw characters of greater emotional complexity, but the general format of his works, at least after 1800, did not differ markedly from his rival's. His most praised contributions to the mélodrame were L'Illustre aveugle (1806) and L'Ermite du Mont-Pausilyse (1823). Ducange, a novelist and editor as well as a dramatist, achieved his first success in 1819 with Calas. His most popular work was Trente ans ou la Vie d'un joueur (1827), which was frequently revived for the following twenty years. Its title indicates how little Ducange shared Pixérécourt's respect for the unities. Among the minor mélodrame writers of this period the most popular were J. G. A. Cuvelier, who helped develop the pantomime dialoguée, Hector Chaussin, also a writer of vaudevilles, and best known for his Maria (1800), and Boirie, whose most popular work was Les Deux forcats (1822).

Before tracing the histories of the boulevard theatres which presented the mélodrames and other less dominant genres during the Empire and Restoration, a few words might be given to their less fortunate rivals, the theatres which Napoleon closed in 1807. Although the number of minor houses had been far greater during some period of the Revolution, there were only seventeen left in Paris when Napoleon's decree reduced their number to eight. The strongest and most influential were preserved, but there were a few regrettable losses among the victims. The Délassements-Comiques, after a long period of instability, had been reorganized as late as 1805 by a new director, Anicet Lapôtre, and was deprived of an opportunity to profit from this. The Jeunes-Elèves, built just after 1800 for actors between the ages of six and sixteen, had already proven a valuable training ground, producing in its brief career Firmin and Rose Dupuis for the Comédie, and Virginie Déjazet, who became one of the most popular actresses of the Restoration.

Perhaps the most interesting venture closed in 1807 was the former Molière, which about 1800 had become the Variétés Nationales et Etrangères. Despite the title, few translations were given here until 1806, when Boursault became director, changed the theatre's name to the Variétés Etrangères, and began to capitalize on the growing public interest in foreign literatures. His opening manifesto promised that works of Sheridan, Garrick, Schiller, Calderon, and Goldoni would be given, that Aristotle's unities would be defied, that the audience would be taken from country to country "as in the Arabian Nights," and that characters might if necessary age fifty years during an intermission.[20] Very little of this ambitious program was accomplished in the year before the Variétés was closed, for the majority of the sixty translations presented were from Augustus von Kotzebue, whose works were sufficiently similar to those of Pixérécourt and Caigniez to guarantee him great popularity on the boulevard.

The four minor houses left open in 1807 were the Ambigu-Comique, the Gaîté, the Vaudeville, and the Variétés. The first two, the longest established of all the boulevard houses, were also by tradition, and now by decree, the centers of the _mélodrame._ The Ambigu, like many of its rivals, was nearly ruined before the Revolution ended, but then its direction fell into the hands of Labanette Corse, an actor whose phenomenal success in the play _Madame Angot_, the story of a _parvenu_ fishwife, brought fortune both to him and to the theatre. Even greater fortune followed, however, as Corse began producing the plays of Pixérécourt and Caigniez. In the sixteen years of his directorship, Corse accumulated a fortune astonishing for a boulevard entertainer and assembled a company unequalled in the _mélodrame_. The greatest favorite was Révaland, who played villains and tyrants. The designer, Daguerre, was one of the period's outstanding scenic artists, and dreamed of "putting every phenomenon of nature" on this little stage scarcely 12 meters deep and 17 wide. A spectator of the time describes a typical Daguerre setting for Mélesville and Delestre-Poirson's _Le Sage:_

> the summit of a high mountain amid the ruins of a gothic chapel. In the moonlight appeared an immense vista broken by a wandering river, reflecting repeatedly the brilliant stars. Passing clouds at times cast heavy shadows and at times thinned to mere wisps, disclosing the luminous disc which brought the scene into new clarity.[21]

After Corse's death in 1816 the theatre declined, but it entered a new period of prosperity after 1823 under the direction of Audinot, son of the Ambigu's founder. A series of blows in 1826 and 1827 then brought this revival to an abrupt end: the death of Audinot, the departure of his _régisseur général_, author, and scenic superintendant Varez, and a devastating fire resulting from a pyrotechnic display in a new _mélodrame_. Audinot's widow reopened the venture in 1829, but without great success.

The Gaîté at the beginning of the century was under the direction of Ribié, an entrepreneur who had guided it through the closing years of the Revolution. Like Corse, he was hospitable to the early _mélodrames_, as he had been to the _pantomimes dialoguées_, but he was less noted for their production than was his successor Bourguignon, who came in 1808. Bourguignon's first act was to commission a new building to replace the dark, smoky old house which had served the Gaîté since 1760. The elegant new hall was stocked with theatrical machinery which Bourguignon had purchased from the Cité, a theatre specializing in spectacle which had been closed by the decree of 1807. The opening production, Hapdé's *Siège de la Gaîté*, like most which followed, relied heavily on this machinery and was designed by the popular Gué. Bourguignon and his wife, who assumed the direction after his death in 1816 and retained it until 1825, also looked to Pixérécourt and his followers as their chief source of scripts. Their most popular actors were Lafargue, who later went on to tragic roles at the Odéon, and Marty, director of the theatre after 1825.

One of the most frequented new theatres of the Revolutionary period had proved to be the Vaudeville, founded in 1792 by Piis and Barré to present this form of light comedy richly decorated with song. During the Consulate, the *vaudeville* continued to rival the new *mélodrame* in audience esteem. Before Napoleon came to power, *vaudevilles* had frequently been based on social issues, class questions and political concerns, causing not a few disputes with the various parties in power since the founding of the theatre. After about 1804, however, the genre turned away from political and social concerns. The more intellectual offerings now frequently concerned literary figures: Rabelais, Scarron, Molière, Voltaire, Rousseau, or less noted contributors to the tradition of the boulevards such as Piron, Favart, or Pannard. The program was rounded out by less pretentious works in the *poissard* and *grivois* genres, broad depictions of the lower classes, and by parodies and reviews. The most popular actors here during the Napoleonic period were Joly in the *poissard* plays and Jenny Vertpré in the more literary works. Among the authors most often presented were Capelle, Armand Gouffé, Laujon, Desaugiers, and the two directors, but the one who raised the *vaudeville* to great popular success and even to a certain literary respectability was Eugène Scribe.

Scribe became interested in the theatre while a student at the Collège Sainte-Barbe, where he met Germain Delavigne, then an aspiring playwright. Upon graduation Scribe, in accordance with his parents' wishes, began studying for the law, but collaborated with Delavigne in writing *vaudevilles* in his free time. Their first produced work was a failure at the Vaudeville in 1811 and the directors did not encourage them to try again. Scribe was now fascinated by the theatre, however, and the following year achieved success on his own with a *vaudeville* called *L'Auberge*. In 1813 he experimented unsuccessfully with both *mélodrame* and comic opera, but a return to vaudeville called Une Nuit de la Garde Nationale in 1814 proved the first in a series of undisputed triumphs. In this vaudeville and its successors, Scribe revolutionized the genre by breaking away from traditional subjects and stock characters to present sketches of contemporary life in brilliantly articulated plots with witty dialogue and graceful verse. In his hands, the vaudeville drew steadily nearer to otherwise neglected traditional comedy. The departure of Scribe in 1819 was a serious blow for the Vaudeville, but it continued to attract the lesser bourgeoisie with parodies, staged anecdotes, light fables, and sentimental pieces all closely related to the scènes populaires and proverbes presented in the popular private theatricals of the Revolution. It is not surprising, therefore, to find that Henry Monnier, long popular as a private entertainer, should have achieved one of the Vaudeville's few major successes between 1819 and the 1850s in Duvert, Brazier, and Dupeuty's La Famille improvisée (1831), in which he played five different roles.

The last of the minor houses left open by the decree of 1807 was the Variétés. The plays presented here were among the least distinguished in the capital--casual potpourris of gross buffoonery, snatches of vaudeville, and crude puns. Yet the theatre possessed some of the city's most popular actors: Tiercelin, Dubois, Volange, Duval, and above all Brunet, whose fame was such that he was considered one of the essential sights of the city for visiting tourists. Thus, despite the undistinguished plays presented, the Variétés proved so serious a rival for the nearby Comédie that while Napoleon did not close it in 1807, he required the theatre to find a more remote location. An elegant new home, seating 1600, was inaugurated the same year on the Boulevard Montmartre, and the major houses were doubtless chagrined to discover that the popularity of the Variétés was if anything even greater after its forced move. In 1809 the theatre gained an important new actor in Potier, whom Talma called the most complete comic artist he had known. Prosperity had little effect on the repertoire, despite the pledge of the opening program in the new theatre: "Let us sometimes abuse the truth, but never offend decency." The grivois programs, despite the censors, drew down regular charges of lapses of taste, and only the protection of influential patrons seems to have preserved the theatre. Members of polite society affected never to attend the Variétés, but the new building had been thoughtfully provided with a large number of grilled boxes, and the demand from spectators who wished to see, but not be seen, was always great.

A number of new minor theatres appeared after Napoleon's restrictions were revoked in 1815, but even during the Empire, two significant theatres successfully challenged the 1807 ruling and were allowed to open. Franconi, director of the Cirque Olympique, chose to interpret the decree as inapplicable to his own establishment, since it was a circus, not a theatre. The authorities accepted this argument, for much of Franconi's program was still based on performing animals, especially on trained horses, an entertainment idea borrowed from the English director Astley. The elaborate pantomimes and spectacles presented at the Cirque nonetheless bordered on the dramatic. Ambigu and Gaîté writers like Cuvelier were represented there, and even Alexandre Dumas consented to write a _Caligula_ for Franconi in which Caligula's horse Incitatus had the leading role. Nothing really was lacking to make such productions open rivals with other theatres except dialogue, and even that was beginning to appear by the end of the Empire. Emphasis remained on historical and military pageants under the Restoration, but the freedom then allowed the theatre also to present more conventional dramatic fare, and several interesting works looking forward to the romantic period were presented here. Chief among these were Chateaubriand's _Les Martyrs_ and an adaptation of _Othello_, both given in 1818.

The Porte-Saint-Martin was the only theatre closed by the 1807 decree that decided to resist. Its position was strong; it had a large and well-equipped building, it was popular and financially stable, it had previous legislative blessing (an 1806 decree had given it first rights to _mélodrame_ in Paris), and its ballets were often considered superior even to those of the Opéra. After two years of petitions, it was allowed to reopen under the title Jeux Gymniques, and to present "acrobatics, historic tableaux, military displays, and prologues."[22] The theatre submitted to these restrictions, which it naturally interpreted more and more broadly until its approach to regular drama caused it to be closed again in 1811. Reopened under the Restoration by J. T. Merle, the theatre became noted for its spectacular productions, many of them adapted from the English or German. Here the popular designer Ciceri first deserted neoclassic settings for such works as the exotic _Doge de Venise_ (1821) or the gothic _Château de Kenilworth_ (1822). Later, as Ciceri began working at the Opéra and elsewhere, this work was continued by the designer Lefèvre and the machinist Griffe, aided by special effects which Merle brought from England in 1824. An English machinist named Tompkins was brought especially for *Le Monstre et le magicien* (1826), an adaptation of *Frankenstein* with a monster that swallowed ships, set fire to villages, and unleashed tempests, floods, and lightning. For Benjamin and Arago's *Mandrin* (1827) the stage was at one point divided in half, showing a forest and a mysterious cavern. Antier and Nezel's *Le Chasseur noir* (1828) featured a great storm, with water inundating the stage and the hero riding an uprooted tree on the current, illuminated by flashes of lightning. One of the most elaborate of such spectacles was an adaptation in 1828 of Goethe's *Faust* by Merle, Béraud, and Nodier, which used all the bizarre machinery the stage possessed. In the apotheosis the stage, divided in half, showed both hell and paradise.

When Napoleon's restrictions on the boulevard theatres were lifted in 1815, a number of houses were soon ready to reopen. Few of the theatres closed in 1807 had been destroyed or totally forgotten. Some had simply been locked up and deserted, but most were converted into establishments reminiscent of the minor theatres' origins in the previous century. Many became riding halls, dance halls, or cafes, while others retained a theatrical flavor with exhibitions of acrobats, magicians, freaks, animal acts, clown shows, or wax figures. Some went through a whole series of adaptations. The Variétés Palais Royal, for example, sheltered rope-dancers, then marionettes, then a company of trained dogs which achieved a certain success presenting mock *mélodrames* with a large bull-dog playing the villain and a poodle the persecuted heroine. Then came singers, clown shows, and a cafe, all within a period of four years. Yet the general architectural arrangements suitable to theatrical presentation remained unchanged, and when the new order of 1815 allowed the Variétés Palais Royal to reopen as a theatre, it was able to do so almost at once after only minor redecoration.

In addition to such revived ventures, many small new theatres devoted to light entertainment sprang up during the Restoration, and although they produced not a single important artist or lasting play, they contributed distinctly to the theatrical life of the capital. Among the more popular of these new establishments were the Théâtre de Comte, the Théâtre de Madame Saqui, the Petit Lazzari, the Funambules, the Bobino, and the theatres of Montmartre and

Montparnasse. No more literary, but distinctly more significant in the development of theatrical art, were certain new ventures dedicated almost entirely to spectacle. The French had been introduced to panorama theatres, featuring only scenery without actors, as early as 1787 by the English painter Fuller, and in 1799 by the American Robert Fulton, but a permanent panorama was not opened in Paris until 1801. In 1804 Daguerre opened the Théâtre Pittoresque, which maintained its popularity into the 1820s by presenting no plays, only sunrises, seas, gardens, streets, and famous buildings. After the Restoration, other similar experiments appeared. The Diorama, invented by the designers Daguerre and Bouton, opened in 1822 and until 1849 attracted audiences with a huge painting (65 feet long and 42 feet high) variously illuminated for different effects. In 1817 the designer Pierre Alaux opened his Néorama, which showed interiors of famous buildings.

The most important of these spectacle houses in the history of the French theatre was the short-lived Panorama-Dramatique. Alaux was given permission in 1819 to open a theatre "to present dramas, comedies, and vaudevilles, on the condition of never having on stage more than two speaking actors."[23] The theatre, opened in 1821, was not large, though its curtain composed of mirrors probably made it seem so. The machinery-filled stage, however, was a commodious 29 meters deep. The major author for the theatre, under several pseudonyms, was the young Isidore Taylor, just then attracting public attention with the publication of the first volume of his _Voyages pittoresques._ The minor _mélodrames_ which he produced served largely as a pretext for displaying the spectacular settings first of Alaux, then of Gué, Daguerre, and Ciceri, all the major designers of the period. It was Ciceri's designs here in 1822 for _Ali-Pacha_ and _Bertram_ which opened the Opéra to him and truly launched his career. Obviously influenced by the panoramas, these used a curving drop without traditional wings and borders. The theatre proved extremely popular, but even so, its production expenses soon far outstripped its receipts. In 1823 it was forced to close, and its director, designers and authors separated, to be later reunited, as we have seen, when Taylor became director of the Comédie.

Among theatres offering traditional drama, the most important new venture of the Restoration period was unquestionably the Gymnase, founded in 1820 by the actor Delestre-Poirson, who had achieved fame at the Vaudeville in

Scribe's Une Nuit de la Garde Nationale. He convinced Scribe to come with him to the new theatre and to sign a contract to write for no rival house. In ten years Scribe made himself and his producer rich with a series of light comedies lauding home and family. For his interpreters, in addition to Delestre-Poirson, Scribe had a subtle comedian named Perlet, an excellent character actor, Gontier, the buffoon Bernard-Léon, and two outstanding actresses, Virginie Déjazet and Jenny Vertpré. The success of the Gymnase drove other theatres to demand government restrictions on it. Then in 1824 the Gymnase performed before the Duchesse de Berry in Dieppe and so delighted her that she promised Delestre-Poirson her protection, thereby removing all threats to his prosperity. The Gymnase was rechristened the Théâtre de Madame and elevated above its long-established minor rivals to be listed in public announcements just below the royal houses such as the Comédie and Opéra.

A useful summation of minor theatrical activity in Paris at this time is provided in Albert's Les Théâtres des Boulevards. Here is reproduced a survey of the boulevard offerings of March 20, 1825, as a typical evening during the Restoration. Forty plays were offered, at least two and more often three or four at each theatre. Runs were not long in this period, even for major successes, and twelve premieres were announced this evening.[24] It was common practice for new works to be put into rehearsal the day after a premiere, no matter what its success, to be ready to replace it in a few days; really popular works could always be revived later. Programs frequently changed on Sunday, a popular day, and rarely was a program repeated on two successive Sundays. The Gaîté had begun the practice of offering as many as four plays in one evening and its rivals were forced to follow suit, so that in a single evening an audience might see a comedy, a mélodrame, a fairy play, and a farce, for even theatres with one speciality introduced other genres for variety. Dramatic output under these conditions was of course enormous, even if the quality was not particularly high. In the years between 1815 and 1830 the minor houses offered 369 new comedies, 280 new mélodrames, 200 new comic operas, and 1300 new vaudevilles. The declining classic tradition managed in the same period to produce only 72 tragedies.

Notes to Part I

1. L. F. Lejeune, Souvenirs d'un officier de l'Empire (Paris, 1895), I, 216.

2. C. M. Desgranges, Geoffroy et la critique dramatique sous le Consulat et l'Empire (Paris, 1897), p. 378.

3. L. H. Lecomte, Napoléon et le monde dramatique (Paris, 1912), p. 382.

4. J.-L. Geoffroy, Cours de littérature dramatique (Paris, 1836), IV, 233-34.

5. Ibid., VI, 272.

6. E. D. De Manne, Galerie historique des Comédiens de la troupe de Talma (Lyon, 1866), p. 202.

7. Emile Maingot, Le Baron Taylor (Paris, 1963), pp. 47-49.

8. E. Biré, Victor Hugo avant 1830 (Paris, 1883), p. 419.

9. Preface to Médiocre et Rampant, Picard, Oeuvres (Paris, 1821), I, 397.

10. T. Muret, L'Histoire par le théâtre (Paris, 1865), II, 143.

11. P. Porel and G. Monvel, L'Odéon (Paris, 1876-1882), II, 20.

12. Ibid., II, 50.

13. Dec. 16, 1807. Quoted in F. Bapst, Essai sur l'histoire du théâtre (Paris, 1893), p. 530.

14. Quoted in A. Royer, Histoire de l'Opéra (Paris, 1875), p. 117.

15. Geoffroy, Cours, I, 35.

16. G. de Pixérécourt, Théâtre Choisi (Nancy, 1843), IV, 496.

17. V. Hugo, *Oeuvres complètes* (Paris, 1952), XVII, 175.

18. W. G. Hartog, *Guilbert de Pixérécourt* (Paris, 1913), p. 180.

19. J. D. B., *Essai sur l'état actuel des théâtres de Paris* (Paris, 1813), quoted in M. Albert, *Les Théâtres des boulevards* (Paris, 1902), p. 244.

20. N. Brazier, *Chroniques des petits théâtres de Paris* (Paris, 1883), II, 364.

21. De Boisjolin, "Daguerre," *Biographie Universelle*, quoted in M. A. Allevy, *La Mise en Scène en France dans la première moitié du dix-neuvième siècle* (Paris, 1938), pp. 42-43.

22. Albert, *boulevards*, p. 230.

23. Maingot, *Baron Taylor*, p. 43.

24. Albert, *boulevards*, pp. 283-4.

II. THE AGE OF ROMANTICISM 1827-1850

The third and fourth decades of the nineteenth century in France are dominated by the rise and decline of the romantic theatre. Romanticism is of course a word of such immense scope, covering phenomena not only in the theatre and literature but in other arts, and even in politics and philosophy, that definition of it has become almost impossible. In France the major source of romantic ideals was unquestionably Rousseau, and his emphasis on the primacy of emotions, his concern with the natural and organic, and his zeal for political reform are all hallmarks of the romantic spirit. The Revolution, which these ideals helped to shape, seemed to interrupt the development of romanticism in France, since the neoclassic revival came in its wake, but in the long run the Revolution proved a liberating force for the new movement. Old models were broken and a path cleared for the development of a new, individualistic, emotional vision of man. The new bourgeoisie found at least the less extreme manifestations of romanticism more harmonious with their own ideas than the stiff and formal classic tradition, but romantic artists ultimately found them dangerous allies. Emotion for them became sentimentality, romantic vision became entertaining spectacle. Once the classically oriented aristocrats were disposed of, the enemy often became the successful bourgeois.

For almost thirty years, neoclassism held romanticism at bay in France. Rich and varied romantic movements developed in Germany, led by Schlegel, and in England, led by Wordsworth and Coleridge, and burst upon the French stage as a powerful revelation with the coming of English companies in 1827. There was, however, a somewhat subversive French romantic tradition in the minor theatres of the Napoleonic era. In the spectacle houses of the boulevards the evocative settings of romantic drama first appeared, and in the melodramas of Pixérécourt and his followers the influence of the mystery, emotion, and imagination of such writers as Schiller and Scott is apparent. What Hugo and Dumas did in large part was elevate these boulevard offerings to literary respectability, thereby creating the French romantic drama.

Though the symbolic importance of the success of Hugo's Hernani in 1830 was great, romanticism was long overdue in France, and the neoclassicism over which it presumably triumphed was already virtually dead. Once the gates were open, therefore, romanticism swept the major theatres of Paris like a flood, revolutionizing ideas of playwriting, operatic composition, acting, dance, design, and costume. Everywhere classic form and control gave way to emotion and imagination. Napoleon's neoclassic theatre disappeared entirely, but when the romantic flood had passed, the traditional classic drama returned with new power and vitality, in such artists as Rachel. The romantic movement in the French theatre ended almost as suddenly as it had come. By 1840 it was in decline, by 1850 almost as dead as neoclassicism. Its external and physical features were preserved in the seemingly indestructible melodrama and in the spectacle houses of the boulevards, but in the major theatres of Paris the end result of romanticism seemed to be the clearing of a dead classic tradition to prepare the way for more realistic plays of contemporary life. The bourgeoisie which now supported the French theatre had had enough of romantic excesses, and turned with relief to the new "école de bon sens" which promised moderate and moral studies of society. Out of this school, with the aid of the techniques of the popular "well-made" plays of Scribe, would come the social dramas of the Second Empire.

1. The Coming of the English

J. T. Merle, the director of the Porte-Saint-Martin during the Restoration, found English stage machinery and adaptations of English plays and novels so profitable that in July of 1822 he organized with an English entrepreneur named Penley the guest appearance of an entire English company at the Porte-Saint-Martin. Posters all over Paris announced "the tragedy of Othello in five acts by the most celebrated Shakespeare," to be performed by "his Britannic Majesty's most humble servants." Both project and publicity, however, were badly ill-timed. England was still widely hated as a traditional enemy, and the servile reference to the English King added to this bitterness. Even the name Shakespeare was at this time inflammatory. The whole preceding generation, that of the Revolution, knew him only through the genteel and totally misleading adaptations of Ducis, who did not himself know a word of English but worked from the earlier classic adaptations of Laplace and Letourneur. The new generation, however, was forcing a new Shakespeare on its elders--uncontrolled, barbaric, frighteningly similar to the loosely organized productions of the scarcely respectable boulevard theatres. In 1821 Guizot had reworked Letourneur's translations in this new direction, attempting to discover the Shakespeare that Lady Morgan, in the tremendously popular La France (1817), had dared to rank above Voltaire, and even above Racine. Thus even the words "most celebrated" on the posters aroused the wrath of both classicists and nationalists. The performances, the unwitting focus of political and literary furor, were disastrous. Little of Othello could be heard over such shouts as "Down with Shakespeare--he's a flunky of Wellington."[1] Potatoes, eggs and large coins rained down on the actors. The School for Scandal, performed the following evening, fared no better, and the project came to an early close.

This disaster prevented similar experiments for five years, but in the meantime public opinion underwent significant changes. These five years were precisely those of Canning's liberal administration in England, and his policies and sympathies did much to erase the bitterness felt for all things English in France. Shakespeare continued to win new supporters among the French critics. Le Globe in particular, from its founding in 1824, carried on a sustained and influential campaign on his behalf. The novels of Scott and poems of Byron were now enjoying great popularity in France, and persistent rumors came to the country of striking innovations in acting to be seen in the contemporary English theatre. By 1827 a significant portion of the Parisian public was eager to see representatives of the tradition they had scorned five years before.

Merle, sensitive to these changes, began arranging for a second English company some time before 1827, but before his plans were realized, he lost his post and the project was assumed by his successor, Emile Laurent. Interest was now so great that Laurent was able to obtain the Odéon (and subsequently the Italienne) for the visitors, and the receipts of the rest of Paris' major theatres showed a sharp drop in September when the theatre-going public flocked to this new attraction. The basic company was adequate but undistinguished, put together with artists from Covent Garden,

Drury Lane, Haymarket, the Theatre Royal of Dublin, and the Theatre of Bath. During the eleven months which followed, however, this group was regularly supplemented by major stars of the English stage. The company's first Shakespearian production was Hamlet on September 11, with Charles Kemble, who in the week following also gave Romeo and Juliet and Othello.

French interest in Kemble was easy to understand. He came already established as one of the best-known names in the English theatre, famous in his own right and also a member of one of the country's greatest acting families. Somewhat more surprising was the French enthusiasm for his partner, Constance Harriet Smithson, who came to Paris with no particular reputation but by her portrayal of Ophelia aroused at once an admiration somewhat greater than that for Kemble. The complaints made against her in England--her Irish accent and the delicacy of feeling which was said to weaken her interpretation of major tragic roles--apparently caused no difficulty in Paris. The quality in all the English actors which most impressed the French was their realism in the portrayal of emotion, and it is therefore hardly surprising that Miss Smithson's mad scene in Hamlet was of particular interest. Le Globe compared her madness to that of Mlle Mars in Soumet's L'Emilia, noting that Mlle Mars had "more grace and intention" and "understood her madness better" but was "not so truly mad." Le Courrier Français agreed: "Miss Smithson has shown us in Ophelia true madness; despite the efforts of our own actresses and perhaps because of our authors, we have never seen it before. One must go see Miss Smithson."[2] The vogue of Miss Smithson was so great that there was even a coiffure à la miss Smithson which gave its wearer an appropriately mad look by means of a black veil and wisps of straw artistically mixed in the hair. Even after the English tours were concluded, Miss Smithson understandably returned regularly to the scene of her triumph as an actress and even as director of her own English theatre. In 1833 she married Hector Berlioz and only rarely appeared on stage thereafter.

The spring of 1828 saw the arrival of another major actor of the English stage, William Macready, who presented Macbeth and a recent tragedy, Knowles' Virginius. During May and June, Parisians were able to see the greatest of the English romantic actors, Edmund Kean, in a rich selection of roles: Richard III, The Merchant of Venice, King Lear, A New Way to Pay Old Debts, and Payne's Junius

Brutus. In July, Macready returned to present Hamlet, Othello, Jane Shore, and Knowles' William Tell. The effect of this series of productions on the French theatre was enormous. The death of Talma had clearly signaled the end of an era, and the English brought their new and energetic approach to a public seeking enthusiastically, if somewhat desperately, to discover what new direction their theatre should take. The actors, directors, and critics of Paris joined the general public as fascinated spectators of Kean, Kemble, and Macready, so that for twenty years after, these performances were recalled as a point of comparison for new offerings. Never had the French seen such violence, such mad scenes, such stage fighting, such unleashing of emotions. "Our own actors have gone back to school,"[3] wrote Delacroix, and indeed, before the "English season" was completed, English mannerisms could be detected in the acting of the outstanding young actors of the boulevards, Frédérick Lemaître, Bocage, and Marie Dorval. Bocage even developed a sardonic laugh so close to Kean's as almost to suggest parody. Actors at the major theatres were naturally more conservative, but reviews of the time report clear traces of English influence in such artists as Ligier and Mars of the Comédie, Lockroy and Anaïs of the Odéon.

The young romantic school of writers was similarly stirred. In the supercharged atmosphere surrounding the English performances, young Victor Hugo completed Cromwell, embodying his ideas on dramatic reform. Dumas, who comments at length on the English company in his memoirs, began his Christine under their influence, noting that "this was the first time that I had seen real passions on the stage, inspiring men and women of real flesh and blood."[4] Less important writers shared this enthusiasm; Soulié reworked his Roméo et Juliette to give Odéon audiences in 1828 the most "English" Shakespeare the French stage had yet offered. Though the famous Hernani production still lay three years in the future, the overwhelming success of these English performances clearly opened the way not only for that work but for the whole romantic movement in the French theatre.

2. Romanticism at the Comédie, 1825-1837

The success of Pichat's quasi-romantic Léonidas (1825) as the first offering of Baron Taylor's administration at the Comédie, along with Taylor's unconventional background (his only theatrical experience being an association with a boulevard spectacle house), encouraged many to expect the immediate launching of a period of innovation and experiment at the national theatre. In fact, the offerings of 1826 were all rather conservative, and the major successes of the year were traditional comedies such as Picard and Empis' *L'Agiotage*, dealing with the popular Restoration subject of financial speculation.

By 1827, however, Taylor was attempting more striking and unusual works. For Mély-Janin's *Louis XI* special costumes were designed by Auguste Garnerey, and Duponchel and Ciceri of the Opéra were brought in to recreate the fifteenth century on the Comédie stage. Boulevard realism was introduced into comedy for *Les Trois Quartiers* by Picard and Mazères, a play dealing lightly with class conflict. *Le Courrier des théâtres* noted "We are not at the theatre; we see the place itself!"[5]--this several generations before the realist movement.

The same sort of interest which boulevard dramatists such as Pixérécourt had shown early in the century in scenic spectacle and historical exactitude was now clearly entering the Comédie. The trend continued in 1828 with Liadieres' *Walstein* and Ancelot's *Olga*, which infuriated the classicists by interrupting the first act for scene changes. Bitter attacks on Taylor began to appear this year: a memoir by Pierre Victor, a disaffected actor, then Léon Halévy's *Epître-Satire*, a preface by Arnault and another *Epître* by Viennet. Papers, most notably the *Incorruptible*, joined the attack, accusing Taylor of bringing *mélodrame* and *vaudeville* to the national theatre and of wasting huge sums on elegant settings.

Taylor decided that the best way to weaken such charges was by the mounting of a significant revival. He therefore appealed to Charles X to lift the ban on *Le Mariage de Figaro*, the most distinguished of a number of plays with strong emotional ties to the Revolution which had been banned after the assassination of the Duc de Berry in 1827. The permission was granted, and Beaumarchais' work was presented, without a single cut, to enormous acclaim. After this success, Taylor felt his position sufficiently assured to return to romantic experiment with Alexandre Dumas' *Henri III et sa cour*.

Although *Henri III* was Dumas' fourth play, he was

still a virtually unknown dramatist. His earlier works were two insignificant vaudevilles presented at the Ambigu in 1825 and the Porte-Saint-Martin in 1826, and Christine, accepted by the Comédie in 1828 but not presented because of the competition of a similar work at the Odéon. Henri III was the most romantic production yet offered by the Comédie, a sprawling historical pageant with conspicuous borrowing from Schiller and Scott. Classicists were especially appalled by a scene in the second act where one character fired at another with a pea-shooter, and by another in the third when the Duc de Guise crushed his wife's hand with an iron gauntlet, the sort of barbaric act hitherto seen only in English drama. These difficult moments were carried off superbly by the playing of Mlle Mars and of Firmin, the Comédie's usual tragic hero since the death of Talma.

Less than a week after the opening of Henri III a reaction had begun. The major classic dramatists--Arnault, Lemercier, Viennet, Jouy, Andrieux, Jay, and Leroy--submitted a petition to the King which stated in part:

> The death of the actor whose talents vied with those of the most perfect artist of any epoch has brought about more than one injury to the noble art which he upheld. Whether from depravity of taste or from consciousness of their inability to take his place, certain persons associated with the Théâtre-Français have pretended that the type of art in which Talma excelled can no longer be profitably continued; they are seeking to exclude tragedy from the stage and to substitute for it plays composed in imitation of the most eccentric dramas that foreign literature affords--dramas which no one ever dared to produce before except in our lowest theatres.[6]

Despite this petition and a heated battle in the papers (Dumas notes in his Mémoires that ironically the liberal papers of the time were reactionary on such a literary question, and the royalist ones were the patrons of change), the play ran for a quite respectable 38 performances, closing at last only because Mlle Mars insisted on a leave of absence. For the fall, Taylor scheduled Marion de Lorme, a new play by Victor Hugo, whose preface to Cromwell had made him the spokesman of the new school. Taylor urged Hugo to soften his treatment of Louis XIII, but Hugo refused, and during rehearsals the play was banned. Hugo still refused to make any alterations, but promised the Comédie a substitute work before the end of the season. In the meantime, Taylor presented Alfred de Vigny's Le More de Venise (1829), with Mars as Desdémona and Joanny as Othello. The production contained some concessions to classicism, particularly in its simple and severe furnishings, but it was sufficiently romantic to arouse protests throughout its thirteen performances. Classicists complained both of the play's language (the word "handkerchief," never before heard on the serious French stage, was particularly offensive) and its interpretation (the acting followed the "English style," with disturbingly realistic touches in such passages as the drunken scene of Cassio).

Le More de Venise served as a sort of prologue to Hernani, the eagerly-awaited new Hugo play written to replace Marion de Lorme. So completely had Hugo made himself the representative figure of the new school that liberals and conservatives alike looked to this work as a test case for romantic drama as a whole, as if Henri III or Le More de Venise had never been presented. Taylor resolved to spare no pains or expenses for the production, and again called on Ciceri from the Opéra for the most lavish of settings. Hugo himself made preliminary sketches for the settings and planned much of the movement of the actors within them. The movement attempted to capture the informality and fluidity of the English stage by substituting curves and diagonals for the traditional flat back-and-forth downstage movement of the French classic stage. During much of the first act, Hernani was required to stand downstage with his back to the audience, thus anticipating by sixty years one of the standard "shocking" devices of the realistic stage. Such innovations were not surprisingly resisted by the actors of the Comédie, especially since Taylor, anxious to win success for the play, cast his best-known and therefore most conservative actors in the major roles. After the death of Talma, Mlle Mars was the uncontested sovereign of the Comédie and the obvious choice for Dona Sol, despite her age. Hernani and Don Gomez were played by Firmin and Joanny, the joint inheritors of the majority of Talma's roles, and Don Carlos by Michelot, dean of the Comédie School of Declamation. Long trained in classic restraint, these actors found Hugo's attempts at English abandon extremely difficult. Firmin, said the romantic actress Marie Doval later, gave the impression of being beaten standing up, and Mlle Mars' "English" convulsions in the final act were considered spectacular by many, convincing by almost none. Some situations and lines were frankly beyond the talents or taste of the interpreters, and the rehearsals were filled with acrimonious disputes between Hugo, Michelot, and Mars. Dumas, in his *Mémoires,* states that only Joanny of the whole company was really sympathetic toward romanticism, that the rest at heart hated the new school.

A bitter winter delayed the opening, for painters found it impossible to execute Ciceri's enormous settings in unheated lofts, but Hugo's friends and enemies took advantage of the delay to prepare their forces. The claque was by now a well-organized and established part of almost all Parisian theatres, but Hugo did not trust that of the Comédie. The failure in 1828 of his *Amy Robsart* at the Odéon convinced him that a romantic work could not rely even on the claque employed by the theatre to support its offerings. When feelings ran high, it was even possible that a theatre's claque could be bought out by enemies of the work being presented, and *Hernani* could hardly take this risk. At last Taylor consented to make the usual claque tickets available to Hugo's friends, and these small red cards, bearing the password "Hierro" (iron), soon became a most coveted prize among the young artists of Paris, proof that one truly belonged to the inner circle of romantics.

On February 25, 1830, the play at last was ready. The Comédie opened its doors to Hugo's friends at two in the afternoon, probably with a view toward controlling their enthusiasm by giving them an eight-hour wait before the performance. Théophile Gautier, one of the determined band that shared this lengthy but unforgettable wait in the darkened house, gives an account of it in his *Histoire du Romantisme.* With snacks, pranks, and recitations from the play about to be presented, the young disciples of Hugo kept up their enthusiasm until the arrival of the Comédie's more conservative traditional audience gave their energy a focus. The opposing parties were already almost at blows when the curtain rose.

> In a sixteenth century bed chamber, illuminated by a tiny lamp, we saw Dona Josefa, dressed in black, with the body of her skirt sewn in black in the fashion of Isabelle the Catholic, listening to the knocks which must have been made at the secret door by the gallant her mistress was expecting:

Serait-ce déjà lui?--C'est bien à l'escalier
Dérobé...

And already the battle was on.[7]

The opening line of the play, running over into the next in obvious defiance of classic usage, was an affront the conservatives could hardly ignore. At once the house was in an uproar. Through the secret door came a King who talked like a commoner and hid in a cupboard like a thief. Each new act, each scene provided fresh outrages, but Hugo's partisans, a formidable force familiar beforehand with the play and strategically located about the house, managed to shout down protesters. More even battles came after the first three nights when Taylor insisted that the smaller regular claque return and the surplus seats be made available to the general public. The demonstrations were now dominated on some nights by friends of the play and on others by its enemies. The insecurity, and in some cases open hostility of the actors added to the confusion. The egocentric Mlle Mars found it difficult to be less important than the play she was appearing in; she was enraged on opening night when Hugo's untrained claque did not even applaud her entrance. Michelot and others tended to omit or mutter the most offensive lines on difficult nights. Taken as a whole, the Hernani presentations seem to have actually changed few opinions; papers hostile to Hugo remained hostile, and his supporters never wavered. The controversy itself, however, was in a way a victory for the romantics. Audiences may have come to the Comédie in sympathy, antagonism, or from simple curiosity, but they came as they had not come since the death of Talma. After such a success, it was clear to all that the romantic drama would have to be dealt with as a new force in the French theatre.

Shortly after seeing Hernani launched, Taylor left for Egypt on a mission to obtain for the French government the obelisk which now stands in the Place de la Concorde. The actors, whose absences he had often protested, were now forced to protest his own, and to call for a commissioner to serve in his place. Hugo and Dumas were suggested, but the choice fell to the less controversial Edouard Mazères. Like most of the lesser Restoration authors, Mazères had built his reputation upon collaborations, and he was primarily known to Comédie audiences as the co-author with Picard of Les Trois Quartiers (1827). His one important success on his own had been Le Jeune Mari (1826), concerning a rich old woman enamored of a young wastrel.

Despite his long association with the theatre, Mazères' administrative skill was slight, and he found the theatre in a situation far from promising. The charges of the classicists that Taylor was ruining the Comédie had some basis in fact. The lavish productions of recent years had attracted audiences, but had left the theatre in 1830 with debts amounting to some 600,000 francs. The July Revolution that year further undermined the theatre, for censorship was again repealed and all restrictions on the rival minor houses withdrawn. Once again the Comédie lost its audiences to the offerings of these rivals--to insignificant but popular occasional plays, anticlerical plays, and political (now largely Bonapartist) plays. Mazères' interest in romanticism does not seem to have been strong, but that school offered him the best hope of meeting increased competition. Here also he could take advantage of at least one aspect of the new freedom, since the disappearance of the censor made available several previously banned romantic works. Hugo's _Marion de Lorme_ would have been a logical choice, but after his difficulties with the Comédie company over _Hernani_, Hugo had decided to have his next production mounted by the Porte-Saint-Martin. Mazères therefore began rehearsals on another previously banned work, Dumas' _Antony_. Difficulties arose immediately. Mars and Firmin disputed endlessly with Dumas, as they had with Hugo; finally Mars left, claiming illness, with no indication of when she might return. Hugo then convinced the discouraged Dumas that their works would always be presented half-heartedly at the Comédie, and _Antony_ in turn was withdrawn for presentation later at the Porte-Saint-Martin.

The two great romantics had thus barely conquered the Comédie when they felt obliged to desert it. Others followed, and the Comédie found itself losing first its new dramatists, then its audiences, and finally its actors. Michelot and Firmin announced that they were going to follow Mlle Mars into a self-imposed exile. Mazères was on the brink of declaring bankruptcy when Taylor returned. Though he had been gone only six months, he found that all of his gains since 1827 had been wiped out. The theatre's debt, heavy enough under his own administration, had enormously increased, and no new stimulant, such as romanticism had earlier provided, was now at hand to regain lost audiences.

Taylor began by solidifying his company, convincing

discouraged members to stay and Mlle Mars to return. He then began the difficult task of winning back his audience by lowering prices and seeking attractive new scripts. The writer whom he found most useful was Casimir Delavigne, a quasi-romantic who had presented his early works to the Comédie, then had been driven to the Odéon by the triumph of the bolder innovators, Hugo and Dumas. The departure of these rivals made him eager to return to the Comédie, bringing with him several still-popular earlier works: _L'École des Vieillards_ (1819), _Les Vêpres siciliennes_ (1819), _Le Paria_ (1821), and _Marino Faliero_ (1829). He also brought a new work, _Louis XI_ (1831), in which for the first time he employed a cautious mixing of genres. The Delavigne works gained a modest success, but otherwise little now went right for Taylor. Some interest was aroused by the historical authenticity of Pyat and Théo's _Les Romans chez eux_ (1832), which featured not only accurate and elaborate costumes, but an attempted reconstruction of Roman speech, gestures, even eating habits. Unhappily, in the course of the play the Emperor Claudius was described as a good ruler for the Romans because he was big, fat, and stupid. The authorities took this as an attack on Louis-Philippe and quickly removed this interesting experiment from the boards.

A censor was now appointed to supervise the Comédie offerings, adding another complication to Taylor's task. He managed to win Hugo back to the Comédie with his _Le Roi s'amuse_, only to have the censor forbid it. A cholera epidemic in 1832 hurt all the theatres, but proved nearly fatal for the Comédie, and in 1833 Taylor abandoned the struggle, and a new administrator was sought.

At this critical period, the actors requested that the administration be turned over to a director, for the first time since the days of Molière. Their choice was Jouslin de la Salle, formerly director of the Porte-Saint-Martin, then of the Odéon, and since 1830 the general _régisseur_ of the Comédie. The selection proved a wise one, for though the new administration was brief (1833 to 1837), it restored the Comédie to financial stability. There were several reasons for this success. First, Jouslin de la Salle was well aware of the uses of publicity. Dumas says that he never had a failure during his management, recalling as an illustration a play by Delavigne that steadily lost customers for each of its first four performances, then enjoyed a run on seats when the director announced that the next six showings were sold out in advance.

Next, Jouslin de la Salle weakened the smaller theatres as sources of competition by introducing to the Comédie even more boulevard influence than had Taylor (though he managed this without ever drawing the criticism Taylor suffered for "debasing" the national theatre). The first evidence of such influence came in the composition of programs. The 1830's saw the development of extremely lengthy spectacles on the boulevards, despite an 1834 ruling requiring theatres to close at 11 p.m. Ten or fifteen-act presentations plus reviews were not at all uncommon at such houses as the Funambules or the Ambigu. Though the Comédie never reached these extremes, a typical bill under Jouslin de la Salle might offer *Phèdre*, a one-act comedy, the third act of *Marie Stuart*, and the second act of *Le Mariage de Figaro*. The sort of scenic realism sought on the boulevard was attempted in the 1834 revival of Diderot's *Le Père de famille*, which boasted the first contemporary exact setting at the Comédie. Historical accuracy was carried to new extremes in Dumas' *Caligula* (1837). The dramatist even requested horses, that popular extra now considered almost standard in such spectacles in other theatres, but the Comédiens would not go that far. After a series of bitter quarrels, Dumas let Caligula's chariot be drawn instead by allegorical girls representing the hours of the day and night (though he still created something of a scandal by selling souvenir medallions in the lobby during the run of the play).

Even more striking was the appearance during this administration of boulevard actors at the national theatre. The first was Pierre Bocage, who had tried unsuccessfully twice before to enter the Comédie. After an unsuccessful debut in 1821, he had retired to the provinces to develop his skill, returning to appear at the Odéon in 1826. A quiet, ascetic actor, he gradually discovered that the roles for which he was best suited were the subdued and melancholy heroes of certain of the *mélodrames*. He achieved his first great success in such a role in Ancelot's *L'Homme du monde* (1827), and this encouraged him to attempt the Comédie again in 1828. Dramas suited to his interpretation were even rarer at the Comédie than at the Odéon, however, and after a few discouraging attempts at the traditional Comédie repertoire, Bocage left for the more congenial Gaîté. A series of successes in such works as Sauvage's *Newgate ou les Voleurs de Londres* (1829) proved that Bocage had indeed discovered his *métier*. The coming of Hugo and Dumas to the boulevards gave him then the opportunity to display his talents in plays of more significance. Crosnier, director of the Porte-Saint-Martin, invited Bocage to appear there in Dumas' Antony (1831) and La Tour de Nesle (1832). He was now at the peak of his career, and contemporary descriptions all agree on the power of his quiet intensity:

> Still young and of high stature, his visage lit by eyes glowing with somber fire, a muffled voice which, in scenes of passion, vibrated brilliantly, his words now calculatedly slow and now violently staccato, a nervous and febrile spirit, an exalted and yet concentrated poetic sense, all gave an ardent and melancholy fire to his playing which had a real and unique attractiveness for spectators.[8]

Bocage's triumphs at the Porte-Saint-Martin assured him recognition as a major romantic actor, and led Jouslin de la Salle to invite him to try his fortunes once again at the Comédie. He remained this time for a full year, bringing new audiences to the theatre but serving also as a focus of conflict. His fellow actors shunned him and complained constantly to the director that Bocage was infecting the theatre with "the poisonous air of the boulevards."[9] Bocage eventually found the animosity too wearing and resigned to return to the Porte-Saint-Martin.

Jouslin de la Salle, not discouraged by this failure, next sought out Marie Dorval, the most noted of the boulevard actresses. Her career was in a number of ways parallel to Bocage's. She too had begun acting in the provinces, indeed her parents were itinerant players. She also had experienced a brief and rather uncongenial encounter with the Comédie, attempting to learn the classic tradition under Lafon in the Conservatoire. In 1818 she joined the company of the Porte-Saint-Martin, and during the next decade contributed greatly to bringing that theatre to pre-eminence among the boulevard houses. Her talent, Gautier observed, was:

> all empassioned; not that she neglected art, but her art came from inspiration. She did not calculate her playing gesture by gesture, or plan out her entrances and exits with a pencil on paper; she put herself into the situation of her role, wed it completely, became it, and acted as the character herself would act. The simplest phrase, an

> interjection, an oh! a mon dieu! she gave with unexpected and electrifying effect, such as the author himself never suspected. She had cries of poignant reality, sobs to break the heart, intonations so natural, tears so sincere, that the theatre was forgotten and one could not believe that the grief was assumed.[10]

This passionate, imaginative, and emotional style made her the perfect partner for the great actors of the Porte-Saint-Martin, Bocage and Frédérick Lemaître. She had shared Bocage's triumph in Dumas' _Antony_, and Jouslin de la Salle was able to tempt her from the theatre where she had made her reputation only by promising to feature her in a revival of this work at the Comédie. Classicists at the Comédie and outside, however, were even more opposed to Dorval than they had been to Bocage. The _Constitutionnel_ urged that "the Théâtre-Français should not descend to these grotesque and immoral exhibitions which are the shame of our times, an affront to public modesty, and a deadly influence in our society,"[11] and the committee of actors empowered to determine the repertoire of the Comédie saw to it that _Antony_ was not presented.

The committee also rejected Alfred de Vigny's _Chatterton_, though it had little of the violence or the romantic turns which many found offensive in _Antony_. The refusal therefore was apparently directed as much against Mme Dorval as against the play, since she was known to be Vigny's mistress, and it was assumed, correctly, that if the play were accepted, he would insist on having her in the leading role of Kitty Bell, Chatterton's landlady. This time, however, the classicists were thwarted, for Louis Philippe himself was interested in Vigny's work, and demanded early in 1835 that the Comédie accept both play and actress. Dorval's gentle and pathetic interpretation became one of her most famous, and insured the success of the play. For the final scene, she requested a staircase down which she half-slid, half-fell to a crumpled heap at the bottom. Her fellow actors, whom she had not warned, were scandalized, many critics fulminated against this "boulevard trick," but audiences were enthralled. Saint-Beuve reported that most of the spectators, himself included, found tears running down their cheeks.[12] The play had one of the longest runs during this administration, and doubtless would have run longer still had not Ligier and Mlle Mars used their influence to promote a revival of Lafosse's _Manlius Capitolinus_ in its place.

From this time on, Mlle Mars was recognized as the leader of the forces within the Comédie opposed to Mme Dorval, and the conflict between the two actresses equalled the notoriety of the Duchesnois-George dispute earlier in the century. In July the Variétés even presented a play by Dumersan called Les Marsistes et les Dorvalistes. The first and only appearance of these powerful rivals in the same play gave to Hugo's Angelo, tyran de Padoue (1835) an interest which so weak an effort would surely not otherwise have obtained. Hugo had planned the two major female roles in this work for Marie Dorval and his protegée, Juliette Drouet, but gave way to the wishes of the Comédie in respect to Mlle Mars. Since the dispute was ultimately over a preference in styles, the confrontation predictably decided little; supporters of Mme Dorval praised her feeling, those of Mlle Mars her spirit. In later tests, where the two appeared at different times in the same role, it was usually found that each was strongest in the scenes where the other was weak. Dorval carried on the battle until 1837, then renounced the national theatre to return to the boulevards.

Though he attempted to restore Hugo, Dumas, and Vigny to the Comédie, Jouslin de la Salle relied far more for his basic repertoire on the popular Casimir Delavigne and Eugène Scribe. Delavigne continued under Jouslin de la Salle's administration to produce his insignificant but popular hybrids of classic and romantic elements--Les Enfants d'Édouard in 1833 and Don Juan d'Austriche in 1835. The Comédie public seems to have ignored the complaints of many critics, such as Gustave Planché of the Revue des deux mondes, who dismissed such works as "flippant and foolish treatments of history."

Scribe appealed to much the same audience as Delavigne--the bourgeoisie that had appeared as a social force in 1815 and which by 1830 had become a major element in French society. Delavigne inspired their loftier passions with liberal social ideals, not without thinly veiled attacks on clericalism and more heavily veiled ones on a strong monarchy. This cautious social moralizing, along with an avoidance of romantic extremes, marks Delavigne as a kind of precursor of the école de bon sens. Scribe's goals were much less elevated. His speciality was clean, light, family entertainment, written in approachable everyday language. The audiences which had supported him at the Gymnase now followed him to the Comédie, a theatre few of them would have thought of attending earlier. Although a few of Scribe's comedies had appeared at the major theatre in the 1820s, it was Bertrand et Raton (1833) which established him as an important Comédie writer, and incidentally set a pattern for comedies of political intrigue which was followed by Scribe himself and by others for a decade after. There is a direct line of descent from Bertrand et Raton to such later Scribean successes as L'Ambitieux (1834), Les Indépendants (1837), and the most popular of all the offerings in this genre, Un Verre d'eau (1840).

Bertrand et Raton also aided Scribe by diverting attention from the tremendous scandal which surrounded his Dix Ans de la vie d'une femme (1832), which shocked many by its realistic portrayal of a case of marital infidelity. Scribe was hardly the first Parisian dramatist to give serious treatment to such a theme. During the Revolution, Beaumarchais' Mère coupable dealt with a similar problem, and Kotzebue's triangle drama, Misanthropie et Repentir, enjoyed a great vogue early in the nineteenth century. Dumas' Antony was the best known of a large number of romantic dramas of unfaithful or at least strongly tempted wives and husbands. Scribe's good bourgeois audiences were appalled, however, to find their favored author dabbling in such salacious material. He probably did not fully redeem himself with many outraged families until 1834, when the Comédie gave his Passion secrète, showing a woman sorely tempted, and with good reason, who was saved however from sin at the last moment. Scribe was careful after this experience to consider the inclinations of his audience, and from the mid-1830's until after 1850 he dominated the French stage, with a far greater following in Paris and abroad than Hugo, Dumas, or Vigny.

3. Romanticism at the Opéra, 1827-1849

The year 1827 was marked at the Opéra by major developments in the dance and in scenic design. The romantic ballet achieved its full flowering overnight with the debut of Marie Taglioni. Her harmony of movement, her effortless grace, her ability to weave intricate pointe work into a unified presentation with never a suggestion of pure technical display, all this was new to her audience, and they were dazzled. For the sixth performance of her debut, the future Opéra director Duponchel threw flowers to her, the first ever thrown on the Opéra stage. The Figaro announced with remarkable clairvoyance: "Here is romanticism applied to the ballet,"[13] for Mlle Taglioni indeed became the greatest ballerina of the new school.

The same year saw the beginning of ballets conceived in part by a professional scenarist. Previously, the choreographer had developed his own action, generally from a play, novel, or comic opera, but the ballet now shook off this derivative character thanks to the popular Scribe, who began to write independent scenarios for dance. He thus completed the revolution begun a decade before by Schenitzhoeffer, who began the practice of conceiving new music for Opéra ballets. La Somnambule (1827) established this new pattern, with music by Hérold, scenario by Scribe, and choreography by Auber. Its leading ballerina was Pauline Montessu.

In the area of scene design, a major reorganization of the Opéra artists gave Ciceri full freedom and launched him on the most influential part of his remarkable career. His studio in the Menus-Plaisirs now worked constantly, training many of the other major designers of the period--Léger, Gigun, Gosse, Philastre, Cambon, Desplèchin, and Charles Séchan, who later founded a school of his own.

Ciceri's period of greatest influence was launched by his designs for La Muette de Portici (1828). An important group of artists contributed to this major success. The script was by the popular librettists Scribe and Delavigne, their first attempt at grand opera, and the music was by Auber, who with this work outdistanced his rivals Boiëldieu and Hérold to be acclaimed as the outstanding French composer of the period. The retirement of Rossini the following year made him the favored author of both the Opéra and the Opéra-Comique. No part of the production drew so much attention, however, as Ciceri's settings, the most elaborate and spectacular any member of the Opéra audience could remember. The crowning effect was the most ambitious example of what was at this time a common spectacle in Parisian theatres--an eruption of Vesuvius. Daguerre's Diorama had begun the fad early in 1827, and soon inspired a Vesuvius designed by Gué for Pixérécourt's Les Ruines de Pompéi at the Gaîté, and another at the Opéra-Comique for Lafortelle and Carafa's Monsaniello. As if all this local volcanic activity were not sufficient, there was envious talk in Paris of an even more spectacular stage Vesuvius on display at

Milan's La Scala for Pacini's Ultimo giorno di Pompeia. Ciceri was sent by the Opéra to Italy to see how the designer Sanquirico had achieved this effect, with the result that Ciceri, combining Sanquirico's devices with the techniques of the diorama, was indeed able to offer the Opéra the most impressive eruption yet mounted. The machinists Ciceri employed, Gromaine and Chatizelle, remained his trusted assistants thereafter, and made spectacular effects an important part of all his designs.

There were also noteworthy side effects of Ciceri's Vesuvius project. He brought back from Italy additional suggestions for local color, so that Hippolyte Lecomte's Neapolitan costumes for the production brought a new aspect of the "picturesque" to the Opéra. The preparation for the final scene was so elaborate that the Opéra was forced to introduce an intermission between the fourth and fifth acts--the first such intermission the theatre had seen. More elaborate productions confirmed this practice; during Rossini's Guillaume Tell, the following year, the curtain had to be lowered for intermissions several times to allow placement of the production's crags, precipices, and Alpine bridges. Ciceri demonstrated his versatility by turning from such romanticized natural settings, first to a realm of pure fantasy for the fairy ballet La Belle au bois dormant (1829), which added to his reputation and that of Mlle Taglioni, and then to settings modeled on the works of Boucher and Watteau for the ballet Manon Lescault (1830) by Scribe, Aumer, and Halévy. As Gautier observed, "the time of purely ocular spectacles had come."[14]

Thus, in the areas of ballet and scene design at least, the Opéra may be said to have entered the romantic period as early as 1827, but the administration most closely associated with that movement is that of Dr. Véron, who arrived in 1830. Since 1816 the theatre had been managed by royal supervisors, none of them notably possessed either of artistic or business acumen. This system was abandoned in 1830 and the older arrangement of private directors operating at their own financial risk was revived. Dr. Véron, the first of these, was a Restoration bourgeois with colossal personal wealth, a necessary qualification for any potential director of this debt-ridden theatre. Like his contemporary, Taylor at the Comédie, Véron recognized that the classic tradition would have to be set aside to attract audiences, and he therefore encouraged the trend already begun toward great spectacles at the Opéra. For scripts he turned usually to

Scribe and his collaborators, for music to Meyerbeer, but almost all emphasis was placed on the decorations, for which Véron engaged Duponchel, already famous on the boulevards as a creator of spectacle theatre. Ciceri now turned his attention more particularly to painting, while Duponchel worked on technical effects. Another important change took place in dance at this same time. The growing importance of Scribe convinced Aumer that ballet was slipping from the control of the choreographer and in 1830 he resigned, just one year after Gardel had retired as instructor of dance for the Opéra. With the last vestiges of the old tradition gone, Véron insured that ballet would take a new direction by engaging Jean Coralli, choreographer of the Porte-Saint-Martin.

A whole new coalition of artists was thus assembled for Véron's first major offering, Scribe and Delavigne's Robert le Diable (1831), a triumphant success. Duponchel was given unlimited funds for the setting, which Véron first visualized as a sort of fantasy Olympus, then allowed his designer to bring closer to romanticized reality. Ciceri conceived an elaborate medieval cloister, with all the effects which perspective and the new gas lighting could achieve, as a setting for Coralli's "Ballet of the Dead Nuns," led by Taglioni, the first dance sequence expressing the full power of romanticism at the Opéra. The massive setting was Ciceri's most famous, remembered for the rest of the century. Later sets were grander or more striking, but the cloister of Robert le Diable clearly marked the change from the old classic settings concentrating on detail to the new romantic ones working with mass and sweeping effects. Duponchel introduced a number of new technical effects as well, most notably English traps for the appearance and disappearance of supernatural characters. Almost the only voice raised against all this display was that of the composer Meyerbeer, who complained justifiably but futilely that his music had been pushed to the background.

The success of Robert le Diable encouraged Véron to present other works whose supernatural themes could justify similar romantic display. Schneitzhoeffer's La Sylphide (1832) sealed the triumph and set the style for romantic ballet--the love of a spirit for a mortal after this became the almost invariable subject of such works, and moonlight, sylvan glades, and ethereal sprites the hallmarks of the genre. Taglioni's personal triumph and that of her anti-classic style were complete. Henceforth Véron ignored the

the traditional "types" of ballet and considered Taglioni his star for any major part, much to the dismay of her rivals, Noblet, Legallois, and Montessu. Her male partner was Jean Perrot, whose debut in 1830 restored some interest in male dancing when the great performers of the Empire, Albert and Paul the aerialist, were almost forgotten. Ciceri's forest scene was one of his masterpieces, Eugène Lami's costumes were equally outstanding (though evidence is lacking to support the tradition that he invented the tutu for this production), and Duponchel first made elaborate use of vols --flying devices for the actors.

La Tentation (1832), by Coralli, Halévy, and Gide, was less distinguished in music and conception but even more elaborate in physical production. Duponchel called upon his sub-designers for six huge scenes. The first was an elaborate but traditional painted hermitage scene in an Oriental desert, executed by Edmond Bertin; but the second, the interior of a volcano designed by Lami, astonished audiences with the first three-dimensional setting on the Opéra stage, a gigantic realistic stairway, ablaze with flame and disappearing into the flies, flanked by two enormous monsters. Down it rushed an army of hundreds of demons, costumed by Paul Lormier with inspiration from Hieronymous Bosch, to perform a hellish orgy before their master Astaroth. Subsequent settings were scarcely less staggering: a fantastic chateau in a snowy park by Roqueplan, an Oriental harem by Feuchères, and a celestial temple with golden stairs by Paul Delaroche. Pauline Duvernay, a debutante whom Véron was hoping to develop into another Taglioni, somehow managed to hold her own against the designers and achieve a measure of personal success.

The costumes for such productions received a care hitherto unknown at the Opéra and, allowing for romantic exaggeration, were the most historically accurate that theatre had yet seen. Certain actors designed their own costumes or called on noted painters such as Delacroix or Raffet, but the majority of the Opéra costumes were conceived by Paul Lormier, Eugène Lami, and Louis Boulanger. For La Tentation, Lormier produced some 700 designs. A masked ball in the climactic scene of Gustave III allowed Duponchel to put hundreds of extras on stage in every conceiveable type of dress, but the major costumes were of the period and place of the play--18th century Sweden. Great care was now similarly taken on properties; for a revival of Don Giovanni in 1834 an exact copy was made, from an original in the

Musée d'Artillerie, of a sword presumably given to the Spaniard by François I.

Early in 1834 Véron added some Spanish dancers to La Muette de Portici, and critical response to this new bit of local color encouraged him to seek a dancer who could oppose the ethereal style of Taglioni with the dashing and earthy dance of Spain. He discovered her in Fanny Elssler, who was launched with great publicity in Coralli, Nourrit, and Schneitzhoeffer's La Tempête (1834) where she was an immediate success. Magnificent sets and costumes by Duponchel, Ciceri and their co-workers contributed to this success.

The coming of Fanny Elssler was significant as an indication of romanticism's gradual development toward realism, a shift which was felt at the same time in settings and costumes. The "exotic" settings of earlier years were now less favored than "accurate" ones, a shift clearly seen in Scribe and Halévy's La Juive (1835), Duponchel's apogee and the best known opera of the time. All the major painters of the theatre--Séchan, Desplechin, Feuchères, Ciceri, Cambon, Dierterle, Philastre--were called upon for the five immense settings, and unprecedented attention was given to historical detail. Paul Lormier designed the costumes directly from the works of Paul Palliot, a 17th century historiographer. Duponchel introduced huge but carefully trained crowds and borrowed the horses of the Cirque Olympique for a magnificent triumphal march. Altogether, the production cost 150,000 francs, more than any previous Opéra offering, 30,000 of it spent on the historically accurate armor alone. The sort of display assembled for La Juive could not soon be repeated, however, for on the one hand even the large audiences Véron had brought to the Opéra could not support such expense, and on the other, criticism was growing of his emphasis on spectacle over music. Some critics referred contemptuously to such offerings as "Duponchellerie," while others now began speaking of the theatre as the "Opéra-Franconi."[15]

The retirement of Véron in the summer of 1835 offered an opportunity to change this emphasis, but in fact Duponchel, so closely tied to Véron's policies, was selected as his successor. Coralli and Gide's Le Diable boiteux (1836) was quite in the tradition of Véron's offerings, a spectacular fantasy ballet capitalizing on the current vogue for things Spanish. Fanny Elssler's performance in it proved her a worthy rival of Taglioni, who maintained the more spiritual side of romanticism in La Fille du Danube the same year. Meyerbeer's Les Huguenots (1836) was greeted as the masterpiece of romantic opera, and its use of contrast and the picturesque indeed exceeded that of its predecessors, though its physical mounting was somewhat less elaborate. Mlle Falcon established herself in this work as Meyerbeer's major interpreter, while male leads were sung by Adolphe Nourrit, now close to retirement, and Gustave Duprez, who was soon to replace him.

The popularity of Duprez compensated for the loss of Nourrit, but Duponchel was widely criticized for the simultaneous loss of Mlle Taglioni, whose contract he allowed to lapse when he found working with her too difficult. He retained Elssler, however, and should have been able to survive the criticism had he continued to manage the theatre with Véron's administrative skill. Duponchel's real interest remained in settings, unfortunately. The theatre's resources dwindled rapidly, and his difficulties in administration now prevented Duponchel from presenting the spectacles he most preferred. When Hugo came in 1836 with a proposal for La Esmeralda, requiring a full-scale painting of Notre Dame to unroll slowly as a backdrop while Quasimodo pantomimed climbing its face, Duponchel dismissed this as too expensive, though it was the sort of effect he had made his specialty a few years before. When the work was finally presented, he stressed authenticity rather than spectacle with the result that the audience hissed settings by Philastre and Cambon which they considered depressing and costumes by Boulanger which were judged sordid. Audiences which had been drawn to the Opéra primarily for the visual displays now began to desert it for such houses as the Cirque-Olympique and Porte-Saint-Martin.

A series of failures for Elssler led many to accuse Duponchel of destroying the ballet to favor the opera, though the opera was itself in scarcely less difficulty. The insecurity of the administration seemed reflected in its authors. Halévy's Guido et Ginevra (1838) was far inferior to La Juive, and Auber's Lac des fées (1839) to La Muette de Portici. Fortunately, as French opera declined, new inspiration again appeared from Italy, this time in the work of one of Rossini's disciples, Donizetti, whose Les Martyrs had been banned in his own country before enjoying a considerable success in French translation in 1840. The same year he produced a purely French work, La Favorite, which introduced an important new ballerina, Carlotta Grisi. Her success was particularly gratifying to Duponchel since Fanny Elssler's health now frequently kept her from the stage. Rosina Stoltz, however, was the Opéra artist most associated with Donizetti's work, making it her own as Mlle Falcon had made Meyerbeer's hers.

In 1840 also, Duponchel decided to return to his position as scenic director, and the directorship of the Opéra passed to Léon Pillet. Pillet's administration presented several important operas--Rossini's Otello (1844), Donizetti's Lucie de Lammermoor (1846)--but in general he allowed his selection of repertoire to be controlled by his soprano Mme Stoltz, whose selections were all too rarely disinterested ones. Public interest in opera, already weakened, declined still further. The ballet, on the other hand, remained generally prosperous. Gautier was inspired by Carlotta Grisi to create a scenario which he brought to the Opéra's new ballet composer, Vernoy de Saint-Georges, for adaptation to the stage. The resulting Giselle (1841) became Grisi's great role, as La Sylphide had been Taglioni's. All the elements of romantic ballet were to be found in this durable work--a rustic first act full of local color, balanced by a mysterious supernatural forest scene in the second; a fragile heroine with an aura of the unearthly; a hopeless love; lyric agony; and a final apotheosis and purification. The composer was Adam, the designers Ciceri and Lormier.

The next decade at the Opéra belonged largely to Grisi, and the ballets in which she appeared were considered both by administration and audiences as the theatre's major efforts. Ciceri, Philastre, and Cambon even returned to the scenic spectacle of Véron's days for such works as Saint-Georges and Adam's La Jolie Fille de Gand (1842) and Gautier and Coralli's La Péri (1843). The ballets of the early 1840's were generally designed to demonstrate Grisi's daring leaps and graceful technique, but Mazilier and Adam's Le Diable à quatre (1845) showed a different side of her talent, by reviving the old light comic ballet of pre-romantic days. Opéra audiences were delighted by this demonstration of Grisi's range, but the genre itself had lost its attractiveness. When Mazilier attempted to repeat his success in Paquita (1846), his choreography was no longer considered quaint, but merely old-fashioned.

Paquita was one of Grisi's last presentations and her retirement, together with Mme Stoltz's in 1847, removed the two main supports of Pillet; he retired in his turn the following year. Duponchel encouraged the journalist Nestor Roqueplan to assume the directorship, and between them a valiant effort was made to revivify the Opéra. The company was restructured and important new artists engaged, most notably the dancer Fanny Cerrito and her husband Arthur Saint-Léon, but the decline of romanticism was well under way, and only occasional echoes of happier years cheered the Opéra of the Second Empire. Roqueplan resigned in 1849, having mounted only one significant offering, Meyerbeer's _Le Prophète_ (1849). The ballet suffered a slower decline than the romantic opera. Saint-Georges and Gautier continued as scenarists, but no poet after Gautier interested himself in this genre, and after the retirement of Adam in 1856, it was several years before the Opéra could find another ballet composer. Thus, though ballet remained important at the Opéra until after 1870, it never again in the century reached the heights it attained during the romantic period.

4. Romanticism at the Odéon and Porte-Saint-Martin, 1828-1848

The visit of the English company to the Odéon in 1828 was one of the few bright spots in a series of catastrophic seasons. Bernard's successors after 1826--Frédérick du Petit-Méré, Thomas Sauvage, Frédérick Lemétheyer --experienced crisis after crisis, despite occasional successes such as Castil-Blaze's adaptation of Mozart's _Don Giovanni_ (1827) and the romantic precursors, _Amy Robsart_ (1828) by Hugo and Paul Foucher and _Roméo et Juliette_ (1828) by Soulié. The company declined steadily. Joanny, Samson, and Périer departed before 1826; Lockroy, Beauvallet, and Mlle Anaïs, all the stars of _Roméo et Juliette_, had within a year after that success left for the Porte-Saint-Martin, the Ambigu, and the Comédie. The Opéra-Comique took away Duprez, the theatre's most popular singer. Thus, when the directorship was assumed by Charles-Jean Harel in 1829 the company was so depleted that most plays could not even be cast, and the theatre was more frequently closed than open.

Harel was the Odéon administrator most associated with the romantic movement, like Taylor at the Comédie and Véron at the Opéra, but Harel never achieved the honor, or even the respectability of these contemporaries. Even among Paris' generally impoverished theatre directors he was notorious not only for the number of his creditors, but for his ability in eluding them. On several occasions he was forced to make his escape by running onto the stage and vanishing through a trap door. The fact that the Odéon could be entrusted to so erratic an administrator is an indication of the desperateness of its situation in 1829. The selection, all the same, proved a wise one. Harel for the first time found himself engaged in an undertaking worthy of his imagination and abilities. His changes in the theatre were sudden, sweeping, and quite effective in regaining the departed audiences. He collaborated with Ciceri in a complete redecoration of the house, cut prices, and brought a whole group of new actors and authors into the theatre. The most important of these was the former tragedienne of the Comédie, Mlle George, now Harel's mistress and the star of a company he had assembled for provincial tours. Lockroy, Ligier, and Mlle Noblet were other significant additions to the Odéon company.

Her eccentric career had not harmed Mlle George's fame. She was generally considered the greatest tragic actress of France, as Mars was considered the greatest player of comedy. Even the extra weight which George had gained during her travels only added to her dignity as a tragic queen. A whole series of romantic historical dramas were written for her. "How many fat queens and oversized empresses we have disinterred from history for her benefit!"[16] exclaimed Gautier. Yet her first role at the Odéon, Dumas' Christine, owed no such inspiration to her. Dumas had written it in 1827, only to see it pushed aside the following year by rival, but unsuccessful, works by Soulié at the Odéon and Brault at the Comédie. At George's request, Harel obtained the play from Dumas and presented it in March of 1830, just one month after Hernani at the Comédie. The classicists who had been demonstrating against Hugo's work now divided their wrath between it and Christine. Dumas, too, was obliged to provide himself with a loyal claque for an opening night almost as tumultuous as that a month before at the Comédie. The play, with leading roles for George and Lockroy, was a great success, and an auspicious beginning for Harel's administration. It also demonstrated that Harel shared the interest of Taylor and Véron in spectacular presentation. All the publicity for Christine noted proudly that he had expended 30,000 francs for the historically accurate costumes by Louis Boulanger and the six huge settings by Ciceri.

Musset's La Nuit Vénitienne, offered in the fall, did not prove attractive, and Harel urged Dumas to create a historical pageant on the life of Napoleon, which he felt both by its subject and its opportunity for scenic elaboration would guarantee him a success. The July Revolution in 1830 which overthrew the Bourbons and restored many aspects of Revolutionary and Empire France encouraged a nostalgia in the theatres for the Napoleonic era. The former persecutor of the minor theatres was therefore now presented in many of them as an embodiment of the nation and its glory. Some theatres presented a whole series of such plays with an actor who made the playing of Napoleon his specialty--Chevallier at the Jeux-Gymnastics, Cazot at the Variétés, Génot at the Opéra-Comique, Gobert at the Porte-Saint-Martin, Béranger at the Vaudeville, Joseph at the Gaîté. Such actors tended for publicity purposes to play this role in public as well as on the stage, so that for some time Napoleons were a common sight on the streets of Paris, stalking alone, scowling, hair combed forward, and hand thrust in coat. Few incidents in the Emperor's life escaped dramatization, requiring a good deal of research on the part of directors, for the public was becoming accustomed to historical exactitude and old soldiers delighted in catching up minor errors in the military spectacles. The Ambigu showed a typical concern when it employed Marchand, who had been Napoleon's valet, to give advice to the theatre's costumer.

According to Dumas, Harel was the first Parisian director to conceive the idea of a Napoleon play after the July Revolution, but Dumas was himself not interested in creating such a play and Harel's rage and frustration grew as he argued vainly with Dumas, month after month, and saw his rivals, one by one, attracting the public with the sort of play he had first imagined. At last, near the end of 1830 Harel invited Dumas to a party, then literally locked him in until the play was written. Under these conditions, Dumas produced the 9000-line drama in a week, and it was ready for presentation at last in January of 1831.

The part of Napoleon in this work was played by a young actor named Frédérick Lemaître, destined to become one of the outstanding artists of the century. His career began early and humbly, as a lion in an 1816 production of Pyrame et Thisbé at the Variétés. Better opportunities then attracted him to the Funambules, where he was seen by the actor Michelot and encouraged to enter the Conservatoire. Here, despite the efforts of Michelot and Lafon, he resisted classical training so successfully that in 1819, when he applied to the Odéon, only one vote was cast in his favor. Interestingly enough, however, that one vote was from Talma, whose place in the public esteem Lemaître would ultimately assume. He was finally accepted in 1820, but his roles were small, his prospects slight. By 1823 he was back on the boulevards at the Ambigu, where he gained his first major success. Cast as the villain Robert Macaire in a third-rate melodrama, L'Auberge des Adrets, Lemaître conceived the idea of exaggerating the clichés and encouraging the audience's laughter. Only Firmin, the actor who played his cohort Bertrand, was in on the plot; their exaggerated costumes and delivery were as much a surprise to their fellow actors as they were to the public and to the stunned authors. Overnight, Lemaître became famous, and the character of the dashing and unscrupulous Macaire was ever after associated with him. A lesser but significant triumph in the melodrama Cagliostro (1825) caused several papers to begin referring to him as "the Talma of the boulevards."

In 1827 the Ambigu burned and Lemaître was engaged by Montguet of the Porte-Saint-Martin. His first performance there was in the leading part of Victor Ducange's Trente Ans ou la Vie d'un joueur, which became the most popular melodrama of the period in France and a great favorite in England. The spreading of the action over thirty years allowed Lemaître to demonstrate the range of his talent by portraying the same character at various ages as well as in successive stages of degeneration. The gambler's wife Amélie was portrayed by Marie Dorval, whose passionate, inspired style seemed a perfect match for Lemaître's. A series of successes followed in 1828 and 1829 for Lemaître and Dorval. Jules Janin considered that these two players, working together, carried out "a complete revolution in the art of drama."

> The audience, used to the shrill tones of melodrama, with its shouting and uproar, looked at each other in astonishment, moved and delighted by such simplicity and grace. Frédérick Lemaître was then a handsome young man, admirably suited for his art, fiery, passionate, violent and proud, while Mme Dorval, with her slightly stooped figure, had everything necessary to command the deepest compassion.[17]

Baron Taylor was so impressed by these productions that he offered Lemaître a position at the Comédie, but the actor's reputation was now such that he considered the minor position of a pensionnaire at the national theatre a step down, and he refused. Probably he would have remained on the boulevards permanently had not the bankruptcy first of the Porte-Saint-Martin, then of the recently opened Ambigu, both in 1830, driven him to accept an offer from Harel at the Odéon.

Lemaître made his Odéon debut just before the July Revolution, so that he was establishing his reputation there during the same months that Harel was pursuing Dumas for the Napoleon script. His debut in Les Vêpres siciliennes proved him a worthy partner for Mlle George. He followed this with successful revivals of Ducis' Hamlet and Othello, but his greatest popularity was gained in contemporary drama, such as Empis and Mazères' La Mère et la fille (1830). His portrayal of Dumas' Napoleon was not one of Lemaître's great parts, but it was a success achieved against obstacles as formidable as any he had faced thus far in his career. First, he had to convince an audience some of which could compare him to the Emperor himself and most of which had at least seen a variety of other Napoleonic interpreters at other theatres. A second and probably more formidable obstacle was the rest of the production, which the publicity emphasized had cost Harel one hundred thousand francs. The audience had been asked to wear their National Guard uniforms and an orchestra played military marches in each interval. Applause greeted the spectacular settings of each of the drama's twenty-three scenes, with particular acclaim given to the burning of Moscow and the crossing of the Beresina, scenes consisting almost entirely of spectacle. The horses from Franconi's circus, which Dumas had been refused by the Comédie, were of course found here in abundance. Not surprisingly, Harel was criticized by many for debasing a major house, and some papers, recalling the term "Duponchellerie" which had been applied to similar spectacle at the Opéra, began to suggest that a related disease, "Harelisme," was now infecting the Odéon.[18] The trend was a general one, however, as E. N. Viollet-le-Duc noted in his Précis de l'art dramatique (1830):

> Although the material part of the setting did not at first seem to us to be integral to the study of dramatic art, we later considered that we might perhaps be reproached for omitting this accessory

> .... No one even questions whether increasing perfection in setting means progress in the art. We must submit to the necessity... for it would today be risking the fate of a dramatic work to abandon it to the talent of the author alone, without asking the aid of the painter, the machinist, the tailor, and the extras.[19]

Rather ironically, while the Odéon was presenting Dumas' immense historical pageant, the Porte-Saint-Martin, traditionally the home of spectacle drama, was preparing a conventional literary work by the same author. The Porte-Saint-Martin had gained a new director, Crosnier, in 1828, and he encouraged Dumas to bring his _Antony_ to the boulevards when it ran into difficulties at the Comédie. This shocking drama, dealing with the forbidden subjects of bastardy and adultery in a contemporary setting, and admirably acted by Bocage and Marie Dorval, was one of the great successes of the romantic drama. Its famous climax showed such drama at its most passionate and melodramatic. The outcast Antony, caught _in flagrante delicto_ with Adèle, a married woman, stabs her and throws the dagger at the feet of her husband with a line that was as widely quoted and admired in the period as the notorious opening of _Hernani_: "She resisted me, so I killed her!" Only the social upheaval of the period made possible so violent a departure from what had hitherto been the accepted norms, and even so, opinion was sharply divided as to the merit of the work. Lemaître said the fourth act of _Antony_ as played by Dorval and Bocage was the finest thing he had ever seen, and the _Figaro_ noted that Dorval "cried as people do cry, with genuine tears; she shrieked as people do shriek, cursed as women do curse, tearing her hair, casting her flowers aside, rumpling up her dress to the knees without any consideration for the standards of the Conservatoire." All this passion was lost on the _Constitutionnel_, however, which complained glumly: "For some time we have not been able to take our daughters to the theatre; now we can no longer take our wives."[20] In 1834 when censorship was restored, one of the first plays to disappear was _Antony_, but its outspoken treatment of forbidden subjects nonetheless made it the herald of the problem plays of the next generation.

After Dumas, the Porte-Saint-Martin played host to Hugo, but the eagerly awaited _Marion de Lorme_ (1831) proved something of a disappointment. Dorval, who had refused an offer from the Comédie to remain the boulevard's chief interpreter of romantic drama, once again justified that title, but her fellow-actors were less successful. Gobert had so associated himself with Napoleon that the audience refused to accept him as Louis XIII, and Bocage's melancholy mien, so effective in Antony, did not suit the role of Didier. Moreover, the opening was overshadowed by rumors that Crosnier had just sold the theatre--Crosnier, who had brought Hugo and Dumas to the boulevard and centered the attention of the literary world on the Porte-Saint-Martin. Fears that an impotent or reactionary administration might follow seemed confirmed when Crosnier's successor was announced, a minor entrepreneur named Léry. Yet just two months later, in October of 1831, the theatre's prospects brightened. It was announced that Léry had in turn sold the theatre to Harel.

Harel's exact motives for purchasing the Porte-Saint-Martin have been much disputed, but it is clear that the directorship of the Odéon had for some time been growing increasingly irksome to him. While Crosnier was praised for bringing the major romantics to his theatre on the boulevard, Harel, like Taylor, was often condemned for bringing boulevard influence to a major theatre. Moreover, Harel's passion for scenic display was expensive and since the accession of Louis Philippe the Odéon subsidy had steadily diminished. A major success would have relieved this problem, but Dumas' promising Napoleon play barely paid its own way. Then came Vigny's La Maréchal d'Ancre, which its author had conceived for his mistress Marie Dorval at the Porte-Saint-Martin, but which Crosnier, already committed to Antony and Marion de Lorme, was not able to accept. The play probably benefited, for the leading role was less romantic than tragic, and so more within the range of the Odéon's Mlle George than Marie Dorval's, yet its success was modest, and of little aid in Harel's financial difficulties. There were, finally, rumors that Harel's purchase of the Porte-Saint-Martin was actually the idea of Mlle George, who felt disposed to dispute the leadership of the new school with Dorval and could best do this in the theatre which was now the center of romanticism, rather than relying on the occasional works of romantic tone such as La Maréchal d'Ancre which chance brought to the Odéon.

The purchase worked to Harel's advantage as well as to the theatre's. The Porte-Saint-Martin had at this time no rival in Paris, except perhaps the Comédie itself. No other theatre recovered so quickly from the general financial crisis of 1830. No other had so varied a repertoire, or appealed to so wide a spectrum of the public. Diplomatic circles favored the Opéra, students the Odéon, small bourgeoisie the Vaudeville and Variétés, but everyone, save a few embittered classicists, came to the Porte-Saint-Martin. By directing two theatres, Harel could balance profits and casts between them, and the combined companies provided him with a group of actors at least equal to the Comédie company, and even superior in the interpretation of contemporary works. These resources allowed Harel to present two new plays by Dumas almost simultaneously near the end of 1831: *Charles VII chez ses grands vassaux* at the Odéon and *Richard Darlington* at the Porte-Saint-Martin. Both plays placed strong emphasis on scenic display. Real armor was borrowed from the Musée d'Artillerie and a variety of live animals and birds appeared in a hunting scene in *Charles VII*. Séchan, a pupil of Ciceri and later founder of his own school, designed elaborate English interiors and exteriors for *Richard Darlington*, which was based on a novel by Scott.

Mlle George appeared with Ligier in *Charles VII*, and the obvious choice to play opposite Lemaître in *Richard Darlington* would have been Marie Dorval. Few doubted, therefore, when Harel assigned the female lead to the relatively obscure Louise Noblet that this was the opening move in a campaign planned by Harel and Mlle George to remove Dorval from her pre-eminence in the theatre. Mlle Noblet acquitted herself well, but the honors of *Richard Darlington* went to Lemaître, who made this villainous politician one of his greatest creations. The scene just after his murder of Jenny (Mlle Noblet) by pushing her from a balcony was as famous a moment in the romantic theatre as Marie Dorval's fall in *Chatterton*. Legouvé has left a graphic description of it:

> He had placed in the wings a jet of colored light which, falling on his face, turned him absolutely green. Then, to complete the effect, he arranged with the actress playing Jenny that in fleeing terrified toward the balcony she would let drop her muslin veil. This veil, lying on the ground, was the first object that struck Frédérick's eyes as he came back on stage. Another man would have trembled to see this veil, as if seeing Jenny's spirit. But what did Frédérick do? He ran to the veil, hastily snatched it up and thrust it into his pocket like a handkerchief. At this moment his new father-in-law rapped at the door, and he

> went to open it with that insolent ease which only he could assume, while the end of the veil fluttered from his pocket. It was terrifying![21]

Despite the advantages in controlling two theatres, Harel, like all Parisian directors, found 1832 a most difficult year. In addition to continuing political turmoil, the capital now suffered a cholera epidemic, and though Harel did not hesitate to advertise that no case of the disease could be traced to any theatre, attendance was slight. Dumas tells of one occasion when the Odéon company was forced to play before a single patron who refused to have his money returned. Happily, Dumas reports, he made the mistake of hissing, and police were called to turn him out for disturbing the performance. The total failure of Saint-Hilaire's Dik-Rajah (1832) convinced Harel that he could no longer afford to manage the Odéon. Not only were expenses ruinous and audiences small, but Harel suffered his severest criticism yet for mounting a play in France's second national theatre in which one of the major performers was an elephant. The departure of Harel merely increased the Odéon's problems, however, since he took almost everything with him--actors, scenery, and repertoire. The government, to keep the theatre open at all, had little choice other than to turn it into an alternate house where Paris' other theatres could from time to time perform, and it operated under this arrangement until 1841.

The large company at Harel's disposal allowed him to be rather cavalier in his treatment of even his best actors. He kept Marie Dorval in secondary parts, doubtless to please Mlle George, he quarrelled with Lemaître, and actually dismissed Bocage. Dumas, who insisted on Bocage for his Teresa (1832), was forced to rent the Ventadour for a special production. Bocage was supported by Dumas' mistress, Ida Ferrier, and a company accustomed to presenting only comic opera; even Dumas later classed this production among his worst. Later in the year, however, Harel rehired Bocage to appear opposite Mlle George in Dumas' Tour de Nesle, one of the greatest successes of the romantic theatre. Dumas, at Harel's request, had reworked this drama from a play submitted to the Porte-Saint-Martin by an unknown young dramatist, Frédérick Gaillardet. A bitter dispute arose as to which author was really responsible for the success of the play, a dispute judiciously encouraged by Harel, who sensed its publicity value, and which led finally to an inconclusive duel between the embittered authors. The truth seems to be that Gaillardet provided the basic plot and Dumas most of the touches of flamboyant melodrama which make the play so striking an example of the genre. Dumas' own description of a single scene gives a suggestion of the whole:

> The end of the second act had a terrific effect. Buridan leaping from the window into the Seine, Marguerite tearing off her mask to reveal her blood-stained cheek, and crying 'Show me your face and then let me die--that's what you said, isn't it? Then it shall be as you desire... Regard, and die!'--all this had a striking and terrible effect. And when after the orgy, the flight, the assassination, the laughter subsiding into groans, the man flung into the river, the lover of a night mercilessly murdered by his royal mistress--when after all this, the unexpected and calm voice of the night watch was heard calling 'Three o'clock and all's well. Sleep quietly, people of Paris,' the audience burst into a storm of applause.[22]

Lemaître, who had left Paris as a result of the epidemic, was convinced that Harel and Mlle George had mounted the play at this time and hired Bocage as a personal affront to him, especially when Dumas admitted that he had written the part of Buridan with Lemaître in mind. Not until Bocage went to the Comédie near the end of 1832 did Lemaître have an opportunity to prove the superiority of his interpretation.

Harel's next major offering was Hugo's Lucrèce Borgia (1833) which the director's scenic display and the talents of Mlle George and Lemaître made the rage of Paris for several months. The romantic drama had never come closer to mélodrame than this, in situations, in settings, even in means of production, for Hugo allowed Harel to use music for entrances, exits, and high points in the action. These major successes by Dumas and Hugo made Harel's Porte-Saint-Martin unquestionably the center of the Paris theatre, but his dominance was shortlived. The long-expected break between Harel and Dorval and Lemaître was not far off, stimulated by the Marquis de Custine's Béatrix Cenci (1833). The play had been first accepted, then refused by the Comédie, and Harel agreed to take it only if the author would bear all expenses. The Marquis agreed, but demanded in return that the major roles be given to Lemaître and Marie Dorval. Harel sought the approval of

Mlle George, who accepted this choice of her rival so willingly that many speculated that she expected Dorval, who had made her reputation in prose drama, would suffer a crushing failure in poetic tragedy. If so, she was quite mistaken, for the play was very warmly received. If her motives were unclear before, they became unmistakable now. She demanded that Harel close the successful work after three performances. He complied, but at enormous cost, both financial and professional. The frustrated public protested. Ciceri, who had created luxurious settings with the generous support of the Marquis, was enraged. Dorval left immediately on tour, and not long after accepted an offer to enter the Comédie. Lemaître actually came to blows with Harel and vowed never to return to his theatre.

Fortunately for Harel, Bocage had already become disillusioned with the Comédie and was willing to return to the Porte-Saint-Martin for Hugo's _Marie Tudor_ (1833). Mlle George, of course, had a major role, but Hugo had created a second female part, almost as large, which he insisted be given to Juliette Drouet, who had played a minor part in _Lucrèce Borgia_ and subsequently became the dramatist's mistress. Juliette's talent was apparently slight anyway, and the combined animosity of Bocage, Harel, and Mlle George so undermined her confidence that her performance was greeted by devastating reviews. Her first major part was also her last, and Hugo, blaming her failure on Harel and the other actors, left the Porte-Saint-Martin for good.

Not even Mlle George profited from this new disaster, since the departure of Hugo left Harel heavily dependent upon Dumas, and Dumas supported his own protegée, Ida Ferrier. Her appearance with Bocage and Lockroy in Dumas' _Angèle_ (1833) and _Catherine Howard_ (1834) proved her superior at least to Juliette Drouet, but neither play won much critical acclaim. Dumas was clearly repeating the techniques of his previous successes; the decline of the romantic drama, and of Harel's Porte-Saint-Martin, was under way. The desperate director sought to attract audiences by enormous spectacles, but the sort of productions upon which he had built his fortune now rapidly consumed it. Each such undertaking left the theatre poorer than before: Dumas' _Don Juan de Marana_ (1836), a gargantuan seven-hour fairy spectacle which launched the career of the actor Mélingue; _La Guerre des servantes_ (1837) by Théaulon and Alboise, with settings by Philastre and Cambon; and Mallian's _La Fille de l'Emir_ (1839), featuring a travelling menagerie. When in 1839

Balzac appeared with an offer to write a play based on the character Vautrin from his Le Père Goriot, Harel seized on this as a last opportunity to save his theatre, even though it meant reconciling himself with his old enemy Frédérick Lemaître, who Balzac insisted must play the leading role. When Vautrin was finally completed, even Balzac privately admitted it was a very weak play, but what turned it into a disaster was the appearance of Lemaître in the fourth act wearing a wig which made him closely resemble the King. Lemaître later denied that he was aware of any resemblance until the audience pointed it out, while Balzac insisted that Lemaître planned the effort as an act of vengeance on his old enemy Harel. Whatever the truth, Louis-Philippe had the play banned at once on the grounds of immorality, and Harel, already on the brink of bankruptcy, retired from his directorship and departed on tour with Mlle George. The Porte-Saint-Martin was closed, its outstanding company dispersed.

The theatre again came to prominence for a brilliant, brief period the following year when two brothers, Théodore and Hippolyte Cogniard, reopened it for a series of revivals of the great successes of the romantic theatre with Marie Dorval and Frédérick Lemaître. Unhappily, they could find no significant new works to present once these revivals were over. For the rest of their administration, which lasted until 1848, they alternated spectacular ballets and fairy plays with mediocre dramas and melodramas such as Eugène Sue and Prosper Goubaux' Les Mystères de Paris (1844), Adolphe Dennery's Marie-Jeanne (1845), and Félix Pyat's Le Chiffonnier de Paris (1847), productions made significant only by the brilliant interpretations of Dorval or Lemaître.

In 1841, after eight years of presenting visiting companies, the Odéon was reorganized as an independent venture, and during the 1840's it presented dramatists and plays distincly more important than those offered by the Porte-Saint-Martin, though never with great financial success. Of the four administrations of this period, the most significant was unquestionably that of A. Lireux, from 1842 to 1845. He worked unceasingly in all genres, presenting more new plays during his three-year directorship than any other theatre in Paris offered during the entire decade. None of the great romantics, but other authors associated with the Porte-Saint-Martin such as Balzac and Harel, now appeared here.

Lireux was particularly interested in encouraging new dramatists, and most of the memorable works of his administration were by previously unknown authors. Paul Meurice and Auguste Vacquerie, writing together under the name Léon Marcel, produced a series of interesting works. Falstaff (1842), a triumph for the actor Louis Monrose, showed their ability at adapting Shakespeare to the French stage, and in 1844 they gained further success with an adaptation of Antigone. For this notable production, Lireux converted the Odéon so far as possible into a Greek stage, with a false forestage built for the orchestra, and the prompter's box covered with grapes, olive branches, and ivy to suggest Dionysiac observances. The curtain fell instead of rising to open the play, in imitation of Roman practice, and there were even choric dances, to the music of Mendelssohn.

The theatrical career of Léon Gozlan was most successfully launched in 1842 with La Main droite et la main gauche, which had been banned at a boulevard theatre the year before because authorities feared it might cause offense to Queen Victoria. The charge apparently came from the English setting of the play rather than its plot, a comic-opera dilemma of a Queen who is torn between marriage with a Prince and with an adventurer. In any case, the censor's objections disappeared when Gozlan changed the setting to Sweden, and the controversy doubtless increased the play's popularity. The major roles were taken by Bocage and Marie Dorval, who for the next few years appeared here as well as at the Porte-Saint-Martin.

The two most important dramatists introduced by Lireux were surely François Ponsard and Emile Augier, whose plays at the Odéon served as a sort of transition between the romantic theatre and that of the Second Empire. Ponsard's Lucrèce (1843) was a minor historical drama of early Rome, clearly the work of a student of literature rather than of the theatre. Its scholarship was sound, its language subdued but pleasant, and its plot totally lacking in tension, surprise, reversals, even distinct character delineation. Lireux, however, was clever enough to capitalize on these defects and announce the work as a symbol of return to "reasonable" theatre after the excesses of romanticism. He did not hesitate to call Ponsard a new Racine and invite the literary and artistic world of Paris to private readings before the opening. The romantics, of course, rallied their forces to condemn the work, and the resulting controversy guaranteed the work a large audience, whatever its merits.

The opening recalled that of Hernani, with the official claque absent and the theatre filled with partisan groups. Lireux's gamble succeeded. The play won wide praise from the general public and the literary world. The Académie awarded Ponsard a prize, and the government increased the Odéon subvention in recognition of the success. The play itself quickly faded. Revived in the fall, it created little stir and, after another undistinguished revival at the Comédie in 1848, totally disappeared from the stage. Its initial success doubtless owed something to the excellent interpretations of Dorval and Bocage, but surely more important was its symbolic function as a rejection of the romantic drama. The public enthusiasm for Lucrèce seems clearly to have been based less on an appreciation of the merits of that play than on a desire for a new direction in the theatre. Within the next few years a series of works by Ponsard and others continued to stress regular structure, simple and natural situations, and an unaffected tone. Achille Ricourt identified them as a new movement with the term the école du bon sens.

Ultimately the only truly important member of this school was Émile Augier, who became one of the major dramatists of the Second Empire. Lireux, who had been ready enough to promote Ponsard, was ironically unaware of Augier's promise, but the Parisian critics were more perceptive. La Ciguë (1844), a little comedy set in classic Greece, was widely praised as an important new contribution to the école du bon sens. Among its warmest admirers was Jules Sandeau, critic of the Revue de Paris, who later collaborated with Augier. Ponsard's second tragedy, Agnès de Méranie (1846), was a complete failure, but Augier went on from success to success with Homme de bien (1845) l'Aventurière (1848) and Gabrielle (1849). Such works clearly looked forward to Second Empire social drama, while the romantic drama was quietly disappearing.

5. Théâtre-Italien and Opéra-Comique, 1830-1850

During the 1830's, as one may see in the Parisian novels of Balzac and Mérimée, the Théâtre-Italien was much in vogue, rivaling even the Opéra as the preferred resort of society. This popularity was largely due to two men: Severini, who became regisseur in 1825, and Robert, who became director in 1830. Before assuming his charge,

Robert visited Italy to discover new composers, singers and musicians, even gaining the aid of Rossini in his search. He arranged to share his performers with the Italian Opera in London, and could thus considerably increase the attractiveness of his offers to them. His return to Paris was therefore shortly followed by a series of important debuts: Luigi Lablanche, the great bass, in 1830, Tamburini and Giulia Grisi in 1832. Nor did Robert confine his search for talent to Italy; in addition to the Grisis, the Persianis, the Albertazzis, and the Marios, his company included the Russian Ivanoff, the Swedish Mlle Schultz, and the Austrian Mlle Ungher.

Most of the operas presented by this theatre were the work of Donizetti and Bellini, the popular and fecund composers who served as a bridge in Italian opera between the greater geniuses, Rossini and Verdi. Anna Bolena (1830) was Donizetti's first great success, and also the first work which showed his musical independence from his master Rossini. The older composer's retirement from the theatre the year before, of course, made this triumph by Donizetti the more striking and significant. Anna Bolena was presented in Paris and London the following year, bringing further fame not only to its composer but to Lablanche, its major interpreter. Mario Faliero (1835) and Lucia di Lammermoor (1836) continued Donizetti's popularity. Yet in Paris an even greater following was inspired by Bellini, whose La Sonnambula shared with Anna Bolena the honors of the year 1831. Thereafter almost every season saw a new Bellini success. A fire in 1837 almost totally destroyed the Italien, and its company sought refuge at the Odéon, which was at this time without a troupe of its own. They remained there until 1841, when the Ventadour was remodeled for their use. At the Odéon they added to their repertoire Bellini's last success, Beatrice, and Donizetti's Roberto Devereux, L'Elisir d'amore and Lucrezia Borgia. Though the company remained an outstanding one, the departure of Robert in 1839 ended this most productive period.

During the early 1840s the Italien continued to rely on the works of Donizetti, but public interest in such offerings as Don Pasquale (1843) was slight. The new director, Vatel, sought in Italy a fresh impetus for his declining theatre, and thus introduced the first works of Giuseppi Verdi to Paris: Nabucco in 1845, Ernani and I Due Foscari in 1846. The Verdi productions did stimulate some interest, but not enough to rescue an otherwise disastrous administration. By 1850 the theatre's fortunes were so low that no French entrepreneur could be found to direct it, so it became a kind of extension of the Italian Theatre in London, under the direction of the English administrator, Lumley.

The years 1827 to 1832 were very difficult ones for the Opéra-Comique, but some stability came with Crosnier, who as director of the Porte-Saint-Martin had brought the major dramatists of the romantic movement to the boulevards. Between 1834 and 1845 he gave the Opéra-Comique a commanding lead in Paris' lyric theatre. For his libretti he relied almost entirely on the prolific Eugène Scribe, who by 1835 was better known in Paris and abroad than Vigny or even Hugo. The same composers now supplied the Opéra-Comique that supplied the Opéra. Auber was the favored author in both houses, the high point of his collaboration with Scribe being Le Domino noir in 1837. The other major composers were Halévy and Adam. Donizetti was represented by La Fille du régiment (1840), and Louis Clapisson, a follower of Adam, made a promising debut with La Figurante (1838) followed by a major success with Scribe in Le Code noir (1842).

To present these works, Crosnier assembled an outstanding company, headed by Roger, Mocker, Henri, and Mme Henri Potier, and by 1840 had made the theatre so profitable that he could commission the architect Charpentier to build a new Salle Favart to house it. The brief administration (1845-1848) of Crosnier's successor André Basset was unable to sustain this remarkable productivity. The single major new work was Berlioz' Damnation de Faust (1846), which, despite the talents of Roger, Hermann-Léon, and Mme Hortense Maillard, failed upon its first presentation and had to await a more favorable verdict in later revivals. The theatre-going public of 1846 much preferred the insubstantial Gibby la cornemeuse of Clapisson, Leuven, and Brunswick.

6. Rachel and the Comédie, 1837-1858

In 1837 Jouslin de la Salle, suspected of financial manipulation, was forced to resign as director of the Comédie. The government's concern over the theatre's economic condition was clearly reflected in the selection of the new administrator. Several candidates who were dramatists or theatre artists were passed over in favor of Vedel, a financier. Whatever the expectations, his directorship was a short and stormy one. By 1838 he was engaged in open battle with his actors, the bitterness of which contributed greatly to the establishment in 1840 of a protective union for actors similar to that organized by authors in 1829. The same year Buloz, the editor of the Revue des Deux-Mondes, took Vedel's place. Yet Vedel's brief administration ultimately proved one of the most significant of this generation, for it saw the first triumphs of Rachel, indisputably the most prominent and influential member of the company since Talma.

Rachel was born Elisabeth Félix in Switzerland in 1821 and came to Paris with her family in 1830. She began her public career singing in cafés, then in 1837 was accepted by the Gymnase. The Scribean comedies there were poorly suited to her thin body and rich, deep voice, but Samson of the Comédie sensed in her a gift for classic tragedy, and arranged for her to present a series of classic revivals at the Comédie in the summer of 1838, beginning as Camille in Horace. For all of these revivals, audiences were small and dispirited. It was the middle of summer, and then as now, Paris was hot and deserted. Some critics, most notably Dr. Véron, spoke in praise of the debutant, but the influential Journal des Débats remained silent. Fréderic Soulié was its summer editor, and as a dedicated opponent of classic tragedy, he saw nothing significant in this new interpreter.

It was a different story when Jules Janin, the regular critic, returned from Italy in the fall. His enthusiasm for Rachel brought the Comédie crowds such as it had not seen in years; by October, the theatre was as popular as in the golden days of Talma and Mlle Mars. Even Louis Philippe, who was never particularly interested in the theatre, came to see and congratulate the new star. Rachel's three-year contract was cancelled on October 1 and renewed with doubled salary. Revivals of Cinna, Andromaque, Iphigénie en Aulide, Tancrède, and Mithridate added to her glory and to her income. Urged by her mercenary father, she demanded constant salary increases, from eight to twelve to twenty thousand francs annually. Even her supporters, Samson and Janin, protested, but Vedel met every request, thereby considerably hastening the collapse of his administration.

Buloz, who succeeded Vedel in 1839, was much less

tractable and had, moreover, a distinct inclination toward bringing back romanticism. Rachel was now given fewer new roles and her creations were greeted with less enthusiasm. Doubtless this reaction came in part from enemies envious of her rapid success, but Rachel herself seemed for several years after 1839 to have lost something of the spirit which had propelled her to her dominant position at the Comédie. She created only a single role in 1839, Esther, a calm, mild, quietly suffering figure which was coldly received by both critics and public. Her aloofness and lack of feeling in this and subsequent works were strongly condemned. She was accused of repeating herself, and even Janin cruelly remarked that in Mithridate she presented "one of her three characters."[23]

Guyon, another actor with an inclination toward classic drama, made an impressive debut in the fall of 1840, but the genre gained little by his arrival since he clearly lacked the power to serve as a regular partner for Rachel. As Gautier was later to observe, Rachel was never fortunate enough to find a male actor to complement her as Lemaître had complemented Dorval. Assured of her superiority, Rachel generally performed with all the worst faults of an egocentric star, ignoring all others with her on stage. The Comédie could do little, since Rachel was now its single major talent; this same fall saw the farewell appearance of Mlle Mars the younger, Rachel's only possible female competition. Despite her uncooperativeness, Rachel could demand and receive for 1841 a salary of 60, 000 francs (an amount equal to that received by the prime minister Guizot the same year for governing the nation) and a leave of three months to spend on tour in England.

Little wonder that she returned in the fall of 1841 to enemies more numerous and hostile than ever. Janin and other critics attempted to humble her by supporting a young rival, Mlle Maxime. The inevitable confrontation between the two took place in October in a revival of Marie Stuart with Maxime as Elizabeth, Rachel as Mary. Mlle Maxime's defeat was complete, her supporters reduced to silence. She remained with the theatre for another ten years, and was only once proposed for a major role. This was in 1843 when the Comédie presented Hugo's last play, Les Burgraves. A leading part in a Hugo play would have been unthinkable for Rachel, and the Comédie countered Hugo's suggestion of Mlle George or Dorval with Mlle Maxime. Eventually, a compromise was reached with Mme Mélingue of the Porte-

Saint-Martin, who soon after was made a *sociétaire*. Hugo, anticipating another *Hernani*, is said to have sent to the painter Nanteuil for three hundred young men, only to be told "youth is a thing of the past." The tumult of *Hernani* did apparently belong to another era, for the opening of *Les Burgraves* was quiet, pleasant, and almost insignificant. So little public interest was aroused, in fact, that Maurice Levaillent called this opening the Waterloo of romantic drama.

The popularity which Rachel restored to the classics was doubtless one of the causes contributing to the decline of the romantic drama, but the virtual failure of *Les Burgraves* actually came during a period when the great actress too was having difficulty maintaining her hold on the public. Audiences found her totally unacceptable as Chimène in an 1842 revival of *Le Cid*, her first creation as a *sociétaire*. Her flawless delivery actually worked against her in Thomas Corneille's mediocre *Ariane* and Lemercier's *Frédégonde et Brunehaut* by emphasizing every flaw in their versification. She first presented *Phèdre* in 1843, but lacked the maturity which would eventually make this her greatest role. Many still remembered Duchesnois, dead ten years before, and their comparison was rarely in Rachel's favor. Her first parts in new plays written especially for her, Mme de Girardin's *Judith* (1843) and *Catherine II* (1844), were total failures.

Then, in 1845, two major successes returned Rachel to the popularity of her first years at the Comédie. First came *Virginie*, by Latour de St. Ybors, a minor contributor to the *école de bon sens*, Rachel's first clear success in a work by a contemporary author. Shortly after, *Phèdre* was revived, and Rachel's mature interpretation was generally accepted as one of the great roles of the century. George Henry Lewes has left a stirring description of her effect:

> Her entrance as she appeared, wasting away with the fire that consumed her, standing on the verge of the grave, her face pallid, her eyes hot, her arms and hands emaciated, filled us with a ghastly horror; and the slow, deep, mournful toning of the apostrophe to the sun, especially in that closing line:
>
> *Soleil, je te viens voir pour la dernière fois*
>
> produced a thrill such as no *spoken* language

> seemed capable of producing: one looks to music only for such emotion.... In the second act, where she declares her passion, Rachel was transcendent. There was a subtle indication of the *diseased* passion, of its fiery but unhealthy--irresistible and yet odious--character, in the febrile energy with which she portrayed it. It was terrible in its vehemence and abandonment; eloquent in its horror; fierce and rapid, as if the thoughts were crowding upon her brain in tumult, and varied with such amazing compass of tones, that when she left the scene our nerves were quivering with excitement almost unsupportable.[24]

These two great successes were not an unmixed blessing for the Comédie, however, since Rachel's demands increased in proportion to her fame. She now began adding extended tours to the burden of her huge salary, removing from the theatre its major source of income. In 1846 she toured Holland and England for five months, and returned only to request a two-month leave for illness. When this was refused, Rachel attempted to resign, but was refused on the grounds that the Moscow Decree required ten years' service and a year's notice from a *sociétaire*. This was Rachel's first serious quarrel with the Comédie since her majority had freed her from her avaricious father, but such quarrels became all too common in the years that followed. The Comédie suffered another blow in 1846--the loss of Joanny, its major tragic actor. Now, even when Rachel was available, she lacked a leading man. This clearly contributed to the failure of a revival of *Tancrède* in 1846, but *Athalie*, in 1847, which Rachel could carry alone, succeeded even though the actress felt it necessary to cover her youth with what many deplored as a disfiguring amount of makeup.

The continuing quarrel between Rachel and the Comédie was overshadowed in the late 1840's by other events at the theatre. In 1845 Mlle Mars' replacement, Mme Arnould-Plessy, created a scandal in the theatre at least as great as any of Rachel's by departing without permission on an extended Russian tour. Her replacement, Mme Allan-Despréaux, was no more adequate a substitute for Mlle Mars than Mme Arnould-Plessy had been, but Mme Allan brought into the theatre a talent far surpassing her own by reintroducing it to Musset.

Musset's work had been first produced at the Odéon

in 1830, but La Nuit Vénitienne was so great a failure then that Musset renounced the theatre completely. He vowed never to submit another play for production and turned instead to writing light dramatic dialogues for private society gatherings. Between 1833 and 1837 the Revue des deux mondes published a series of these playlets, but neither Musset nor any one else at that time viewed them as possible material for the stage. Some years later Mme Allan, in St. Petersburg, saw a comedy which delighted her in a small Russian theatre. She asked for a French translation and found to her surprise that the play was originally French but had never been produced in its own language. It was Musset's Un Caprice from the Revue des deux mondes. Mme Allan then offered the original work with great success at the French theatre in St. Petersburg and insisted on reviving it at the Comédie when she came to Paris in 1847. Musset hesitated and then agreed, and the resulting production established him overnight as a significant dramatist. Gautier wrote:

> This short work given Saturday at the Comédie was a real literary event. Many huge works trumpeted a month in advance are not worth a line of this delightful three-person comedy, marvelously interpreted by Brindeau, Mlles Allan and Judith. Since Marivaux, whose wit was his genius, nothing has been produced at the Comédie so fine, so delicate, so gently playful as this little masterpiece, hidden in the pages of a review, that the Russians of St. Petersburg, that snowy Athens, had to discover for us.[25]

Un Caprice enjoyed a far longer run than any other new offering of 1847 and the hitherto ignored playlets from the Revue des deux mondes suddenly became most attractive to the Comédie. It was hardly a propitious time for Musset to be discovered. The revolutionary year of 1848 seemed an unlikely background for these delicate fancies, as Got observed uneasily in his Journal for June 19:

> The Théâtre-Français plays every evening, and for the last month has been calmly rehearsing Il ne faut jurer de rien, that great and charming proverbe by M. Alfred de Musset. Charming, surely, but what interest can it have beside that immense drama which is now swirling about us?[26]

Yet *Il ne faut jurer de rien* and *Il faut qu'une porte soit ouverte ou fermée* were the great successes of this year of barricades, toppling governments and civil strife. These and the lesser successes of *Le Chandelier* at the Théâtre Historique and *André del Sarto* at the Comédie this same year--all from the *Revue des deux mondes*--encouraged Musset at last to write a new play specifically for the theatre, *Louison* (1849). Thanks to his new reputation it was respectfully received, but it was clearly inferior to the earlier works. Musset's later productions bore out this strange situation: his dramas written expressly for the theatre seemed stiff and constrained; the great successes, *Les Caprices de Marianne* (presented in 1851), *On ne badine pas avec l'amour* (1861), and *Fantasio* (1866), were all dramas that had originally appeared in the *Revue des deux mondes*, written when their author had no hopes of ever seeing them on the stage.

The uprisings of 1848 resulted in many theatres being rechristened with their old Revolutionary names, so that the Comédie again became the République, and the Odéon the Nation. As in 1790, critics urged the theatres to respond to the new era with stirring patriotic drama, and as before, the theatres generally responded with insignificant occasional pieces. Though the Comédie avoided this degradation, Rachel appealed to the spirit of the times by regularly appearing at intermissions to sing the *Marseillaise*. This gained her the approval of the populace but further antagonized such critics as Janin. Her disputes with her fellows continued too. Her required ten-year period of service at the Comédie was completed in 1848, and she again attempted to resign, but was forced to remain another year. Fortunately, this continuing controversy had no adverse affect on her art. Her 1849 revival of *Andromaque* was one of the most brilliant of her career. Two very different successes followed, *Le Moineau de Lesbie*, a light comedy by Armand Bathet, and Scribe and Legouvé's *Adrienne Lecouvreur*, which proved that Rachel's powerful interpretation could be effective with prose as well as with poetry. Late in 1849 she again attempted to leave the Comédie, and a bitter legal battle followed. In its midst a new administrator, Arsène Houssaye, took charge. His leniency with leaves of absence apparently placated Rachel, who remained at least nominally with the theatre. Still, the years of her greatest triumphs were now past. Audience interest shifted to political pieces and to modern drama. The old charges that Rachel was too cold, too intellectual, were raised again. The high point of

1852 for her, significantly, was not in Paris but during her summer leave, when she performed with great acclaim before the King of Prussia, the Emperor Nicholas, and a host of lesser nobility. The next year saw her last major success, in a modern comedy, Mme de Girardin's Lady Tartuffe.

Rachel's final two years at the Comédie were darkened by new and ever more bitter legal disputes. The old problem of resignation from the society underlay most of these. At one point Rachel refused to create any new parts, much to the dismay of Legouvé, who had created a Medea particularly for her. Doubtless the most bitter blow of these last years for Rachel, however, was the appearance of Mme Ristori at the Théâtre-Italien. Despite the language barrier, the Italian actress created a stir such as the theatre world of Paris had not seen since Rachel's own discovery. Here was no Mlle Maxime to be destroyed by a single superior interpretation, but a major rival, the first that Rachel had ever encountered. At her request, Houssaye filled the spring of 1855 with revivals of her greatest works. Once again, public and critics united in praise of her ability, but not at the expense of Ristori. There was general agreement that the two great actresses were so different in approach that no comparison derogatory to either could justifiably be made. Ristori, who made a point of attending a number of Rachel's performances, attempted to define the difference in their styles:

> We were following two totally opposite ways; we had two different manners of expression. She could inflame an audience with her outbursts, though academic, so beautiful was her diction, so stately her acting. In the most passionate situations her expressions, her poses, everything was regulated by the rules of the traditional French school; nevertheless the power of her voice, the fascination of her looks were such that one had to admire and applaud her.
>
> We Italians, in playing tragedy, do not admit that in culminating points of passion, the body should remain in repose; and in fact, when one is struck either with a sudden grief or joy, is it not a natural instinct to carry one's hands to the head? Well then, in the Italian school, we maintain that one of the principal objects in acting is to portray

life and reality, what nature shows us.[27]

It soon became clear to Rachel that despite her great ability she would henceforth be forced to share her public with the star of the Italien. Exhausted by this battle, she left Paris on a major tour which took her first to England and then to America. In the fall in America she contracted the illness that led to her death, but despite her growing weakness, she continued the tour. She returned to Europe in 1856, but never to act again, and died in the south of France in 1858. Jules Janin, her first important supporter and later one of her bitterest critics, delivered the major oration at her funeral. Her old teacher, Samson, was refused permission to speak by Rachel's family, but his claim was so clear that no other artist from the Comédie wished to replace him. Thus Rachel went to her grave, as she had lived, estranged from the theatre for which her career had done so much.

7. Minor Theatres and the End of Romanticism, 1830-1850

By 1830 the boulevard theatres had enjoyed fifteen years of relative ease and prosperity. Their repertoires and companies had become steadily more respectable, and so had their surroundings. The rough paving was smoothed, wooden barriers were erected to control each theatre's queues, marquees offered protection from the rain, the humble dwellings previously mixed in with the theatres had been replaced by elegant town houses and cafés. When Charles X did away with the fair booths in the district, this destroyed the air of a perpetual carnival which had characterized this part of Paris ever since the Revolution. During the day, the quarter was now as peaceful as any, coming to life only after five, when lines for the theatres began to form. Major houses like the Comédie now opened at seven in the evening, but the long programs on the boulevards required earlier openings--5:15 or 5:30. Even so, a police decree of 1834, demanding that all theatres be closed by 11:00 p.m., met with considerable protest.

Although each theatre had its own character, clientele, and favored authors, the minor houses taken as a whole drew audiences from all social classes, from the royal family to the humblest laborers. The demonstrative audiences of the turn of the century had disappeared, shamed into silence by the increasingly powerful claque. Every theatre now had a well-organized claque, the chief a personage almost as important as the director himself. The chief attended rehearsals, planned applause, and sat in the middle of the house among his employees, who by 1830 had largely driven out the old inhabitants of the pit. The claques were composed of both sexes, for while men could excel in sheer volume of noise, women were useful for laughter, weeping, even judiciously planned fainting. The claque produced many varieties of applause, generally adapted to the importance of the actor performing, but young or insecure actors could make special arrangements, and often did. Indeed, even silence could be purchased, if one wished to weaken a rival's effect. The resulting corruption, together with the loss of the attentive and experienced pit audience, which often could not afford balcony seats, brought bitter complaints against the claque, but the institution remained, even in the face of a law of 1831 specifically designed to reduce the number of complimentary tickets given out by the theatres.

The major boulevard home of the romantic drama was of course the Porte-Saint-Martin, but two other far less successful houses, the Ambigu and the Gaîté, were involved in the production of similar works. Their major authors were Joseph Bouchardy and Anicet Bourgeois, who replaced the _mélodrames_ of Cuvelier and Loaisel-Tréogate with the _drame_, a more realistic but equally emotionalized study of contemporary life. The old Ambigu burned down in 1827. A new house opened in 1829, one of the most attractive in the capital, but expenses were great, the company old, the public bored. Brief appearances by Lemaître and Marie Dorval did not improve the situation, but M. de Cés-Caupenne, the director from 1830 to 1838, managed to keep his venture alive by a prolific if undistinguished offering of _drames_ such as Benjamin's _Six degrés du crime_ (1831) and Fontan and Herbin's _Jeanne de Flandre_ (1835). His only great success came in 1837 with Bouchardy's _Gaspardo le pêcheur_. A series of directors filled the years 1838 to 1840, but amid these unsettled conditions the theatre managed to present two important successes: Bouchardy's _Lazare le pâtre_ and _Le Naufrage de la Méduse_, which seems to have gained most of its popularity from its major setting, based on the painting by Géricault.

This lesson was not lost on the Ambigu's next director, Antony Béraud. Between 1841 and 1848 he placed new emphasis on the physical production, with the result that the fortunes of the theatre steadily improved. In the first years of his administration he presented scenes of domestic life similar to those offered by his predecessors, but with noticeably more attention to the reproduction of realistic detail in both the acting and the design. This early manifestation of realism was not so revolutionary as it might appear. On the design side, the romantics had long been concerned with historical accuracy in period dramas, as Pixérécourt had been before them, and the contemporary concerns of the *drame* naturally led to similarly painstaking reproductions of modern settings. In his *Histoire de l'art dramatique* Gautier observed: "We are no longer in a time when the inscription *a magnificent palace* suffices for the illusion. Shakespeare and his contemporaries asked for no more; but that was Shakespeare and the Elizabethans, and we bourgeois of 1840 have rather lazier imaginations."[28]

In acting, Talma himself had introduced realistic notes even into such formal works as *Britannicus*, and Lemaître, Bocage, and Dorval had made natural acting standard on the boulevard, stressing spontaneity as well as passion. In such successful works as Dupeuty and Cormon's *Paris la nuit* (1842) and Dennery and Grangé's *Bohémiens de Paris* (1843), Béraud merely emphasized trends already clearly in evidence in the Parisian theatre. By 1845 Charles Maurice in the *Courrier des théâtres* noted actors at the Ambigu and elsewhere sitting on tables and the arms of chairs, speaking while lying down, and turning their backs to the audience, all this forty years before Antoine.

In the later years of his administration, Béraud turned away from dramas of contemporary life to historical subjects. After the enormous success of Dumas' *Les Mousquetaires* (1845), with Mélingue and Lacressonnière in the leading roles, the Ambigu presented *Louis XVI et Marie-Antoinette*, then *Napoléon et Josephine*, and finally works in which the historical subject served merely as an excuse for spectacle--Dennery and Denaux' *Le Juif errant*, Bourgeois' *Quatre Fils Aymon*, Paul Foucher's *Notre-Dame de Paris*--little different from the boulevard extravaganzas of the 1820s.

The Gaîté's first great success of this period was a *drame*, *Latude ou Trente-cinq ans de captivité* (1834), the theatre's most popular offering since the heyday of the *mélodrames* twenty years before. The success was providential for the theatre, since it burned in 1835 and only the great profits from Latude allowed a speedy rebuilding. M. de Cés-Caupenne attempted for a few years to manage both the Ambigu and the Gaîté, but found this ultimately unprofitable. He was followed in 1838 by Montigny, and in 1844 by Meyer. Under their direction the theatre followed the Ambigu in turning more to spectacular drama, and enjoyed a series of successes, some of which were revived through the rest of the century: Bouchardy's Le Sonneur de Saint-Paul (1838) and La Grâce de Dieu (1841), Dennery and Clairville's Sept Châteaux du diable (1844), and Bourgeois and Masson's Marceau (1848).

The Cirque Olympique during these years was the major theatre devoted entirely to spectacle. The historical pageants so popular after 1830 naturally reached their apogee here, in the only house which could comfortably present a Napoleonic battle, complete with horses. Its directors, the Franconi brothers, had been presenting spectacular pantomime drama here since the beginning of the century, but a fire in 1826 led them to rebuild the theatre for even more extravagant offerings. The architect Boula described his work as "modelled on a Roman circus" but the new Cirque was in fact an elaborately equipped stage with an arena in place of the orchestra and moveable ramps connecting the two. The theatre had a permanent company of 100 actors and 30 horses, but scenic display remained the major concern, and required a large staff of its own, headed by Ferdinand Laloue and including the scenic artists Philastre and Cambon, two of Ciceri's best students, the machinist Sacré, and the lighting designer Desmarais. There was even a full-time employee, Laurent, engaged in scenic research. These collaborators brought to the Cirque audiences of the 1830s an ever more dazzling series of wonders. Forty settings were designed for Prosper Saint-Almer's La République, l'Empire, et les Cent Jours (1832). Zazezizozu (1834) by Pujol and Desnoyer, from the popular genre of fairy plays, featured an infernal ballet in an enchanted palace, great battles, and underwater spectacle. The public was now becoming increasingly interested in how these miracles were achieved, and theatre journals such as the Revue du théâtre and the Monde dramatique began about 1835 to publish regular articles on technical aspects of the theatre. Almost every major new production at the Cirque introduced new wonders. A version of Tasso's Jérusalem délivrée (1836) presented divine and infernal scenes with monsters, knights, tourneys, parades, and enchanted forests. Bourgeois' Austerlitz (1837) included a panorama which showed almost the entire city of Paris. Pixérécourt and Brazier's _Bijou, enfant de Paris_ (1838) featured a cascade of water which turned into burning lava. Laloue's own _Pilules du diable_ (1839) had a train, one of the first to be seen in the theatre, which rolled onto the stage and exploded. Little wonder that journals of the time reported that at the Cirque cries of "machinist" eventually replaced those of "author" at the end of a production.

The _comédie bourgeoise_, comedy of everyday life written in prose with occasional rhymed couplets, was at this time the standard fare at four houses: the Gymnase, the Vaudeville, the Palais-Royal, and the Variétés. The Gymnase had been so popular under the Restoration that audiences after 1830 tended to associate it with the previous regime, and it suffered accordingly. Caricaturists of the time pictured the typical patron of the Gymnase as an old _beau_, wrinkled, perfumed, in silk stockings, still delighted at the old Restoration comedies that other houses spurned. The loss of Scribe to the Comédie was a great blow for the theatre, but his former collaborators Mélesville and Bayard gradually began winning back the theatre's public. The great star of the Gymnase now was the protean comic Bouffé who played Joseph in Bayard's _Le Gamin de Paris_ (1835) to set a boulevard record--100 consecutive performances. For serious roles, the director Poirson was fortunate enough to obtain Bocage, who was apparently finding less and less demand for his intense, personal interpretation in the lavish spectacles Harel was now producing at the Porte-Saint-Martin. By 1840, however, the Gymnase was again in difficulty. It could offer no satisfactory actress to Bayard for his _Premières Armes de Richelieu_ (1839), and thus lost its most popular author to the Palais-Royal, where Virginie Déjazet made the work a major success. Poirson quarreled with Bocage over his untraditional interpretations, especially when these involved what some critics characterized as "English devices" such as playing scenes with his back to the audience. The result was that Bocage deserted the Gymnase for the Odéon. Finally, in 1842, Poirson came under the interdiction of the Société des auteurs et compositeurs dramatiques, a protective association constituted in 1829 on the initiative of Scribe. Poirson fought the ban for two years, then resigned the devastated theatre to Lemoine-Montigny, a minor writer of melodrama, who made peace with the Société and began rebuilding. He engaged three important new actors: Bressant, Rose Chéri (whom he eventually married) and, most notably, Geoffroy of the Palais-Royal. Major authors returned to the theatre and the 1840's saw the Gymnase again among the most popular of Paris' theatres with such successes as Scribe's Geneviève (1846).

The Vaudeville and the Variétés appealed in general to less sophisticated audiences than the Gymnase, and so mixed a variety of simpler genres with their conventional comedies. Light fables, occasional anecdotes, broad farces and parodies were common. The Variétés was closer to the old fair theatres, its intrigues simpler, its jokes broader. Parody, for example, tended to be literary at the Vaudeville, as in Harlani ou la Contrainte par cor, while the Variétés favored slapstick burlesque, as in Hernani, bêtise romantique. Both houses had popular companies during this period, though the Variétés had more stars. Virginie Déjazet spent the 1820s here, and was dismissed by the director Brunet when she aroused the artistic jealousy of the theatre's established leading lady, Mlle Pauline. She returned to the theatre in the 1840s, however, during the administration of Roqueplan. Frédérick Lemaître, at odds with the Ambigu and Porte-Saint-Martin, appeared here in one of his great roles, Dumas' Kean (1836), but this specialist in dramas of passion and fury found little to stimulate him in the Variétés repertoire, and soon departed. The actor Odry enjoyed a tremendous vogue in 1838 with Les Saltimbanques and Les Trois Epiciers. Then, finally, in the 1840s, Roqueplan managed to engage Bouffé, the star of the Gymnase. Against such competition, and with a disastrous fire in 1838, the Vaudeville steadily diminished in significance.

The first new theatre opened under the July monarchy was the Palais-Royal, on the site of the former Variétés-Montansier. The change in government brought no real relaxation of theatre restrictions, but the entrepreneur Dormeuil advanced his project by arguing that he was not really opening a new theatre but reopening an old one, never officially closed. Napoleon's concern in 1809 had been simply to remove a powerful and near-by competitor to his favored Comédie, and once Montansier's company had gone, their theatre remained an occasional haven for rope-dancers, pantomimes, and exhibitions of curiosities, which posed no threat to the national theatre. Louis-Philippe accepted Dormeuil's argument, and for the next two decades this theatre enjoyed a steady success. Its standard authors were Mélesville, Brazier, and particularly the team of Bayard and Dumanoir which produced such popular comedies as Les Premières Armes de Richelieu (1838) and Le Vicomte de Letorières (1841). Most of their scripts were primarily vehicles for Virginie Déjazet, the company's leading actress, whose sprightly interpretations of young women, and even more, of young men, were among Paris' leading theatre attractions. Later in the century, Jules Claretie sought to capture her style:

> A woman of wit beneath the woman of talent--a talent based on a piquant and bantering grace, on a touch of malice, on raillery, on an indefinable nimbleness, a smartness, a pertness which seemed to belong to the eighteenth century rather than the nineteenth.... Déjazet created a completely individual and totally charming genre, a false genre some have called it, as artificial as the travesties that it used almost to excess. But the art was no more false on the contrary than that of Watteau, Eisen, Moreau the younger, the whole art of the last century, composed of a piquant elegance and an unexpected artfulness.[29]

By 1830 the boulevard possessed in addition to regular theatres a great number of minor establishments featuring acrobatic displays, pantomimes and marionettes. The Revolution of 1830 raised certain of these to respectability, as the Revolution of 1789 had done for certain of the fair houses. The Théâtre de Mme Saqui, established in 1814, now rechristened itself the Délassements-Comiques and presented vaudevilles, melodramas, dramas, even the classics. M. Comte's theatre, also opened in 1814, so expanded that it was called the little Porte-Saint-Martin until it took the new title of Bouffés. Among the many such small houses that achieved a brief prominence during these years, two made a major impact on the theatrical life of the capital--the Funambules and the Folies-Dramatiques.

When Frédérick Lemaître served his 1816-1818 apprenticeship at the Funambules, that tiny theatre was itself in its first years, next door to and competing with Mme Saqui. The venture was unpromising enough in those days, but even before Lemaître left, the director Bertrand had set his theatre on the path that would lead to fame by hiring the Débureaus, a family of acrobats. In 1819, Gaspard-Baptiste Débureau began to play Pierrots, gradually surpassing his rivals in pantomime both at his own and the rival Saqui theatre. His greatest early challenge came in 1824 when the Funambules engaged a rival "English" clown, Clément

Philippe Laurent, but after a period of strife, the two became close friends and by 1827 were regularly appearing together. Le Boeuf enragé (1827), one of the house's greatest pantomimes, set the pattern for later successes and was itself revived for twenty years with Débureau playing the Pierrot Gilles, and Laurent Arléquin. The reputation of the theatre began to spread as we may see from a contemporary review in the Pandore:

> M. Laurent is an extraordinary man, I assure you; he writes plays, stages them, paints scenery and plays the leading roles. All that he does demonstrates the highest intelligence; his imitations of English pantomimes are witty; his talent as an actor is far preferable to that of twenty famous tragedians or comedians I might mention. As Arléquin M. Laurent is particularly fine.
>
> M. Débureau has a reputation as great as his comrade and he is neither author, nor designer, nor machinist. He is only Gilles: that in itself tells you something of the superiority of his unique talent! I was enchanted by him and I would give five famous comedians, small actors with large pretensions, for him, simple, modest, and perfect in this difficult genre. Gilles, you see, is a character whose infinite nuances are not at all easy to render! Simple as a child, cowardly, crafty, lazy, mischievous by instinct, obliging, mocking, greedy, thieving, swaggering, grasping, bungling, cunning in schemes which might lead to the gratification of his tastes, a naive and farcical Satan. Assuredly this is one of the drollest creations in all farce. [30]

In 1828 the critic Charles Nodier discovered Débureau and brought Nerval, Gautier, and other leaders of the new romantic school to applaud. He also brought a pantomime, Le Songe d'or, which achieved so great a success that the names Débureau and Laurent became known all over Paris. Marchand de salade (1829), Ma mère l'oie (1830) and Les Vingt-six Infortunes de Pierrot (1830) were further triumphs for Débureau, while Laurent's fortunes began to dim. Jules Janin's Débureau, histoire du théâtre à quatre sous firmly tied the Funambules in the public mind with its Pierrot and helped to establish him as an institution. Shortly after, Laurent went to the Cirque Olympique, leaving the field to his triumphant former partner.

For several years Débureau continued to portray his lovesick, languishing, and yet potentially cruel Pierrot with such success that the romantic Pierrot has become accepted as the traditional interpretation of the role. Then in 1836 the public of the Funambules was astonished to find its beloved Pierrot actually on trial for murder. The actor's assault on a man who had pursued him and his wife with insults and abuse was considered justified by the court and Débureau was acquitted, but his career went into eclipse for several years and the Funambules began to turn from pantomime to spectacle drama. During the 1840s Débureau's fame returned but his death in 1846 ended the great years of the Funambules. Paul Legrand attempted for a time to carry on his tradition, then Débureau's own son Charles appeared with somewhat more success, but the public recognized both for what they were--pale imitations of an unrecapturable original.

The tiny Folies-Dramatiques was one of the new houses which opened in 1830. Like many minor theatres, it offered a staggering range of genres--fairy plays, patriotic spectacles, vaudevilles, dramas, farce-comedies, and melodramas--but was noteworthy for achieving popular success in almost all of them, so that Mourier, its director, died a wealthy man in 1857. The theatre's major claim to renown, however, was its presentation of the work generally acknowledged, at least by its contemporaries, as the outstanding play of the period, Robert Macaire (1834). Mourier's opportunity came when Harel at the Porte-Saint-Martin quarreled with Frédérick Lemaître, dismissed him, and attempted to band together all Parisian theatres to prevent him from finding another position. Only Mourier refused, so Lemaître came to him with Robert Macaire, a sequel to the famous Auberge des Adrets largely conceived by the actor himself. Public response to the play was enormous. Critics of the time saw in Robert Macaire the symbol for a whole era when graft and greed seemed to abound everywhere under the guise of philanthropy and respectability. Arsène Houssaye said that Macaire was "you, me, everybody--even the King," an observation echoed by Chateaubriand.[31] A later generation called Robert Macaire the nineteenth century Mariage de Figaro, Honoré Daumier based one of his greatest series of cartoons on the adventures of Lemaître's anti-hero, and Flaubert called him the greatest dramatic type since Don Juan. A record-breaking run seemed assured, but other developments intervened.

The new regime followed the by now familiar pattern of abolishing censorship, then gradually restoring it under the mounting pressure of bolder and bolder works. The boulevard houses were not long in producing anti-clerical and even anti-goverment plays once the censor disappeared. By 1831 a law had to be passed to protect living persons from being presented on stage. Though the same law made recommendations on the morality and patriotism of staged works, enforcement was not strict, and a stronger regulation was encouraged by the outcry of both classicists and romanticists, each heaping charges of corruption and obscenity on the others' work. An attempted assassination of the King in 1835 gave a pretext for stronger government control, and a Board of Censors was selected. Few works were actually banned by this rather cautious Board, but Robert Macaire, with its free-wheeling assault on the society of the time, was their first victim. Lemaître's brief career at the Folies was thus abruptly ended. He made his peace with Harel and returned briefly to the Porte-Saint-Martin, then went on to the Variétés to create another of his great roles, Dumas' Kean, in 1836.

By the year 1837, romantic drama was in full decline. After the failure of Dumas' Caligula, the Comédie was unwilling to proceed with plans to revive Hernani and premiere Hugo's Ruy Blas. Marie Dorval, tired of the battle with Mars, went to join Bocage at the little Gymnase, leaving the field to her classically oriented rival. Mars was quick to follow up this victory with a series of extremely successful revivals of Molière, and there was talk of bringing Mlle George back to similarly revive classic tragedy. The Duc d'Orléans urged Hugo to return to the theatre, offering him the privilege of establishing a new home for drama, comedy, and vaudeville.

Hugo and Dumas were delighted; in their own theatre romanticism might regain its lost impetus. The organization they turned over to Anténor Joly, a disciple of Hugo and editor of the theatrical magazine Vert-Vert. After much searching, he selected the Salle Ventadour for the venture. It was remodeled and opened as the Théâtre de la Renaissance in November of 1838. The troupe was not ideal--Bocage and Dorval in particular were missing, tied by contract to the Gymnase--but Dumas, who had just been working with Lemaître in Kean, pursuaded him to head the new company. Lemaître brought his protegée, Atala Beauchêne, and Hugo and Dumas insisted on including their stage-struck mistresses, Ida Ferrier and Juliette Drouet. The opening production was Hugo's Ruy Blas, and after a bitter dispute, Atala Beauchêne, doubtless the most talented of the three mistresses, carried off the leading female role of Maria de Neuberg. The play belonged largely to Lemaître, however, and allowed him to display the full range of his magnificent talents. Hugo had unqualified praise for his interpreter: "For old men, he is Lekain and Garrick in one; for us, his contemporaries, he combines the actions of Kean with the emotion of Talma."[32] Lemaître's effect in this play was so great that thirty years later Mélingue refused to revive it, fearing that some would still compare his interpretation with his great predecessor's.

Never again did the Renaissance equal this opening production, and even Ruy Blas created division within the theatre. Fernand de Villeneuve, Joly's partner and the financial backer of the Renaissance, was convinced from the outset that the public had had enough of romanticism and worked steadily to convert the theatre to comic opera. Whenever Ruy Blas was presented, therefore, the heating worked improperly, the orchestra played out of tune, members of the claque hissed--problems never present when a musical play was offered. Far more discouraging, however, was the total failure of the drama which replaced Ruy Blas, Dumas' L'Alchimiste (1839), a stiff, clumsy drama in verse which not even Lemaître could save. Shortly after, the theatre's major actor departed and Villeneuve got his wish. The Renaissance lasted only two more years, but its offerings during that time were entirely musical comedies.

After the failure of Les Burgraves at the Comédie in 1843, Hugo dealt no more with the theatre, but Dumas attempted one final time to revivify the romantic drama in a new home. He commissioned Séchan and Dieterle to design the Théâtre-Historique on the boulevard Saint-Michel in a new form particularly suited for spectacular productions. The house was oval in form, but cut not at the end, but at the widest point, creating a stage almost double the ordinary size. The director was Hippolyte Hostein, a former regisseur of the Ambigu, and his troupe included many of the best actors of the boulevards. Marie Dorval joined the company a few months after its formation in 1847, though Bocage was now committed to the Odéon and Lemaître to the Porte-Saint-Martin, where he was enjoying a huge success with Félix

Pyat's Le Chiffonnier de Paris, a piece of sentimental socialism concerning a virtuous rag-picker.

Interest in Dumas' venture was great, with a line forming for tickets twenty-four hours (or according to some reports, two days) before the opening. The first production, La Reine Margot, established the reputation of Mélingue, the last of the major romantic actors, who remained the idol of the boulevard for twenty years. It also set the style for almost all later Théâtre-Historique productions. The settings, designed by Cambon and Desplechin, were lavish--full of gold, draperies, and plumes. Everything about the production was huge, even its length, for the twelve acts lasted from six in the evening until almost dawn. A sizeable crowd of anxious friends and relatives gathered at the theatre before the play was over on its opening night, convinced that there had been some disaster.

Le Chevalier de Maison-Rouge (1847) by Dumas and Auguste Maquet was an even greater success, running for an unheard-of 134 consecutive evenings. A mob of sans-culottes was needed and Dumas' regisseur Achille hired hundreds of extras for each performance. Dumas himself supervised their costume and herded them onto the stage to create what were hailed as the most imposing and delirious mob scenes ever witnessed in the theatre. There were even rumors later that many of the workers who took part in the rebellion of 1848 had learned techniques of mob violence under the direction of Dumas at the Théâtre-Historique.

All the Parisian theatres naturally suffered during the period of political upheaval between the abdication under duress of Louis Philippe in February of 1848 and the election of Louis Napoleon Bonaparte as the new President in December. The Historique, however, did not find its public returning as political stability was restored. New and ambitious productions came in rapid succession, but expenses were great, and each production attracted smaller audiences. Mélingue's most famous role came at this time, Dumas' Monte Cristo. This work was, if not the greatest, at any rate the longest of the Historique's overblown spectacles, and had to be presented on two successive evenings. Cham, a cartoonist of the period, showed a young man going into the theatre, and coming out old, lame, and half-blind. Aside from the length, the only really notable thing about the production seems to have been the interpretation of Mélingue, and even he was criticized by many as presenting a kind of parody of Lemaître and Bocage. Certainly he seems to have relied less on depth of feeling than on grimace and skill at quick-change. The empty display at the Historique drew criticism, too. In 1849 Théodore de Banville expressed a typical reaction: "I am not among those who demand that the five acts of Le Cid occur in the same place... but at the same time I protest with all my strength against the abuse of gadgets, cardboard, and golden paper into which M. Dumas and M. Hostein have plunged us up to our necks."[33]

The cycle was nearly over; romanticism was returning to spectacle and melodrama, and its writers and interpreters to the minor boulevard houses. Marie Dorval achieved her last triumph in Dennery's melodrama Marie-Jeanne, at the Porte-Saint-Martin in 1846. When Hostein arranged for her to appear in a revival of the work two years later, the house was empty, and Dorval died the following year, almost totally forgotten. In 1850 Lemaître appeared in his last great romantic role, Lamartine's Toussaint L'Ouverture, at the Porte-Saint-Martin. Shortly afterwards that theatre, so long the refuge of romanticism, closed its doors. During the same summer the Historique expired. It subsequently reopened as the Théâtre-Lyrique, an important and influential theatre, but one which never again offered a work which might be considered romantic.

The evolving political situation doubtless had its effect on the last days of romanticism. Hugo and Dumas had received a certain support from the old regime. Deprived of that, and frightened by Louis-Napoleon's dictatorial aspirations, both felt obliged to leave France. When the new President dissolved the Assembly and ordered the arrest of prominent political opponents, Lemaître and others followed their example. Still, the defeat of the later experiments by Hugo and Dumas, and the success of such minor rivals as Ponsard showed clearly that the impetus of the romantic movement had died well before the Revolution of 1848 gave the politics, and the culture, of the nation a new direction.

Notes to Part II

1. V. Leathers, British Entertainers in France (Toronto, 1959), pp. 58-61.

2. J. L. Borgerhoff, Le Théâtre Anglais à Paris sous la

Restauration (Paris, 1913), p. 90.

3. E. Delacroix, *Lettres* (Paris, 1880), Sept. 26, 1827 (misdated 1828 in this volume).

4. A. Dumas, *Mémoires* (Paris, 1888), IV, 280.

5. June 4, 1827, quoted in M. A. Allevy, *La Mise en scène en France dans la première moitié du dix-neuvième siècle* (Paris, 1938), p. 80

6. Dumas, *Mémoires*, V, 138.

7. T. Gautier, *Histoire du romantisme* (Paris, 1874), p. 107.

8. C. De Manne and O. Ménétrier, *Galerie historique des acteurs français* (Lyon, 1877), pp. 251-52.

9. J. Plunkett, *Fantômes et souvenirs de la Porte-Saint-Martin* (Paris, 1946), p. 88.

10. T. Gautier, *Histoire d'art dramatique depuis vingt-cinq ans* (Paris, 1858-59), VI, 104.

11. J. Valmy-Baysse, *Naissance et vie de la Comédie Française* (Paris, 1945), p. 221.

12. M. Descotes, *Le Drame romantique et ses grands créateurs* (Paris, 1955), pp. 281-82.

13. August 13, 1827, quoted in I. Guest, *The Romantic Ballet in Paris* (London, 1966), p. 79.

14. Gautier, *art dramatique*, II, 174.

15. G. Bapst, *Essai sur l'histoire du théâtre* (Paris, 1893), pp. 552-53.

16. Gautier, *art dramatique*, I, 50.

17. J. Janin, *Histoire de la littérature dramatique* (Paris, 1853-58), VI, 156.

18. Bapst, *Essai*, p. 550.

19. Allevy, *La Mise en scène*, p. 144.

20. *Figaro*, May 4, 1831, quoted in A. Maurois, *The Titans* (trans. G. Hopkins, New York, 1957), p. 104.

21. E. Legouvé, *Soixante ans de souvenirs* (Paris, 1886), II, 32.

22. Dumas, *Mémoires*, IX, 180.

23. Mme de B-----, *Mlle Rachel et l'avenir du théâtre français* (Paris, 1839), p. 106.

24. J. Foster and G. H. Lewes, *Dramatic Essays* (London, 1896), pp. 84-85.

25. Gautier, *art dramatique*, V, 190.

26. E. Got, *Journal* (Paris, 1910), II, 239.

27. A. Ristori, *Memoires and Artistic Studies* (trans. G. Mantelli, New York, 1907), p. 31.

28. Gautier, *art dramatique*, II, 96.

29. J. Claretie, *Profils de théâtre* (Paris, 1902), pp. 34-35.

30. July 19, 1828, quoted in L. Pericaud, *Le Théâtre des Funambules* (Paris, 1897), p. 78.

31. A. Houssaye, *Les Confessions* (Paris, 1885), II, 253-54.

32. V. Hugo, *Oeuvres* (Paris, 1952), XVII, 175.

33. *Dix décembre*, November 12, 1849, quoted in Allevy, *Mise en scène*, p. 167.

III. SOCIAL DRAMA AND OPERETTA 1850-1870

The two decades of the Second Empire saw the development of two new theatrical genres which together created a strikingly complementary view of that dark yet dazzling society. On the one hand were the grim moralities of the early realists, on the other the glittering fantasy of Offenbach's operettas. The realistic social drama of Augier and Dumas *fils* was the clearest reflection yet of the concerns of the new affluent French middle class; the tension between new money and old social positions, financial speculation, the threat posed to family life by illicit liaisons and the courtesans of high society were its most frequent subjects. There was plenty of villainy in such drama, but its basic moral position, founded on an enlightened mercantilism and the sanctity of the family, was clear. The plays were sentimental, even melodramatic at times, but their subjects were immediate, the settings and character types drawn from their audience's own milieu. However artificial they may seem today, they were authentic enough to their first observers, and with such works came a new concern for realism in acting and in physical surroundings.

This new drama worked its way slowly into the Comédie, which in 1850 was largely controlled by the popular but more mechanical plays of Scribe and his school. The major homes of the social drama in its first decade were the Gymnase and the Vaudeville, both real rivals of the national theatre. Hugo, fleeing the stifling conditions of the Comédie, had opened the possibility of major literary movements developing outside the national houses, and the Gymnase and Vaudeville of the Second Empire confirmed that possibility. Montigny, the influential director of the former, prepared the way for more famous directors later in the century through his concern for realistic detail and his control of the entire production. Ironically, by the time the new social drama was admitted to the Comédie in the 1860s its youthful force was spent, its major works already created.

The light-hearted operettas of Offenbach poked

cautious fun at the pompous court and the military ambitions of Napoleon III, but such humor was dangerous, and the more obvious targets of operetta amusement were the Greek myths, with classic heroes converted into buffoon figures suspiciously similar at times to contemporary Parisians. Both comic opera and the comedies with songs called *vaudevilles* doubtless contributed to the operetta's development, but its attitude and its subjects tie it firmly to the Second Empire, when it had its greatest vogue and produced its more durable works. There is more than a little truth in Hugo's assertion that the Second Empire was merely a grotesque parody of the First, and it seems oddly appropriate that the court of Napoleon III should be regaled by burlesque treatments of the classic themes which the court of Napoleon I regarded with the utmost reverence.

By 1880 the operetta and social drama were well-established and popular forms, but both had become almost as sterile and repetitive as the melodramas, spectacle dramas and *vaudevilles* which made up most of the rest of Parisian theatre fare. A number of writers, most notably Zola, attempted to find a new approach to theatre in the 1860s, but with little success.

1. Social drama at the Gymnase and Vaudeville, 1850-1861

Ponsard's *école de bon sens* served as a kind of transition between Scribe and the new generation. The only important writer to come out of this school was Emile Augier, who has already been mentioned as the author of a series of realistic little verse comedies in the 1840s. This series continued on into the Second Empire with *Gabrielle* (1849), *Le Joueur de flute* (1850), *Diane* (1852) and *Philiberte* (1853). Most of Augier's later concerns are clearly anticipated in these early works--class struggle, the role of the courtesan in society, defense of the home against the menace of adultery. The most successful was *Gabrielle*, generally considered the outstanding product of the *école de bon sens*. In both form and content it took sharp issue with Scribe. A generation of French audiences had found marital infidelity a minor, amusing matter on the stage. Augier returned to the sentimental morality of Kotzebue, spiritedly defending hearth and home. The simple but highly emotional story of *Gabrielle* is that of a thoughtless young husband who allows his wife to drift toward an affair with a friend. He awakens in time, however, paints for the tempted couple the agonies of illicit love, and convinces them to part. The wife throws herself into her husband's arms with the famous curtain line: "O père de famille! ô poëte! Je t'aime!"

Though the work was poetic in structure, Augier sought his poetry in the commonplace, and nothing in Gabrielle caused such a sensation as its language. The romantic dramatists had, of course, opened the way to prosaic concerns in poetic drama, but nothing in the romantic theatre approached such interchanges as that which closed the first scene of Gabrielle:

> JULLIEN: Gabrielle.
>
> GABRILLE: Plaît-il?
>
> JULLIEN: Hors chez nous, où voit-on/Chemise de mari n'avoir pas de bouton?
>
> GABRIELLE: Ah! Mettez un épingle!
>
> JULLIEN: Il faut que je te gronde;/Mon linge est dans l'état le plus pitieux du monde.[1]

Yet the new realism was established as a major force not by Augier but by an author who was relatively unknown, although he bore a famous name: Alexandre Dumas fils, the natural son of the romantic dramatist. Aside from a certain minor notoriety in bohemian circles, his only claims to attention before 1852 were a standard debutant volume of verse called Péchés de jeunesse, a short lyric drama played as a curtain-raiser at the Historique in 1848, and a few hastily written novels. From one of the latter he made a play, La Dame aux camélias, which the elder Dumas planned to present at the Historique. When the Historique was forced to close before the new play was offered, no other boulevard theatre seemed interested; some said it was not stageworthy, others that it was not moral. Dumas fils took the play to the popular Virginie Déjazet, hoping to interest her in the leading role. She refused it, but admitted being deeply moved by his work and then made a striking prediction. The play could be a great success, she told Dumas,

> But for that to happen, three things are necessary: a revolution which will destroy censorship;

> Fechter in the role of Armand, and me not playing Marguerite, for I would be quite ridiculous. For me to play the role, you would have to change to a Louis XV setting, give me some verses to sing, and let me marry my lover at the end. I wept too much in reading your play to want to change it. [2]

Déjazet proved a remarkable prophetess. In 1850 Bouffé, the new director of the Vaudeville, agreed to present the play and engaged Fechter to play Armand. The role of Marguerite still presented a difficulty but Fechter arranged for the return of Marie Doche, a young actress who had gone to London in dissatisfaction with the roles she had been offered in Paris. The third obstacle, the censor, still remained, for despite the reputation of Dumas and his father, the minister Léon Faucher pronounced the work too immoral for a public theatre. Then came the revolution, and with it a new minister, the duc de Morny, who attended a rehearsal and approved the play three days after his appointment.

La Dame aux camélias was clearly a brilliant success from its opening act. Actors and audience were caught in a rising tide of emotion. Near the end of the fourth act Fechter, who had never laid a hand on Mme Doche during rehearsals, was so involved that he remembered a suggestion from Dumas which he had previously disregarded as too extreme, seized Mme Doche by the wrists and threw her to the floor. Then he rushed from the room, slamming the door so violently that a candelabra was thrown down from one of the tables. Little wonder that at the end of the act Mme Doche fainted away in earnest. The audience was ecstatic, and when the play was finished, showered the author with boquets which, observed Gautier, they "tore from their bosoms, drenched in tears."

Surely no French play of the century has been so frequently revived as La Dame aux camélias, and in our own century, when sentiment has tended to be viewed with condescension, Camille has come to be commonly associated with excessive, even melodramatic emotionality. Such a reaction would have seemed strange indeed to the audiences of the play's own time. Granted, men and women wept openly and profusely at the play, but even with this emotional appeal, it was a bold step toward realism in the French drama. No one had yet dealt with contemporary society in so daring a way on the stage, and no one had more successfully captured the details of contemporary life than Dumas. The new realism which Augier had tentatively suggested was here placed powerfully before the public for the first time. Little wonder that La Dame aux camélias produced a tremor in the theatre as severe as that produced in the novel by Madame Bovary five years later. The critic Weiss called them both daughters of the 1851 revolution and argued that Dumas' play was a striking forecast of the social and philosophical tendencies in the later part of the century. Dumas fils' critics charged him with immorality, but in fact the play was concerned with morality of a new kind:

> Georges Duval is a sort of police superintendant for this morality; he recommends it less as something just in itself than as an all-powerful force which must be obeyed no matter what and which has always the last word, if only through the harm it causes to those who defy it. Morality appears here as a 'cause' or a 'law' of the same order as electricity or gravity. No more divine transport of souls; now the proprieties, the social niceties, the unyielding and presumably legitimate omnipotence of things and people who stand above the outlaws--those without capital or social position. No more ideals; instead, the fitting together of facts. No more right to happiness; instead, the fatality of conditions and circumstances. That is what literature and philosophy have been telling us ever since.[3]

With La Dame aux camélias the French stage left the world of the romantics as clearly as they had departed from the classic tradition, and embarked on the path that led to the dramas of Zola, Becque, and Ibsen.

When Augier's Philiberte appeared in 1853, many critics remarked that it had more in common with Dumas fils than with Ponsard, despite its poetic form. Augier unquestionably aligned himself with the new movement in 1855 with the prose Mariage d'Olympe. Though this work attacked the sentimentalized courtesan of La Dame aux camélias, for Augier was always a rigid moralist, it shared the earlier play's interest in the realistic depiction of contemporary society.

Until 1861, when Augier's Les Effrontés was presented at the Comédie, the Vaudeville and the Gymnase were the homes of the new movement, just about evenly dividing the works of Augier, Dumas _fils_, and their less significant followers. The great success of _La Dame aux camélias_ restored the Vaudeville to prosperity after two decades of stagnation, so it was hardly surprising that Gautier, its director, deserted the genre for which his theatre had been founded to present modern comedy and realistic drama after 1852. Théodore Barrière and Lambert Thiboust's _Les Filles de marbre_ (1853) proved for a time even more popular than _La Dame aux camélias_, which had clearly inspired it, and Barrière followed this with another great success, _Les Parisiens_ (1854), generally considered his best realistic play.

Dumas _fils_ took his second major work, _Diane de Lys_ (1853), to the Gymnase, at this time a considerably more prosperous and influential theatre than the Vaudeville. Its director, Montigny, was a natural ally for Dumas, since he already had a reputation for encouraging new playwrights, many of them headed in the new direction. Among the works given in the past decade at his theatre had been George Sand's _Le Pressoir_ and _Le Mariage de Victorine_, Balzac's _Mercadet_, Augier's _Philiberte_, and Lambert Thiboust's _Je dine avec ma mère_. Montigny brought far more to the French theatre, however, than an interest in new playwrights. He demanded a care and concentration in rehearsals then almost unknown in Paris, yet demanded a far longer rehearsal period than the few days then commonly employed. Seated in his legendary armchair, he watched incessantly for any false note in a production. He applied a keen analytic mind to the plays he presented, and knew how to make the points in every scene. In him the Parisian stage experienced for the first time the kind of guiding invisible presence we associate with the modern director.

Beyond this, Montigny unquestionably helped lay the foundations for the realistic theatre which developed later in the century. André Beauquesne, in an obituary for Montigny in the _Revue Française_, reports a typical interchange between the director and one of his actors which would not seem out of place in the theatre of Antoine: "Pardon monsieur, but you are giving your speech too well." "What? Too well?" "Yes, it's too effective. Your function here is to give a reply. Give a reply, then."[4] Various authors who worked with Montigny later praised his realistic innovations in movement and setting as well. Dumas _fils_ in _Nouveaux entr'actes_ recalls:

> It was Montigny who first had chairs changed in position by characters while they were speaking, who began ladies knitting during the dialogue when previously they never had anything in their hands but a fan or a handkerchief. He added many little pieces of business to give the dialogue life, to make it appear more realistic, more lively, more rapid.[5]

When Thiers, later in the century, expressed surprise that in Sardou's plays real tea was drunk, and real sugar put into the glasses, the playwright responded:

> Montigny made the first reform by putting a table in the middle of the stage; then chairs had to be placed around the table; and the actors, instead of standing up to speak without looking at each other, sat down and spoke naturally among themselves as we do in real life. When the chairs and table were in place, the setting was arranged as in your study; everywhere were put end tables, writing desks, chairs of all sorts according to the contemporary fashion. My merit, if any is due me, is to have applied Montigny's theories to the historic theatre; I tried to introduce reality into the drama.[6]

Obviously a certain measure of the success of the realistic social drama of the Second Empire was due to Montigny's concern with its physical presentation, and that presentation doubtless helped determine the direction of its development. He can therefore no more be separated from the early works of Augier and Dumas *fils* than the Bancrofts can be separated from the works of that somewhat similar precursor of realism in England at this period, Tom Robertson.

Diane de Lys, Montigny's first production of a work by Dumas *fils*, was a play which might be considered, even before Augier's *Mariage d'Olympe*, as an answer to the sentimentalized view of an illicit union presented in Dumas' first great success, *La Dame aux camélias*. Yet even though it concluded with a deceived husband shooting his wife's lover, the lover remained the more sympathetic character, and the moral ambivalence of the piece kept it under the censor's ban for eight months while Dumas rewrote it. Such rewritings, Dumas was careful to explain, did not damage the heart of the play; at any rate, he resisted Montigny's pleas for a happy ending.

Diane de Lys was dedicated to Rose Chéri, the leading actress of the Gymnase, who had made her debut here in 1842 and married Montigny in 1845. Though she had established her reputation in works of the old school such as Bayard and Charles Lafont's Un Changement de main (1845), and Scribe's La Protegée sans le savoir (1846), she soon made herself the outstanding interpreter of the new. In 1853 she was so successful in Dumas' Diane de Lys and Augier's Philiberte that each author conceived for her a central role in his next work--Antoinette in Le Gendre de M. Poirier and Suzanne in Le Demi-Monde.

Le Gendre de M. Poirier (1854), written by Augier in collaboration with Jules Sandeau, is unquestionably one of the most durable comedies of the period, though its subject is very much of the time. The conflict of social classes is of course a standard theme of social comedy, and the nineteenth century had already produced a whole series of works on this theme, from Picard and Mazères' Les Trois Quartiers (1827) to Sandeau's own Mademoiselle de la Seiglière (1851). The conflict between nouveau riche and improverished aristocracy seemed particularly well suited to the turbulent society of the Second Empire, however, and Sandeau and Augier's story of a wealthy bourgeois' agonies in assimilating an impoverished nobleman into his family enjoyed great popularity. Moreover the play was, by all accounts, excellently interpreted by Montigny's company, now generally regarded as the best in Paris after the Comédie and Odéon. Though Rose Chéri dominated the group, she had excellent male partners in Geoffroy and Bressant. Other important contributors to the company during Montigny's administration were Adolphe Dupuis, Etienne Arnal, and Pierre Lafont, who later went on to the Comédie.

When Dumas' Le Demi-Monde was accepted by Montigny in 1855, Augier went for the first time to the Vaudeville with Le Mariage d'Olympe, the first failure among his mature works. The harshness of its tone gained it many enemies, and its interpretation at the Vaudeville was most likely inferior to that received by earlier Augier works at the Gymnase. Yet Augier and other dramatists blamed the play's lack of success on a public reaction to too many courtesan plays in too short a period. Thus, though the courtesan remained a significant and distinctive feature of Empire society, her sway in the theatre was much reduced after Le Mariage d'Olympe.

Augier did not desert the Vaudeville, and for the next five years he remained the major dramatist of that theatre while Dumas stayed at the Gymnase. The fashionable subject for social drama now shifted from the courtesan to money and speculation, another traditional concern of social comedy with particular significance for the Second Empire. Almost every drama or comedy of this period dealt with financial concerns to some extent, and during the 1850s, as during the 1820s, they moved to a central position. Ponsard's *L'Honneur et l'Argent*, one of the most popular plays of 1853, might be considered the beginning of the series which included Dumas' *La Question d'argent* (1857), and Augier's *La Ceinture dorée* (1855), *Les Lionnes pauvres* (1858), and *Les Effrontés* (1861). The speculators Jean Giraud from *La Question d'argent* and Vernouillet from *Les Effrontés* became as famous, or as notorious, as Augier and Dumas' earlier courtesans. Then, while Augier continued to work the vein of finance, Dumas shifted his attention to comedies and dramas of family relationships, somewhat in the manner of Diderot. *Le Fils naturel* (1858) told of a natural son spurned by his father who turned the tables by becoming famous and refusing in turn, to recognize the repentant gentleman. *Un père prodigue* (1859) showed a rakish count redeeming his honor by defending that of his son.

A number of lesser authors at the Gymnase and Vaudeville presented works similar in themes and approach to those of Augier and Dumas. The most important of these was Octave Feuillet, who first came to the public's attention with Musset-like *proverbes* such as *Péril en la demeure* (1855) at the Comédie, but who gained his greatest successes in the new plays of social realism. The Vaudeville presented his most noted work, *Le Roman d'un jeune homme pauvre* (1858), the Gymnase his *Montjoie* (1863).

During the 1860s a variety of circumstances forced both the Gymnase and the Vaudeville to turn away from social drama. Most important was the loss of the two major dramatists in this genre. Augier was now writing for the Comédie and the Odéon while Dumas, after suffering a nervous breakdown, produced only two plays during the decade: *L'Ami des femmes* (1864) and *Les Idées de Madame Aubry* (1867), a kind of modern morality with a distinct mystical element. A triumvirate of directors took over the Vaudeville in 1861: Benou, in charge of financial matters; Duponchel, the noted designer of the Opéra, in charge of settings; and Dormeuil, the artistic director. Duponchel seems never to have attempted to introduce to the Vaudeville the sort of scenic display associated with his name at the Opéra; settings and interpretation in both serious and comic plays at the Vaudeville seem to have continued in the realistic direction established during the previous decade. Dormeuil revived certain important works of the new drama; Augier's Le Mariage d'Olympe, with Mme Fargueil, achieved its first great success in his 1863 revival. Dormeuil found himself increasingly at odds with his actors, however. Febvre reported that the irritated director "could not understand all the sitting down, and was horrified to see a back."[7] It was apparently with some relief that Dormeuil turned the venture over in 1864 to Beaufort, who was more sympathetic to the new style and who opened his directorship with a revival of Feuillet's Roman d'un jeune homme pauvre.

The emphasis at both the Vaudeville and the Gymnase during this decade was on realistic comedy, however, rather than realistic drama, and the major playwright was Victorien Sardou, who virtually alone filled the places left by the departure of both Augier and Dumas. Though Sardou became a dominant figure in the French theatre of the late nineteenth century, he gained the acceptance of the public only with great difficulty. His first play, La Taverne des étudiants, was so disastrous a failure at the Odéon in 1854 that no director in Paris was willing to risk presenting his next offering. At last the actress Virginie Déjazet rescued the dramatist from this impasse. Sardou offered her his Premières Armes de Figaro, based on Les Premières Armes de Richelieu, the historical drama which had elevated Déjazet to stardom at the Palais-Royal in 1839, and she agreed to use it for the opening production in her own theatre in 1859. Her trust was rewarded by a gratifying success, launching Sardou's career as well as that of the theatre. He continued to write for Déjazet, but after 1859 other Parisian theatres were open to him as well.

In 1860 and again in 1861 Sardou had plays presented at the Déjazet, the Gymnase and the Vaudeville, and by 1862 he was represented even at the Comédie, with La Papillonne. The Vaudeville offerings were the most important of these, with Les Pattes de mouche (1860) proving his skill in a farce based on complicated plotting and Nos Intimes (1861) showing that he could apply to social comedy the same realistic concerns as those in a Dumas drama. The Comédie production of La Papillonne was a near disaster, but Sardou was consoled by two very popular productions at the Gymnase during this same year, La Perle noir and Les Ganaches. These were in turn surpassed by La Famille Benoîton (1865), with the Vaudeville's leading actors, Félix, Parade, and Mme Fargueil. La Famille Benoîton was the last important success at the Theatre for a number of years. In the late 1860s Sardou worked almost exclusively for the Gymnase, and no author appeared at the Vaudeville to replace him. Another blow was a forced relocation in 1869 as a result of Baron Haussmann's urban renewal. The administration of Hermant (1869-1872) at the new theatre did not enjoy a single success.

Sardou, who once reported that he had learned his craft by reading the opening acts of a Scribean play and trying to write the last himself, now found himself again in Scribe's footsteps, as the major author for the Gymnase. He proved as valuable for that theatre as his predecessor had, so that by 1866 Barbey d'Aurevilly could write "the Gymnase is at this moment the real Théâtre Français." The most important Sardou play of these Gymnase years was Nos bons villageois (1867), which satirized provincial life as La Famille Benoîton had satirized the city. To emphasize the parallel, the Gymnase revived the earlier Vaudeville work in 1867, and the two plays together provided one of the major theatrical events associated with the great Exposition of that year. Toward the end of the decade, the Gymnase was fortunate enough to attract other important dramatists. Edouard Pailleron displayed a major comic talent with Le Monde ou l'on s'amuse (1868). Then came Henri Meilhac and Ludovic Halévy with their first full-length comedy, Fanny Lear (1868). This success was followed by an even more popular comédie larmoyante by the same authors, Froufrou (1869). Since the death several years before of Rose Chéri, the Gymnase had possessed no important female interpreter, and the casting of the leading part in Froufrou was very difficult. At the last moment Dumas fils appeared with Aimée Desclée, who had made her debut at the Gymnase in 1856 but had been subsequently performing in Russia and Belgium. The authors and director found her perfect for the part, and the public shared their enthusiasm.

During the next several years the major Gymnase productions were a series of plays by Dumas written for the new star. The bitter but brilliant short comedy, Une Visite de Noces (1871), showed Dumas returning to the old themes of seduction and adultery. La Princesse Georges (1872) was a similar but more complex study. Aimée Desclée portrayed

Séverine, the rather melodramatic heroine who forgives all when her unfaithful husband returns from an affair with another married woman. Though the play was a great success, many critics were offended by the morality of Dumas' motivation, for the erring Prince returns less in repentance than in fear, when the husband he is wronging shoots another of his wife's lovers. Yet the author went further still in La Femme de Claude (1873), Aimée Desclée's last great role before her death. Césarine, the debauched heroine, seduces a student of her scientist husband to obtain the plans for a super-weapon he has invented. She is about to throw the plans to an enemy agent from a window when her husband appears and shoots her. Even the Gymnase public found this grim story impossible to accept and turned with relief to Dumas' later work the same year, Monsieur Alphonse. This lighter and more sentimental piece, reminiscent in tone of Le Fils naturel, came to rank second only to La Dame aux camélias in popularity among Dumas' works. After the death of Aimée Desclée, Dumas again left the theatre for several years, and his next production, L'Etrangère (1876), was presented not at the Gymnase but at the Comédie.

During the 1870s the Vaudeville returned to the sort of light comedies and comedies mixed with song which had been its original fare, and after the departure of Dumas, the Gymnase also turned in this direction. The most popular new writer in this genre to emerge during the decade was Alfred Hennequin. He made his debut at the Vaudeville with Les Trois Chapeaux (1871) and produced several other plays at that theatre before Le Procès Veauradieux (1875), which gained him a reputation as a master of light comedy. Feydeau later called Labiche the master of character, Meilhac of dialogue, and Hennequin of craft. This made Hennequin, even more than the others, an ideal collaborator, and most of his successes, which appeared almost yearly after 1875, were written in conjunction with Delacour or Emile de Najac. In 1878 he began writing for the Variétés, and a few years later for the Palais-Royal, both of which were more traditionally associated with the light entertainment he offered than the Vaudeville or Gymnase.

The loss of Hennequin might have been quite serious for both of these theatres, but fortunately just at this time several of their longer-established dramatists returned with important works. Augier's last two works were presented at the Vaudeville. Madame Caverlet (1876) went even further than Dumas' Femme de Claude in attacking the sanctity of marriage and openly advocating divorce. Les Fourchambault (1878) turned away from the thesis play tradition, but still echoed Dumas in giving a sentimental picture of a natural son who comes to the rescue of his legitimate family.

Comedy rather than drama was the mainstay of both the Gymnase and the Vaudeville during this period, however. Eugène Labiche, who before 1870 had been primarily associated with the Palais-Royal, contributed during this decade to both the Variétés and the Vaudeville. His only great success at the latter theatre was his last play, Le Clé (1877), done in collaboration with Duru. The theatre's most notable production that year was Sardou's Dora, his first undisputed success in almost ten years. A comedy of political intrigue, it returned to the approach of La Famille Benoîton and enjoyed a similar popularity. A minor but significant voice of dissent was that of Emile Zola, who wrote in the Bien public that with this work Sardou had forfeited his literary esteem--an early hint of the antagonism the realists in general would express toward Sardou.

The major comic author of the Gymnase was Pailleron, with L'Age ingrat (1878) and L'Etincelle (1879). Gondinet, in collaboration with François Oswald and Pierre Giffard, contributed Jonathon (1879). The last great success of Montigny's administration was Albert Delpit's most important play, Le Fils de Coralie (1880). Though it ended happily, its relation to the more serious dramas of Augier and Dumas was clear. The hero, the illegitimate son of a prostitute, is denied marriage to the girl he loves when her family discovers his background. She then forces the match by swearing (falsely) that she has already had an affair with him. Lucien Guitry, who had come from the Conservatory to play Armand Duval two years before in a major revival of La Dame aux camélias at the Gymnase, created the title role and proved himself a major new acting talent. Several months after this success Montigny died, and the great years of the Gymnase were over.

In the sixty years since its founding, the theatre had had only two directors, Montigny and his predecessor, Delestre-Poirson--a record unique in Parisian theatre. Montigny himself had directed the theatre for thirty-six years, during which time it was the rival of the Comédie itself in popularity, and the foremost theatre in Paris in the discovery of new talents and innovative staging practices. Both in his encouragement of the social drama of the Second Empire and in his directorial practices--his attention to realistic detail, his use of stage space, his long and careful rehearsal patterns--Montigny may in a real sense be considered the founder of the realistic theatre of the late nineteenth century.

2. The Operetta Theatres, 1848-1880

Operetta is generally considered to have emerged as a distinct genre, separate from comic opera or vaudeville, in 1848 when Florimond Rongé, known as Hervé, presented at the Palais-Royal a one-act parody of the Italian grand opera called *Gargouillada.* Many of the elements associated with the operetta were first combined in this work--the mixture of sung and spoken elements, the fantasy, the almost grotesque buffoonery, and most important of all, the basic irreverence of subject and treatment. Not the least of the attractions of this popular work was the first performance in a theatre of the notorious cancan.

Hervé's success with *Gargouillada* encouraged him to obtain a license for a theatre to present such works regularly. The license for the Folies-concerts, later called the Folies-nouvelles, was a traditional one, with very strong restrictions. Hervé, for example, was to present only one-act plays with no more than two characters. Hervé's response was equally traditional; he worked around the law with such expedients as adding a "singing corpse" to the cast or painting choruses on backdrops behind which additional actors sang. Under these conditions, Hervé wrote the music and Jules Moineaux the libretti for a series of popular mythological burlesques. The success of these encouraged Jacques Offenbach, then director of the orchestra at the Comédie, to submit a work in the same style for Hervé's theatre.

Offenbach's *Oyayaïe* (1854), a broad farce about a double-bass player captured by cannibals, was such a success that Hervé's jealousy was aroused, and Offenbach was informed that he must find another theatre for his future works. He heard of a small abandoned theatre near the Palace of Industry which was being erected for the Exposition of 1855, an excellent location to attract a public, at least while the Exposition was in progress. Offenbach applied at once to the Ministry of the Interior for permission to reopen this little house, but he reckoned without bureaucratic delay and the rival claims of some twenty other entrepreneurs. When he finally obtained his license the Exposition had already opened. Speed now became essential, and Offenbach appealed to Fromental Halévy, his former teacher in composition, to find him a librettist willing to help create a work within three weeks. Fromental's nephew, Ludovic Halévy, accepted the challenge and remained thereafter Offenbach's major collaborator.

Critics who attended the dress rehearsal of Les Deux Aveugles predicted a total failure. The libretto was unquestionably funny and the tunes light and witty, but the basic idea, a quarrel between two sham beggars, was thought too sordid to capture the public fancy. Even Halévy thought the work would fail, but Offenbach's confidence was unshaken, and was triumphantly vindicated on opening night. The public embraced these rogues with an enthusiasm equal to that shown for that earlier great rogue, Lemaître's Macaire. Now Patachon and Giraffier, like Macaire, appeared in all the theatrical reviews, in the cartoons and the skits of the day. Offenbach's music, particularly his Boléro, enjoyed a similar vogue in balls and café-concerts. The tiny Bouffés-Parisiens was packed every night. It could hardly have been a comfortable place. The tiers of seats climbed so steeply that a comic review compared them to a ladder with human beings clinging to each rung, and at the top was a row of boxes so small that patrons could not remove their coats, it was said, unless they opened the door and the window outside in the corridor as well. Yet the vogue for the theatre was so great that these cramped and uncomfortable conditions were generally considered charming and intimate. They doubtless also encouraged an informality between actors and audience that remained even after Offenbach moved to more spacious quarters. Hortense Schneider, later the theatre's leading lady, relied on such close involvement with her audiences that she could exchange quips with them or even pause to laugh at a good sally from the house without creating the impression of a break in the performance.

When winter came and the Exposition closed, Offenbach moved to a somewhat more elegant but scarcely larger theatre, the former Théâtre des Jeunes Elèves. Like Hervé, he had been limited in his first theatre to two actors, but he was allowed four for Ba-ta-clan (1855), the first work in the new Bouffés. This tale of a Chinese king with only twenty-seven subjects showed the influence of the recent Exposition with its mingling of nationalities and introduced a number of themes to which Offenbach and Halévy would frequently return. There was deft parody of grand opera, and particularly of Meyerbeer. There was the exuberant joy of the music which, Jules Janin commented, "gave people of all ages an irresistible urge to dance."[8] And finally, there was the picture of public life in general and court life in particular as an elaborate mummery, a playing of meaningless games of politics and power.

It is perhaps fruitless to speculate how consciously Offenbach and Halévy set out to reflect their society in comic opera terms. It is probably most accurate to assume that their work was a product of a society which in its illusions, its mock pomposity, and its heady pursuit of pleasure had in itself a quality of comic opera. The smoldering dissatisfaction of the workers, the students, and the republicans presented a threat that neither Napoleon III nor any of those who surrounded him could come to terms with intellectually, politically, or emotionally. And so, instead of social reform came the huge public works programs of Baron Haussmann, instead of business reform came a period of reckless financial speculation, instead of a concern with real and contemporary problems came a society of balls, feasts and revels, of romantically remote wars and great celebrations at home --the Peace Congress, the great Expositions, the christening of the Prince Imperial. Offenbach was fortunate in finding in Halévy a shrewd and astute observer of the contemporary scene who could capture its essence without being taken in by its shams or becoming embittered or sardonic in seeing through them. All the affectations, the pomposity of the time appear in his libretti, and yet so does the exuberance, the joy of life which was both a release and a shield from a darker reality. And Offenbach's music, of course, was the perfect accompaniment for this strange blend.

Offenbach produced the works of a number of composers at the Bouffés. There were lesser works of such famous names as Adam, Mozart, and Rossini. There were also new names; in 1856 he held a contest for the best new comic opera and thus introduced to the theatre Charles Lecocq and Georges Bizet. Most of his offerings, however, were from his own pen, which was no great handicap, for he was a prolific author. In 1857 alone he produced twenty operettas, five pantomimes and several cantatas, in addition to carrying out the responsibilities of producer and director. A new license in 1858 allowed him to present longer plays with more actors; the immediate result was the mythological travesty _Orphée aux enfers,_ the first of Offenbach's major works.

It was only a modest success until Jules Janin a month after the opening wrote a review denouncing the production as "a scandal, a sacrilege, a profanation of holy and glorious antiquity."[9] The result of this, as Janin in a cooler mood might have been aware, was to stimulate enormous public interest in the play, which ran for a spectacular 225 performances.

Janin's outrage at Offenbach's cavalier treatment of the Olympic gods seems more than a little surprising when we recall that Hervé had established the operetta with mythological travesties and that such parody had been a common feature of French cartoons and vaudevilles for most of the century. One feels compelled to agree with the critics who have argued that Janin's discomfiture arose less from the mythological than the political echoes of the play. When Archduke Maximilian paid his first visit to Napoleon III's court, he wrote home to Schönbrunn in some dismay: "There is something amateurish and theatrical about the whole thing, and the various roles are played by officials who are not very sure of their parts."[10] The pleasure-loving court of the amorous Jupiter, concerned only with amusement and distraction, trembling only on occasion before an inspired chorus-figure, Public Opinion, clearly had many points of similarity to this. At one point the gods, tired of nectar and ambrosia, are tempted to throw off this world of illusion and turn upon Jupiter with a revolutionary song through which echoes the "Marseillaise," but Offenbach and Halévy were observers, not revolutionaries. The mood subsides, the gaiety returns, the dance goes on. The waltzes and galops from _Orphée_ swept Paris from the Tuileries to the smallest suburban taverns.

By 1860 Offenbach's reputation earned him an invitation to write a work for the Opéra-Comique, long one of his goals. But _Barkouf_, calling for a dog on stage and music imitating his barking, scandalized the critics and did not please the public. Another disappointment came in 1864 when his _Rheinnixen_, a grand opera commissioned for Vienna, proved a complete failure there. Offenbach now returned to the sort of work which had established his fame. _La Belle Hélène_ (1865), presented at the Variétés, was received much as _Orphée_ had been. Classicists complained of its desecration of Homer and the public flocked to it and sang its songs throughout Paris. The court parody seemed clearer here than in _Orphée_ and was given a darker tone by the threat of destruction which hung over the frivolous Trojan court, but this possible implication of the play was understandably officially avoided. Hortense Schneider, who ever since the early days at the first Bouffés had been associated with Offenbach, emerged as a major star with her rich and sensuous interpretation of Hélène. Her fame grew with two more Offenbach comedies on unlikely subjects; Barbe-bleu (1866) transformed horror into uproarious humor and La Grande-Duchesse de Gerolstein (1867) gave Parisians the opportunity to laugh at the rising German militarism under Bismarck. For La Vie Parisienne (1866), at the Palais-Royal, Offenbach and his librettists, Meilhac and Halévy, selected at last a contemporary story, but avoided any mention of the court or contemporary politics. Instead there is developed a picture of the exuberant flow of life in fashionable Paris, full of fancies and improbabilities, but by that very quality catching something of the dream-like state of the city just before the reckoning of 1870.

During the years between the great Expositions of 1855 and 1867 Offenbach was really the only important producer of operettas in Paris. Even Hervé, his predecessor in the genre, had been forced by ill health to retire from the theatre just as Offenbach's career was getting started. After 1867, however, Offenbach had to share the field with a whole group of composers, and half a dozen Parisian theatres were needed to present all their contributions. Hervé returned to the Folies-Dramatiques in 1867 with L'Oeil crevé, and within two years had presented that theatre with three other important successes--Le Petit Faust, Les Turcs, and Chilpéric. All of these works showed a strong influence from Offenbach, though Hervé laid more emphasis on farcical elements. He even found an actress, Blanche d'Antigny, whose style was so close to that of Hortense Schneider that it became almost a parody.

A new composer, Charles Lecocq, emerged to dominate the next decade of operetta as Offenbach had dominated the 1860s. His Fleur-de-thé (1868) attracted favorable attention to a new and rather unimportant little theatre, the Athenée, but he was recognized as a master of the genre with La Fille de Madame Angot, presented at the Folies in 1873. Lecocq and his librettists, Koning, Clairville and Siraudin, had the happy idea of writing a sequel to the adventures of the parvenu fishwife who had so delighted audiences of the Directory, and the resulting satire on the social pretensions of the Second Empire proved more durable than any other operetta of the period except Offenbach's two or three most successful. During the 1870s, Lecocq was associated with the Renaissance, a new theatre built for operetta in 1872. Under the direction of Hostein, and with the librettists Vanloo and Leterrier, Lecocq made this little theatre the center of Parisian operetta for almost a decade. The actress Jeanne Granier, who was as closely associated with Lecocq's work as Hortense Schneider was with Offenbach's, made her debut in the first of his works presented here, Giroflé-Girofla (1874). La Marjolaine (1877) had an elaborate Belgian scene by the designer Cornil which was considered outstanding even in a period of generally lavish settings. The most popular offering of the period was Le Petit Duc (1878), for which Lecocq deserted his usual collaborators to work with those of Offenbach, Meilhac and Halévy.

For Offenbach the 1870s were difficult years. The French defeat of 1870 naturally tarnished the reputation of a composer born in Prussia, and he returned in 1871 from a year of self-imposed exile to find himself condemned by some as a supporter of the Emperor and by others as an agent of the Prussians who had wittingly or unwittingly undermined French spirit with his decadent works. All these trials seem to have affected his next operettas, which proved gloomy and unattractive. Hoping to launch his own operetta theatre once again, Offenbach purchased the Gaîté, only to encounter new difficulties. The now-powerful Société des Auteurs pointed out to Offenbach that it would not allow a director to present his own plays, and for almost a year he was forced to offer unsuccessful dramas at the Gaîté while the more popular of his own works, now coming back into favor, drew audiences to the rival Variétés, Bouffés, Folies, and Renaissance. By 1873 his financial situation was so desperate that the Société relented and permitted the Gaîté to revive Orphée aux enfers. Offenbach took no chances with this revival; he removed any satire likely to offend his audience and shifted the emphasis of the presentation to spectacle and a scantily-clad chorus. A stage machinist trained in London, Godin, added such effects as a dawn on Olympus, represented by the clock of heaven, a blue globe on which a woman stood swinging a pendulum which struck and thus introduced a series of transformations: a procession of hours, then dreams--black, pink, gold, and silver--then grey clouds, changing color and parting to reveal the marble hemisphere and gigantic steps of Olympus. There was a chorus of 120 members and a corps de ballet of sixty-eight. The debutant Louise Théo was praised as Euridice, but the production was essentially what one critic called "an exhibition of legs and décor."[11]

This was followed by a somewhat more respectable success, La Jolie Parfumeuse (1873), a light opera in the manner of Lecocq.

All of the profits from these two works Offenbach put back into a colossal production of a new play by Sardou, La Haine (1874), for which Offenbach wrote incidental music. The production boasted settings as elaborate as any romantic opera and huge, realistic mob scenes, surpassing even those of Dumas at the Historique. "The portrayal of the mob forcing the gate of the castle was scrupulously accurate," Sardou later reported. "Men raised beams, broke down the walls, acted realistically just as workers set to such a task would act." Unfortunately, all this expense and care did not make the production a success, and the defeated Offenbach soon after turned the Gaîté over to a new director, Vizentini.

Freed from the burdens of this venture, Offenbach found his fortunes improving. He created the music for Vizentini's first major success at the Gaîté, a spectacular fairy play, Le Voyage dans la lune (1875), with a script by Vanloo, Leterrier, and Mortier. He then departed for a triumphant series of concerts in America. Once again the old dream of producing a major operatic work returned to him, and in 1877 he began work on Les Contes de Hoffmann. The grotesque and fatalistic subject of the work seemed in these final years more and more suitable to Offenbach as he came to realize that he was engaged in a race with death for the completion of the work. Yet he found time to return once again to the light and witty operettas which had made him famous. La Fille du Tambour-Major (1879) at the Folies and La Belle Lurette (1879) at the Renaissance were extremely popular examples of the old Offenbach spirit. Les Contes de Hoffmann, presented at the Opéra-Comique in February, 1881, was a great success, the fulfillment of Offenbach's dreams. But the composer himself was not present. He had died four months before, shortly after the completion of the manuscript.

3. Comédie and Odéon, 1848-1879

The Empire's new director of the Comédie, Arsène Houssaye, got on well with Rachel, as we have seen, but his relations with the rest of his company were less satisfactory. His leniency with his leading actress may have been part of the cause, and some actors clearly agreed with Jules Janin, who criticized him as too young for the position. More likely, however, the major source of conflict with the sociétaires came simply from their habit of having their own way. Any director would probably have found them a difficult group. Almost at the outset Houssaye was threatened with a mass resignation if he did not give way on certain points, but he cooly proposed advancing the pensionnaires and hiring Odéon and boulevard actors such as Bocage, Lemaître, and Mélingue, and the rebellion quickly dissolved.

The major victims of the tension between director and company were probably young dramatists, since Houssaye expressed an interest in presenting the new authors appearing during the Empire, while his conservative company usually rejected such works. Scribe thus remained the mainstay of the Comédie, collaborating with Legouvé on Les Contes de la Reine de Navarre (1850) and Bataille des dames (1851). Madeleine Brohan made a memorable debut in the former work and established herself as one of the Comédie's outstanding actresses in the title role of Mademoiselle de la Seiglière (1851). Houssaye wrote to the Minister that her appearance was an occasion for "genuine festivity in the house of Molière."

> She has beauty, a golden voice, intelligence and charm.... She was charming yesterday, she is charming today, she will be more charming still tomorrow. She has at once dared to break the bonds of the 'school.' When she shall be a little more of a woman--for she is only seventeen--she will play Celimène better, but she is already fit to play many parts. Hence her advent is a stroke of luck to the Comédie Française which, at Mlle Rachel's return, has some brilliant morrows in store for it. [12]

Interested in staging Molière with the original spectacle, Houssaye borrowed the corps de ballet from his friend Roqueplan at the Opéra and engaged Offenbach to build up the Comédie orchestra. Once again the sociétaires protested, arguing that the acting was being overshadowed, but while their reading committee could veto new plays, they had little control over production of old ones, and Houssaye won on this point. His spectacular productions of L'Amour médecin and Le Médecin malgré lui delighted the public, whatever the company thought of them, and did much to restore the theatre's depleted accounts.

Among the moderns, the most successful authors produced by Houssaye after Scribe were Ponsard and Léon Gozlan. Ponsard's *Charlotte Corday* (1850) was considered his best work, though Rachel felt the modern Ponsard to be beneath her talents and advised Houssaye to feature the less talented Mlle Judith "who has," Rachel explained, "neither personality nor opinions."[13] This haughtiness was suitably rewarded, for Judith achieved a clear success in *Charlotte Corday*, while the sterile neo-classic *Horace et Lydie* (1850), which Ponsard created at Rachel's request, was a failure. After this, not even a classic subject could tempt Rachel to undertake Ponsard's *Ulysse* (1851), and Houssaye again turned to Mlle Judith. She had no more success than Rachel with Ponsard's dull classicism; the only favorable comments on the production were gained by the choruses, created by the then almost unknown composer Charles Gounod. Ponsard subsequently deserted the Comédie for the Odéon and classic tragedy for contemporary comedy.

Léon Gozlan, who wrote spectacular melodramas for the Porte-Saint-Martin such as *Le Livre noir* (1848) and *Pied-de-fer* (1850), created for the Comédie a series of delightful fantasy *proverbes* in the manner of Musset: *La Queue du chien d'Alcibiade* (1850), *La Fin du roman* (1851), *La Pluie et le beau temps* (1861). His full-length contributions to the Comédie were far less distinguished, only the Scribean historical fantasy *Le Gâteau des reines* (1855) achieving a moderate success. With Ponsard gone to the Odéon, Gozlan apparently unable to create a successful major work, and such authors as Dumas *fils* and Augier apparently settled at the Gymnase and Vaudeville, it is little wonder that Houssaye, the would-be innovator, grew increasingly discouraged. The departure of Rachel on tour in 1855 seems to have been a final blow for him, and he retired the following year.

The Odéon during the 1850s struggled to break free of fifteen years' stagnation. Non-musical theatre had regained supremacy during the 1840s but success eluded director after director. The decade saw four administrations, and four bankruptcies. The most recent in this unhappy series, Augustin Vizentini, had to flee the country to escape his creditors in 1848, leaving the Odéon actors to form a society without any director. For two years it remained in this state, with the better actors leaving for other theatres. Then in 1850 Marie-Michel Altaroche, a politician with little theatrical experience, took charge of the insolvent, frequently closed theatre and began to restore it to stability. His first important success was the bizarre and original Contes de Hoffmann (1851) by Jules Barbier and Michel Carré, which later served as the basis for Offenbach's opera. Henry Monnier and Gustave Vaëz' Grandeur et décadence de Monsieur Joseph Prudhomme (1852) was the first important success in a genre that was to become a staple for the Odéon--bourgeois comedy. The company, still suffering from its losses in the past decade, was not outstanding, but the actors Laferrière and Tisserant now gained an appreciable following.

Alphonse Royer, the Odéon director from 1853 to 1856, continued to build on the base Altaroche had established, and had moreover the good fortune to receive Ponsard's modern comedies L'Honneur et l'argent (1853) and La Bourse (1856) when Ponsard left the Comédie. The other high points of this administration were the dramatizations of George Sand's novels, chiefly remembered in later years for their emphasis on realism in the bucolic settings. With Dumas fils, Augier and their contemporaries, the concern for scenic authenticity which had manifested itself in regard to historical subjects during the romantic period shifted, along with the subjects of the plays, to contemporary society. In this respect Sand's works carried on the experimentation begun at the Odéon by François le Champi in 1849, which aroused much interest by its realistic peasant costumes and settings designed by Cambon. Both the Odéon and the Comédie, as early as the 1850s, were also showing a realist interest in revivals of the classics, though of course with only hints of the extremes this interest would involve by the end of the century. Royer's succesor at the Odéon, La Rounat, shared Houssaye's interest in the use of authentic period furniture, but sought also to develop realistic business. In the popular 1857 revival of Tartuffe, for example, Orgon dropped into a chair before the fire upon entering, and Dorine removed his muddy boots during the line, "La campagne à présent n'est pas beaucoup fleurie."

In 1856 Houssaye was replaced at the Comédie by the dramatist Adolphe Dominique Empis. His brief and undistinguished administration clearly felt the loss of Rachel, especially since the Italien during the same years was interspersing its musical offerings with guest appearances by the great Italian actress Ristori. She first appeared in 1855 with the noted Italian actor Ernesto Rossi and other members of the Royal Sardinian company, and her success was so great that for several years after, she returned regularly to the Italien, presenting plays by Goldoni, Maffei, and Alfieri.

Rachel's departure from the Comédie focused more attention on Ristori, especially when in 1856 the Italian actress presented in her own language Legouvé's Medée, a role which Rachel had refused. It was a powerful emotional interpretation, as the actress' own description of the climax indicates:

> At this point I snatch my little Melyant--I raise him--I press him under my arm, while with the other arm I drag Licaon and make an attempt to run. Some of the threatening mob force me to go back. I try in vain to open for myself a passage at the other end, but the cries which come from the palace, 'To death! to death!' force me to look for another way of escape. At that point the mob rushes in like a torrent from every side and tries to take the children from me... with a spring I rush upon the altar of Saturn, dragging both my children with me. The people of Corinth rush upon me, surround me from every side, when a cry of horror bursts forth from them, which announces that the nefarious sacrifice has been accomplished. The people draw back at such a sight and allow Medea to be seen, her eyes haggard, fixed, her body drawn and contracted like a statue of remorse, her two slain children at her feet. [14]

Legouvé now began to beg Ristori to appear for him in a play in French, and after much hesitation she presented his Beatrix at the Odéon in 1861. Though her accent proved something of a distraction, her success was sufficient to justify reviving the work for her later visits to Paris.

At the Comédie Legouvé continued his profitable collaboration with Scribe to produce Les Doigts de fée (1858), though the administration of Empis was the last to make the work of Scribe and his collaborators the basis of the modern repertoire. Edouard Thierry, who became director in 1859, accomplished what Houssaye had hoped but failed to do, bringing into the national theatre younger dramatists, especially those who had gained a reputation in minor theatres during the preceding decade. Augier therefore dominated the premieres of the 1860s as Scribe had dominated those of the 1850s. Les Effrontés (1861) and Le Fils de Giboyer (1862) shared certain characters and themes: speculation, class conflict, and a new concern, to be more fully developed later --anticlericalism. These two works at the Comédie unquestionably established Augier's supremacy among dramatists of the contemporary scene. Such critics as Sarcey, Doumic, and Lemaître united in calling them the Mariage de Figaro of the period--perfect expressions of contemporary political and social feeling. Augier left such concerns temporarily with Maître Guérin (1864), but returned to them again with La Contagion (1866), a general attack on the scepticism of the times, built around two standard Augier characters, the heartless courtesan Navarette and the unscrupulous financier, the Baron d'Estrigaud. A quarrel with the Comédie actors led Augier to take La Contagion to the Odéon, where the volatile but erratic Latin Quarter audience hissed down this work, but as warmly applauded his next political piece, Lions et Rénards (1869), which dealt with the same concerns. The wily Baron is again the central figure in the new play, now pitted against M. de St. Agathe, a representative of clericalism who is in search of political power.

The first major success of Thierry's administration was Le Duc Job (1859) by Léon Laya, who had already received much praise for Les Jeunes Gens (1855). These two light but popular works, called by some critics vaudevilles without the music, placed Laya first among the theatre's modern comic writers, and with La Loi de coeur (1862) remained long in the repertoire. The actor most associated with the plays of Augier and Laya at the Comédie was Edmond Got, who established himself during this decade as the leader among actors of modern comedy. Of him, the critic Montégut observed:

> M. Got has brought a new element to the Comédie, the feeling of reality. Although he understands fully the tradition of his art, he still does not seek his inspiration there; he takes his models from living nature, from the spectacle of contemporary reality. He doesn't compose his roles, he incarnates them, so that his playing possesses a spirit, a vivacity, a seductiveness such as is found in no other contemporary actor. He is truly incomparable in Le Duc Job; one might say that he has plumbed every depth of the character which the author created.[15]

One of Got's greatest triumphs was in L'Illusion comique, for Thierry also shared Houssaye's interest in restoring the original versions of Corneille and Molière to the stage. This interest in a purified text, along with accurate costumes and elaborate but historically exact settings, was carried on after

1871 by Thierry's successor, Perrin.

Got, though the most popular, was of course not the only significant new talent to appear at the Comédie during the Second Empire. In his own area of comedy he was followed in 1860 by Constant Coquelin, an actor of great charm and style who eventually gained a kind of theatrical immortality by his creation at the close of the century of Cyrano de Bergerac. His younger brother, Ernest, joined the Comédie eight years later, building a solid, but lesser reputation on a different comedic approach. Alphonse Daudet in the mid-1870s sought to characterize the two popular brothers:

> The talent of the two brothers is as different as their physique. The one has a deep laugh, the other a long one; Coquelin elder is at ease in the comedy of Molière, Regnard, bold, open comedy, forcing us by its frankness and brilliance to forgive the sometimes unthinking boldness of its gaiety. Add to this the magic of a truly admirable delivery, and a skill that can betray, for M. Coquelin is a man who can make you hear Beethoven when he is playing _Au clair de la lune._ Beside M. Coquelin the elder, M. Coquelin the younger has found the means to make himself applauded in roles where he is admirable in his simplicity, his finesse, his honest drollery. His good humor has nothing to do with that of his brother. It is a colder comedy, more peaceful yet often quite irresistable. With a little training in acrobatics he could become a fine clown.[16]

Two major _jeunes premiers_ came from other theatres; Louis Arsène Delaunay, like Coquelin younger, came from the Odéon, in 1848, and Jean Baptiste Bressant from the Gymnase in 1854. Bressant had been at the Gymnase since 1846, and had, with Rose Chéri, created many of the major works of the new drama there. At the Comédie, he continued to excel in works by Scribe, Augier and Sandeau, but it was said that he always played himself, and the style of the classic works remained beyond him. His health began to fail after 1870, and he retired in 1875. Delaunay began with less striking success than Bressant, but proved ultimately both more flexible and more durable. His range included Musset, Augier, Pailleron, Hugo, and Molière, and to all he brought a freshness and impression of youth which seemed remarkably impervious to his own aging. Aside from his physical charm, he was much praised for his diction, which Sarcey for one considered almost unique:

> Except for Mlle Sarah Bernhardt, whose diction is a natural gift, no actor of our times approaches Delaunay in the exquisite and knowing art with which he delivers a poetic line, giving each word its proper value without ever disturbing the shape of the line; always being careful to maintain the proper harmony of the verse and the sound of the rhyme despite whatever breaks the sense of the line might require. It is pure pleasure to hear the music of this young and caressing voice whether it is performing in the sober, clear, and firm alexandrines of Molière, Corneille, or Piron, or in the poetic prose of Marivaux, or Alfred de Musset. One might say without fear of error that in this respect Delaunay is a virtuoso without an equal in the present time and doubtless with few equals in the past.[17]

In _Henriette Maréchal_ (1865), at the age of 39, he played an eighteen-year-old with great success, looking if anything rather young for the part, and in the 1880s he still maintained his conviction in youthful roles, having long since become affectionately styled "the eternal _jeune premier_" by the Parisian theatre public.

Madeleine Brohan's success in Scribean comedy during the 1850s has already been mentioned. The two other important new female talents of this period at the Comédie were Mme Arnould-Plessy, who returned to major roles in 1855 after a long stay in Russia, and Mme Guyon, who came from the boulevards in 1858 to assume the tragic leads. Both were actresses of distinction, though both naturally suffered by the inevitable comparisons with the departed genius, Rachel. Samson, Geoffroy, Regnier and Provost still had their public, but the emphasis at the Comédie was now on the young, in actors as in dramatists.

Thierry's administration introduced several important new playwrights to the public, though their Comédie debuts were in general more promising than successful. Sardou was the best known of these new talents, having presented successful works at the Déjazet, the Gymnase, and the Vaudeville before the Comédie offered _La Papillonne_ in 1862. Neither it nor Pailleron's Comédie debut, _Le Dernier Quartier_

(1863), was well received, and the disappointed authors returned to the more congenial Gymnase and Vaudeville. Two young poetic dramatists appeared with little fanfare in 1865, Emile Bergerat with *Une Ami* and Théodore de Banville with *La Pomme*. Banville's subsequent *Gringoire* (1866) provided Coquelin with his first important success.

A rather special premiere was *Henriette Maréchal* (1865), the first dramatic work by the noted authors Edmond and Jules de Goncourt. Though the Goncourts styled themselves politically neutral, they took little pains to conceal the pleasure they felt in receiving the attention and encouragement of the Princess Mathilde. This mark of Imperial favor, especially at a time when works by the idolized exile Victor Hugo were being kept from the stage, spurred Republican sympathizers to insure the unfavorable reception of this rather innocuous play. Parisian students formed the heart of the resistance to the government, and shortly before the opening of the Goncourt play a note was circulated in the school of Law signed by the popular leader George Cavalier, called "Pipe-en-bois": "All students of law are invited to gather this Monday evening at the Théâtre-Français to hiss the new play, *Henriette Maréchal*. The curtain must fall after the first act."[18] In fact, the drama was presented to its conclusion, though few lines could be heard above the uproar. Thierry offered the play six times, in a tumult characterized by the *chef de claque* as the worst since *Hernani*, before giving up and cancelling the production. The references to the battle of *Hernani* only further infuriated the students, who considered the Goncourts a symbol of the reactionary forces the honored poet had resisted. Largely to pacify such spirits, Thierry at last arranged for a revival of *Hernani* in 1867.

The riots over *Henriette Maréchal* were an isolated occurance at the Comédie, but the Odéon regularly suffered from such demonstrations. Even plays with no political overtones were hissed from the stage if their authors, like the Goncourts, were considered too friendly with the court. Little wonder that La Rounat, whose administration ran from 1856 until 1867, preferred to offer his explosive Latin Quarter audience innocuous light comedy and verse plays. He particularly favored the now-forgotten poet Louis Bouilhet, author of *La Conjuration d'Amboise* (1866), but more to his credit, he also encouraged the young Pailleron, premiered Musset's *Carmosine* (1865), and presented *Le Marquis de Villemer* (1864), one of George Sand's most popular works.

His company was not a distinguished one, its only important member being Frédéric Febvre, who soon went on to the Comédie.

In 1864 La Rounat conceived the idea of bringing Frédérick Lemaître to the Odéon to play Tartuffe and Harpagon, a recent government ruling having freed the works of Molière for presentation at theatres other than the Comédie. Lemaître was at this time again in the public eye after several years of eclipse. He returned to Paris from his self-imposed exile in 1852, but the decline of the romantic theatre left him with few plays that could demonstrate his abilities, and during the next decade he created no major new roles. Finally, in 1864, Edouard Plouvier's drama _Le Comte de Saulles_ at the Ambigu provided him with a suitable vehicle, and the ageing actor dazzled audiences and critics again as he had done in his youth. Coppée described his impressions in his _Journal_:

> Aged and exhausted by a life of irregularity and excess, he regained the power and agility of his youth. He leaped about, filling the stage with his grand, flowing gestures and his giant strides. He shed real tears and his eyes burned with a passionate fire. His face reddened with authentic anger, went pale with genuine terror, softened with sincere pity. His voice, faint when he began, burst forth with cries, groans, sobs. This was truth itself as life shows it, but truth as it should be revealed to the public, that is to say magnified by art, poetic, moving, and glorious![19]

Shortly after this production, the government awarded the Legion of Honor to Samson, now Dean of the Comédie and the first actor to receive this honor. Not a few journals protested that the award rightfully belonged to Lemaître, and the time seemed right to give the great boulevard actor an opportunity to show his ability at the classic repertoire. La Rounat planned for the Molière presentations to follow _Le Marquis de Villemer_, for which he anticipated a short run, but its great success upset his plans. By the time he was ready to mount a new production, the public interest in Lemaître which had been aroused by _Le Comte de Saulles_ and the Legion of Honor controversy had largely dissipated, and La Rounat feared that he could no longer rely on Lemaître's name to attract audiences. He therefore withdrew his invitation and Lemaître remained on the boulevard, still bringing flashes of his old greatness to small theatres and insignificant plays, until his death in 1876.

As the Second Empire drew toward its close, political demonstrations grew more violent and more common at the Odéon, and the combined administration of La Rounat's successors, Charles Chilly and Duquesnel, from 1867 until 1872, is remembered for little else. Particularly bitter were the protests occasioned in 1868 when Chilly's attempted revival of Ruy Blas was forbidden by the government, though Chilly had the satisfaction of carrying through this project with great success after 1870. The most important work presented during these years was François Coppée's Le Passant (1869), which introduced not only an important new dramatist but an even more important new actress, Sarah Bernhardt.

Bernhardt had made an undistinguished debut seven years before at the Comédie, then almost immediately became involved in one of the typical Comédie artistic quarrels, with Mme Nathalie. As usual, the established actress prevailed, and Bernhardt was dismissed. A series of engagements in small theatres followed; then in 1866, with the support of the actor Pierre Berton, she was engaged at the Odéon. Her debut in Le Jeu de l'amour et du hasard was another failure, but her power and assurance steadily grew. By 1868 her command was such that she successfully quieted a student demonstration which broke out during a revival of Dumas' Kean. Then came Le Passant and her first important creation--the youth Zanetto, a role ideally suited to her slim, boyish figure. Coppée's mistress, Mme Agar, played opposite Sarah, and the delight the dramatist expressed with his two interpretresses was warmly shared by the general public:

> What can I say of Agar, so majestically beautiful in her white satin dress with its flowing train?--What can I say of Sarah, so slim then, so svelte! Sarah, who possessed so completely the suppleness, the lightness, the grace of a youth. How admirably gifted they both were! What nobility of gesture, what deep emotion in my Silvia! What rapture, what delight, what youthful folly in my Zanetto! They both recited marvelously, and I took infinite pleasure in the contrast between Sarah's golden voice and Agar's moving contralto. One word must be used to describe the first inter-

pretation of Le Passant. It was perfection.[20]

Sarah scarcely had time to enjoy her new success when her career, along with the entire theatrical life of the capital, was interrupted by the Franco-Prussian War. The declaration of war on July 18, 1870, had an almost immediate effect on the theatres of Paris. The July 19 performance at the Opéra, featuring Marie Sasse singing the "Marseillaise," became almost legendary. Most of the smaller theatres were able to assure themselves large and enthusiastic audiences by the production of patriotic dramas. For a brief period, the capital enjoyed an almost holiday mood, but then came news of the increasingly catastrophic defeats, culminating in the capture of the Emperor with his entire army at Sedan in September. The lower house of Parliament met as soon as the news arrived, deposed the Emperor and laid the foundations of the Third Republic. During these turbulent days, the theatres were virtually deserted. A police decree of September 9, closing all theatres in Paris, was merely the official recognition of an already-existing situation. Ten days later German troops began to surround the city.

During the fall and winter, with Paris under siege, a number of the larger theatres were pressed into service as emergency hospitals. Enlisted men were cared for in the foyers of the Comédie, officers in the Galerie des bustes, while the former Emperor's box served as temporary quarters for members of the company who had volunteered as substitute nurses. Early in October, Sarah Bernhardt was instrumental in organizing a second hospital at the Odéon, and a third was later established at the Porte-Saint-Martin. All were plagued by shortages of supplies, especially fuel, and even when goods were available, money often was not. As a result, certain theatres began to reopen to present benefits for war victims. Beginning in October, the Comédie offered such productions, in street clothes, almost weekly, though the shortages and the attempt to combine the operation of a theatre and a hospital caused great difficulty. The main stairway was closed so that the audience would not have to come into the theatre past patients, but even so, the audience of Tartuffe on January 19 was terrified by the groans of the actor Seveste, who had been brought in that day badly wounded and who died shortly after. The Odéon began in November leading the same grotesque double existence.

A provisionary armistice allowed the closing of these emergency hospitals at the beginning of February, and the

Comédie soon after reopened for three days a week. By the end of the month, almost half of the regular theatres had reopened. Continuing political turbulence made theatrical production very irregular, however. At the end of February the French government accepted the German terms of surrender and German occupation forces entered Paris. A new menace appeared late in March, when internal revolutionists seized control of Paris, established a radical Commune, and defied the National Assembly, now meeting at Versailles. This insurrectionary government controlled Paris for almost a month, and was at length put down only with considerable loss of life and widespread destruction in the city.

During most of this terrible spring of 1871 only the Comédie, the Gymnase, and the tiny Délassements-Comiques were open. Distribution of parts was difficult with many actors fled from the city, yet receipts were so low and the political situation so uncertain that the Comédie was forced to split its small number, sending the older members under the direction of Got to obtain extra support by a London tour. By summer, however, conditions were returning to normal. Theatrical posters began to reappear in June. Coquelin's younger brother drew good audiences to the Comédie for _L'Aventurière._ Smaller houses reopened, among them the Cluny with Lemaître in a popular revival of _Trente Ans._ In July Got's company returned from London to rejoin their companions at the Comédie, and by fall the theatre world of Paris was ready to resume its interrupted course. Though Edouard Thierry had proved quite satisfactory as a director, protecting the fortunes of the national theatre as best he could, even during the difficult days of the Commune, the new order demanded a new administration, and he was replaced by Emile Perrin, a former director of the Opéra, the Opéra-Comique, and the Lyrique.

Perrin, who had never before managed a non-musical theatre, began his administration cautiously, with standard revivals and few new works. Among the latter, a modest success was attained by Gondinet's _Christiane_ (1871), but Pailleron's _Hélène_ (1872) was a costly failure, which added to Perrin's conservatism. Much more significant in his first years was the new director's search for talented young actors. He encouraged Sophie Croizette, who had been kept back by older tragediennes, after her brilliant debuts, and brought to the Comédie Jean Mounet-Sully and Sarah Bernhardt, surely its two greatest stars in the final third of the century. Mounet-Sully had arrived in Paris in 1863, and after training at the Conservatoire had played in suburban theatres directed by Larochelle. In 1867 he was brought to the Odéon to play Cornouailles in a revival of Ducis' Le Roi Léar with an excellent cast, including Bernhardt and Réjane. After the war, Mounet-Sully considered his Odéon wages insufficient and left to appear in an influential matinee series directed by Ballande at the Gaîté. Here Perrin saw him in 1872 and encouraged him to come to the Comédie. His debut opposite Rosalia Rousseil in Andromaque was a triumph, an evening which Sarcey reported remained fresh in the memories of all patrons of the theatre for years after:

> When he came on stage, his arms bare, superb arms that seemed to be shaped from antique marble, the locks falling in disorder on his brow, his eyes full of oriental melancholy, glowing mysteriously, a cry went up from the entire house--we seemed to see appearing on the stage one of those passionate and ferocious Arabs that Regnault loved to paint. It was a wholly new way of understanding the role and interpreting the character.[21]

Once again, as in the time of Rachel, an actor had been discovered who could almost single-handedly revive the moribund classic tragedy.

For the moment, however, Perrin was more interested in reviving Hugo than Racine. The poet had returned from exile with the fall of the Empire, and never had his fame and popularity been so great as now. Just before his retirement from the Odéon, Chilly mounted in 1872 the previously-banned Ruy Blas. The political situation assured that this production would be a national event, and the Odéon mounted a presentation worthy of the occasion, headed by four of the best actors of the time: Bernhardt, Mélingue, Geoffroy, and Lafontaine. Bernhardt was particularly praised in this, her richest interpretation to date. Sarcey wrote:

> Mlle Sarah Bernhardt has received from nature the gift of melancholy, plaintive dignity. All her movements are noble and harmonious; the long folds of her silvery robe flow about her with poetic grace. Her voice is soft and languishing, her diction so rhythmical, so exquisitely clear that not a syllable is ever lost, even when the words are breathed forth like a caress.[22]

Théodore de Banville wrote simply: "Always, until the end of time, men will recall the image of Sarah Bernhardt when Ruy Blas says: 'She wore a little diadem of silver lace.'"

Perrin at the Comédie naturally felt the reverberations of this success, one of the greatest of the century. Within a few days he had extended an offer to Sarah Bernhardt to join his company and had begun plans for his own major Hugo revival, _Marion de Lorme_. Despite a rather operatic but splendid _mise en scène_, and the talents of Mme Favart, Got, Delaunay, and Mounet-Sully, the 1873 _Marion de Lorme_ was not the success Perrin anticipated. Several years passed, therefore, before he decided to continue his project with the more profitable revivals of _Hernani_ (1878), _Ruy Blas_ (1879), and _Le Roi s'amuse_ (1882). Sarah made her Comédie debut as Chimène opposite Mounet-Sully in _Le Cid_, making as striking a first impression on her audience there as her partner had a few months before. Théodore de Banville saw a new era opening at the national theatre:

> Very tall, thin, endowed with that slimness which we find in so many theatrical heroines, even though it gives such ready ammunition to wits, Mlle Sarah has one of those expressive yet delicate heads that medieval artists painted in the miniatures of their manuscripts. Her profoundly deep eyes, limpid and sparkling, her straight, narrow nose, her red mouth that opens like a flower to expose the whiteness of her teeth, a long and flexible neck--all this gives a striking and unforgettable impression like that rich and transparent coloration which is found in beautiful Dutch women... From Provost she learned pure, elegant, and scrupulously exact diction, but nature gave her a far rarer gift--the quality of being totally and unconsciously lyrical in whatever she attempts. Her voice captures the rhythm and music of poetry as naturally as a lyre... This makes her quite the opposite of other actors and actresses. They, as Talma so rightly explained, are always troubled by real poetry, which locks them in an inexorable bond of words. They are at their best when they obtain the sort of script they can turn to their own ends, a play with lively and well developed situations in which the style is of no importance... Mlle Sarah on the contrary receives all her inspiration and force from poetry, and the nearer she approaches

> the purely lyrical, the greater she is and the more she is herself. Make no mistake, the engagement of Mlle Sarah Bernhardt at the Comédie Française is serious and violently revolutionary. It is poetry entering the home of dramatic art; it is a wolf in the fold.[23]

After the departure of Chilly, his co-director Duquesnel managed the Odéon alone until 1879, placing the major emphasis during these years on spectacle. The loss of Bernhardt was doubtless one reason for this change of emphasis, but Duquesnel could not have been entirely motivated by the weakness of his company, since the Odéon during his administration had the services of several important actors--Porel, Albert Lambert, Lafontaine, and Mme Tessandier. The spectacular Odéon productions of the 1870s were in fact clearly related to trends in staging observable throughout the century, beginning with the elaborate effects of the melodramas and romantic theatre and carrying on through the emphasis on realistic detail found in the mid-century productions of social dramas. The _pièce à grand spectacle_ as presented at the Odéon and elsewhere was considered at the time largely a development of the post-war period, but its debt to these earlier traditions was great.

The _Ruy Blas_ revival of 1872 relied on Hugo's name to attract the public, but it was nonetheless mounted in as lavish a style as the theatre could afford, thus setting an example for future productions, especially for those which had to rely more on such display than on their author's reputation to gain a public. Duquesnel's first major productions, in 1873, were of works by important authors, but clearly audiences came to the Odéon more to see the lavish settings of Lecomte de Lisle's _Les Erinnyes_ than to welcome the Parnassians to the theatre, and the elaborate hunting scenes of _La Jeunesse de Louis XIV_ were a greater attraction than the name Dumas _père_ attached to the play. The success of these offerings then encouraged Duquesnel to embark on a whole series of huge historical dramas. _Les Danitchev_ (1876) by Corvin and Dumas _fils_, writing under the joint pen-name of Pierre Newski, confirmed his appraisal, though its enormous success was surely due in part to a general interest in Russia which followed the signing of the Franco-Russian alliance this year. Still, no such external consideration aided the success in 1877 of Paul Déroulède's _L'Hetman_, a mediocre work clearly made popular by Zarat and Cheret settings of seventeenth century Poland and the scrupulously authentic costumes of Thomas. The following year Zarat, Chéret, and Thomas similarly re-created scenes from eighteenth century France for Joseph Balsamo, a script in which Dumas was said to have some share. Among the eight huge scenes there was even an accurate reconstruction of the Hall of Mirrors at Versailles. Duquesnel more and more found himself the target of the same sort of criticism directed at his predecessor Harel during the romantic period; once again fears were expressed that France's second theatre was being debased by an interest in spectacle. Auguste Vitu was the only important critic in Paris who found any literary merit whatever in Joseph Balsamo. The criticism sharply increased when the success of Duquesnel's spectacles forced him to discontinue evenings devoted to the introduction of new young authors. An arrangement with the director of the Gaîté, Camille Weinschench, to present there matinee revivals of the classics with the combined troupes of these houses, lessened but did not silence the criticism, and in 1879 Duquesnel was forced to resign his position in favor of the previous director of the Odeon, La Rounat.

The major concern of the Comédie during the 1870s was the rivalry between its two popular young actresses, Sarah Bernhardt and Sophie Croizette. The acceptance of Croizette as a sociétaire in 1874, before Bernhardt, created particular bitterness, which flared up that year in the production of Octave Feuillet's Le Sphinx. Feuillet, like his Second Empire predecessors, specialized in rather melodramatic studies of adultery. Julie (1869) had depicted the agony and death of an unfaithful wife, and Le Sphinx's subject was the same, the title referring to a ring worn by the doomed woman and containing her liberating poison. At a period when interest in realism was increasing (Mounet-Sully had created a minor scandal the year before by smoking a cigarette on the Comédie stage in Augier and Sandeau's Jean de Thommeroy), Croizette consulted toxicologists for interesting symptoms to employ during her death scene, and exhibited spasms and agonies never before seen on the national stage. The public was enraptured and the critics appalled. Francisque Sarcey suggested in Le Temps that public interest in this spectacle was similar to that engendered by the guillotine:

> With the aid of certain tricks, whose secret was subsequently revealed in the newspapers, the actress' face suddenly became greenish, horribly decomposed, wrinkled in fearful contractions; her

> glazed and haggard eyes rolled in their sockets, her hands and legs trembled convulsively, and her head was shaken in the convulsions of lockjaw. These terrible spasms lasted only a few seconds but they seemed very long. The whole audience was seized by a shudder of revulsion, and some women cried out in horror. Somebody in the orchestra stalls hissed.[24]

Amid the scandal, Bernhardt could have been forgotten, but her supporters in the audience made sure her applause was equal to that for her more spectacular rival, and she gained extra praise from critics anxious to laud her at Croizette's expense. A realistic influence could also be seen in the settings for this influential production. The first act showed for the first time in the theatre a salon lighted by a luminous ceiling, and the moonlit park of the second act created a sensation.

The great success of 1875 at the Comédie was Henri de Bornier's *La Fille de Roland*, a weak echo of Hugo saved by its patriotic exhortations, its sumptuous archeological settings, and the brilliant interpretations of Bernhardt and Mounet-Sully, whose performances guaranteed the acceptance of both this year as *sociétaires*. Croizette attempted the same sort of physical presentation she had used in *Le Sphinx* for *On ne badine pas avec l'amour*. It was a total failure, and she abandoned Musset thenceforth to Bernhardt. Public desire now ran high for another play matching the talents of the Comédie's leading actresses, and the occasion was offered by Dumas' *L'Etrangère* (1876), his first work written for this theatre. The play was one of its author's weakest efforts, the sentimental tale of a naive heiress lured by "the Stranger," an American adventuress, into marriage with a debauched duke. Misguided innocence is at last rewarded when the duke is killed in a duel and his widow is freed to marry an honest engineer. The rival stars were in conflict from the moment of casting, and all Perrin's good offices were required to keep peace between them. Croizette was given the leading role of the American, Mrs. Clarkson, but in rehearsal it seemed to her that the Duchess, with less lines, had better scenes, and she demanded that the roles be changed. Bernhardt refused, and bitter quarrels ensued. Then, abruptly, Bernhardt gave way. Doubtless she had been considering in secret the possibilities of Croizette's role, and after the exchange she still dominated the play, gaining most of the plaudits from audience and critics, and adding more fuel to her rival's anger.

This victory for Bernhardt was shortly followed by another in Dominique-Alexandre Parodi's Rome vainçue (1876), the first major new classic work of Perrin's administration. Parodi, like de Bornier, attempted to revive the spirit of Hugo in elaborate historical dramas, though with no greater ultimate success. Rome vainçue, his best work, tells of a vestal virgin condemned to death for her love of a Roman soldier. Perrin selected Mounet-Sully and Bernhardt for the leading roles, but Bernhardt rather surprisingly requested not the virgin Opinia but the relatively minor role of the blind grandmother who eventually slew her. Perrin agreed, and gave Mounet-Sully a similarly elderly role to balance her. Their success in these unusual parts added greatly to the reputation of both.

A quite different note was struck in the last major offering of 1876, Erckmann-Chatrian's L'Ami Fritz, a modest study of life in Alsace that Zola later included, somewhat over-enthusiastically, among the precursors of realism in the theatre. The production did in fact allow Perrin to continue the development of realistic staging which had already been seen in Le Sphinx and L'Etrangère, and his attention to this sort of detail was long remembered by the public. Febvre notes in his Journal that the salad in L'Ami Fritz was generally considered the first realistic meal on the Comédie stage, though that honor actually belonged to wine and chicken consumed by Provost and Brindeau in Il ne faut jurer de rien in 1848. At any rate the press, which in general opposed Erckmann-Chatrain as politically suspect authors, dismissed the work as a "comédie gastronomique."[25]

Perrin's notable revival of Hernani in 1878, the year of the Great Exposition, has already been mentioned. The other major event of that year at the Comédie was the return of Augier with his last play, Les Fourchambault. In 1874 he had withdrawn his Madame Caverlet to make way for Dumas' L'Etrangère, taking it to the Vaudeville for the first Augier premiere outside the Comédie in sixteen years. Both Madame Caverlet and Les Fourchambault reflected Augier's long-standing concern with family morals. The former argued for divorce by showing a happy family menaced by the wife's first husband, from whom she had separated but who still had a claim on her according to French law. The latter repeated Augier's condemnation of marriage for money, spiced here by a bit of adultery. An erring husband and his threatened family are saved by the understanding and forgiveness of his former mistress and illegitimate son. Many argued that the sentimental conclusion contradicted Augier's earlier moral position, but his last play remained nonetheless one of his most popular. So great was its success, indeed, that Perrin revived Dumas' _Le Fils naturel_ to capitalize on its similar subject.

Perrin next attempted to revive _L'Aventurière_, but with little cooperation from Sarah Bernhardt. Her few years at the Comédie had seen a steady deterioration in relations between the actress and her director, who found her escapades, such as risking her life in a balloon ascension during the 1878 Exposition, increasingly irritating. Her efforts to force her way into a Comédie tour going to London in 1879 almost led to a cancellation of the entire venture, and Bernhardt went so far as to write an open letter in the _Figaro_ offering her resignation. _L'Aventurière_ came as the climax to all this. The actress argued against the revival, pleading her dislike of Augier, then did not attend rehearsals, pleading illness. The revival was a failure, with particularly bad reviews for its star. This time Perrin accepted his difficult actress's resignation and she departed for the Gaiety Theatre in London, where she had achieved a great success the summer before, then proceeded to a tour of America.

4. Lyric Theatre, 1849-1879

The Second Empire saw French opera evolve from the rather pompous artificiality of Meyerbeer to the lyricism and emotionality of Bizet and Gounod, with the yet unassimilated spirit of Wagner always hovering rather threateningly in the background. The spirit of romanticism, which had already left its mark on the physical settings, the libretti, and the dance, now at last moved clearly into the domain of music itself. Few indications of this change could be seen in the first Opéra administration of the period, that of Nestor Roqueplan, who directed the theatre from 1849 until 1854. True, Gounod made his Opéra debut with _Sapho_ (1851) and in 1850 the overture to _Tannhäuser_ was performed, the first Wagnerian presentation in Paris, but the major Opéra production of the period was Scribe and Auber's _L'Enfant prodigue_ (1850), remarkable only for its _mise en scène_, and lesser offerings were in general no more revolutionary. Roger had come from the Opéra-Comique in 1848 to replace Duprez as the theatre's leading singer, but if his roles changed, the composers he interpreted remained the same--Auber, Adam, and Halévy.

Despite Roqueplan's interest in the ballet, the decline which was to continue throughout the Second Empire in this genre was already clearly under way. Fanny Cerrito and her husband, Arthur Saint-Léon, engaged with such high expectations in 1848, separated in 1851 and only Saint-Léon remained at the Opéra. The real stars of the Opéra ballet in these years were the scenic artist Desplέchin and the chief machinist Victor Sacré. Mazilier's ballets no longer sought the traditional Germanic woods of the romantic period, but increasingly remote and bizarre settings--mythic Iceland in Orfa (1852), mythic Rome in Aelia et Mysis (1853), and 17th century Mexico in Jovita (1853), which challenged Sacré to create a grotto that could collapse at the conclusion of the second act.

Jovita saw the debut of Carolina Rosati, whose success was great and whose dramatic interpretation led such critics as Gautier to compare her with Elssler and Bigottini. Doubtless her ability at mime had much to do with the increasing dramatization of the ballet during her five years at the Opéra. La Fonti (1855), by the same artists who had created Jovita--the choreographer Mazilier, the composer Labarre, and Rosati--was generally considered a work to equal Giselle, La Péri, and Le Diable à quatre. Rosati's greatest success was Le Corsaire (1856) by Mazilier and Adam (his last score), but the ballerina here as always had to share the honors with Sacré, the machinist. The realistic presentation of stage ships became as fashionable at mid-century as volcanoes had been in the 1830s, but that of the final act of Le Corsaire was hailed as superior to any previously achieved; a popular mot was that Crosnier, who had followed Roqueplan as director in 1854, had saved the Opéra with a shipwreck.

Despite this success, Crosnier soon gave way in turn to a new director, Alphonse Royer. The first ballet which Royer presented, Mazilier and Gabrielli's Les Elfes (1856), introduced Amalia Ferraris, whose lightness and mechanical perfection led invariably to a comparison with Taglioni. Ballet audiences soon were divided in their preference between her and Rosati as they had been in the days of Taglioni and Elssler. Royer could not resist the temptation to cast the two together in Mazilier and Auber's Marco-Spada (1858), a widely anticipated confrontation which predictably only confirmed the two camps in their previous preferences. The work was otherwise most notable for one of Sacré's most elaborate effects--for one scene the whole front half of the stage rose with some thirty persons on it to reveal the next scene taking place in a grotto beneath.

In 1858 Ferraris added to her reputation with Sacountala, Gautier's adaptation from the Sanskrit play, choreographed by Lucien Petipa and composed by Ernest Reyer, new to the Opéra. Further impetus was given to the dance by the sudden triumph of a native French ballerina, Emma Livry, who successfully challenged comparison both with Taglioni and Ferraris in a revival of La Sylphide. Every indication seemed to point to the beginning of a new golden age of French ballet, but the renaissance was tragically brief. In 1859 Mazilier retired. Rosati, feeling that Royer was favoring Ferraris, left for Russia. In Offenbach's Le Papillon (1860) Emma Livry found her vehicle to compare with Taglioni's Sylphide and Grisi's Giselle, but in 1862 her scarcely launched career came to a tragic end when her costume caught fire from an open gas jet. She died of the effects of the burns seven months later, barely twenty years old. Shortly after this disaster, Royer retired from the directorship, and his successor, Emile Perrin, was unable to work with Ferraris and cancelled her contract. In just three years, almost all promise for the future development of ballet at the Opéra had disappeared.

From time to time during the 1850s reports reached Paris of a new force in opera developing in the works of Richard Wagner. The composer had come to Paris between 1839 and 1842, attempting without success to gain a hearing for his opera Rienzi and for several of his shorter works. In 1860 he returned as the recognized if somewhat notorious author of four produced operas in Germany: Rienzi, Der fliegende Holländer, Tannhäuser, and Lohengrin, but he found the French capital if anything less responsive than before. Though persons known and respected at the Opéra, such as Gautier and Ernest Reyer, had brought back favorable reports on his work in Germany, a far more influential and determined group found his music detestable and anarchistic. A long and detailed attack by Fétis in the Gazette Musicale of 1852 scored Wagner as "an enemy of melody" and provided the basis for most subsequent anti-Wagnerian articles in France.[26] By 1860, therefore, Wagner found antagonisms so widespread that he was at last driven to rent the Italien for a concert of his work as the only means of putting it before the

Parisian public.

Finally, in 1861, the Austrian Ambassadress, the Princess von Metternich, appealed to Louis Napoleon on Wagner's behalf, and the Emperor himself commanded a production of Tannhäuser at the Opéra. Wagner was therefore given his choice of artists from any theatre in Paris, and extra attention was given to rehearsals of singers and orchestra. Elaborate and costly settings were created by Desplèchin. The production which resulted was of high quality and drew large audiences, but at the same time caused such violent demonstrations against Wagner that after three nights it was forced to close. French nationalists, musical conservatives, enemies of the Empire each had their own motives for desiring the failure of the work, but the anti-Wagner cabal was led on this occasion by the influential Jockey Club, which occupied seven of the ten proscenium boxes and at this time regarded the Opéra as virtually their private theatre. A few years after the Wagner performance Charles Yriarte described these spectators: "The man of fashion at the Opéra ...has no use for the sublime melodies of the great Gluck, he wants the brisk and lively airs of M. Auber, the adorable flutterings of Mlle Fioretti or Mlle Fonta, the fairy-like effects of Giselle and the ethereal pirouettes of the Wilis, the ballonné of Mlle Baratte, the alluring figure of Mlle Morando in travesty."[27] The effect of the revolutionary Tannhäuser on an audience of this delicate taste can readily be imagined. Wagner even committed the sin of putting his ballet in the first act, a boldness no French composer would have risked, so that when the majority of the Jockey Club members arrived fashionably late, the part which they considered the heart of any opera was already over. After the demonstrations which they led forced the closing of the production, several influential critics, most notably Janin and Baudelaire, wrote in Wagner's defense, but the damage was done. After Royer's experience, no director during the next decade cared to risk a production of Wagner, and his works were sampled in Paris only through concert performances such as Pasdeloup's Concerts populaires.

Deprived of the invigorating influence of Wagner, the Opéra of the 1860s continued its pale reworkings of earlier romantic material. Some impetus came from Verdi, but Don Carlos in 1867 was his only major work at the Opéra. All the really important Verdi performances during this period--Il Trovatore (1854), La Traviata (1856), Rigoletto (1857), Ballo in maschera (1861)--occurred at the Italien.

A major vocal talent was discovered in 1862 in Mme Patti, but neither she nor the works of Verdi could bring prosperity to the Italien, which changed directors during the Empire with distressing frequency. When she retired and government subsidy was discontinued in 1870, Italian opera in Paris virtually ceased.

The major new French composers of the Empire were in general not associated with the Opéra either, but with the popular and successful Théâtre-Lyrique, in many respects the most significant musical theatre in Paris at this time. This was a venture entirely of the Empire, opening in 1851 and closing in 1868. Its home was the old Théâtre Historique, which the suburban director Sevestre reopened as a third home of French musical drama. He replaced the statues of Corneille and Molière beside the stage with Lulli and Gluck and premiered new works unsuitable for the Opéra or the Italien, in competition with the Opéra-Comique. His first and most important such success was David's La Perle de Brésil (1851). Sevestre's son Jules succeeded him in 1852 and introduced to the theatre the works of Adam, who became its most often played composer. His major works were Si j'étais roi! (1852) and Le Bijou perdu (1853). Marie Cabal, introduced in the latter work, and the tenor Monjauz formed the basis of this excellent company.

Jules was followed in turn in 1854 by Émile Perrin, formerly director of the Opéra-Comique and later of the Opéra, who greatly improved the theatre's position in Parisian artistic life, but who dealt it a serious blow in 1855 when he left, taking with him Mme Cabal. His successor Pellegrin was fortunate enough to replace Mme Cabal with Caroline-Marie Carvalho, the popular star of the Opéra-Comique, but his ambitious plans for the theatre drove him nonetheless to bankruptcy in half a year. Organizational stability was not restored to the Lyrique for several months more, until the discouraged actors appealed to M. Carvalho, the husband of their new diva, to assume the directorship. His guidance from 1856 until 1860 made the theatre one of the artistic centers of the capital. Clapisson's La Fanchonnette and the last work of Adam, Mam'zelle Geneviève, brilliantly inaugurated the new administration, and the same year saw the introduction of important new artists, Mlle Borghèse and Balanqué. Carvalho next turned his attention to translations, with even greater success. Weber's Obéron dominated the 1857 season and Mozart's Mariage de Figaro proved the theatre's greatest triumph. Meillet appeared as Figaro,

Balanqué as Almaviva, and Mme Carvalho as Chérubin. So great was the renown of this production that little notice was given to the debut of a young French composer the same year, but Charles Gounod's Le Médecin malgré lui did attract sufficient favorable attention to encourage Carvalho to hope for a more marked success with the composer's next work.

Since assuming leadership of the Lyrique, Carvalho had aspired to mount a full-scale opera, and Gounod's Faust (1859) at last gave him the opportunity. There is a legend that Faust, the most durable of the Lyrique's offerings, was at first a failure, but in fact the work enjoyed a quite respectable run. Even so, Carvalho was doubtless chagrined that the work which he rightly considered his outstanding discovery was preceded and followed by revivals which considerably surpassed it in popularity--Mozart's L'Enlèvement au sérail and Gluck's Orphée. Mme Carvalho, of course, created Marguerite, Barbot Faust and Balanqué Mephistopheles. If Faust was a disappointment, Gounod's subsequent Philémon et Baucis (1860) was a disaster, and clearly contributed to Carvalho's decision to leave the Lyrique later the same year.

He returned in 1862, at the request of the company, after an interim administration by Charles Réty which was distinguished primarily by the first French production of Beethoven's Fidelio (1861). During Carvalho's second administration, he relied far more heavily on translations, particularly of authors already introduced by the Théâtre Italien. The enormous success of the French Rigoletto in 1863 led to productions the next year of Norma, Don Pasquale, and La Traviata (called Violetta in French). After the Italians came Mozart with La Flute enchantée (1865) and Don Juan (1866). French premieres seemed rather pale beside such offerings, but here as well the Lyrique easily maintained its supremacy over other Parisian theatres with such works as Bizet's Les Pêcheurs de perles, Berlioz' Les Troyans (both 1863) and Gounod's Roméo et Juliette (1867). The company, led by Mme Carvalho, Mlle Nilsson from Sweden, and MM Michot and Troy, was widely considered the finest musical ensemble in Paris. Receipts were great, but Carvalho's expenses were greater, and mounting deficits forced him at last to close the Lyrique in 1868.

The popularity of the Lyrique and its monopoly on major composers worked great hardship on the Opéra, the Opéra-Comique, and the Italien throughout the Second Empire. The major composers for the first two were the lesser and somewhat old-fashioned figures: Meyerbeer, Grisar, Bazin, and Auber, whose final work, *Rêve d'amour*, was given at the Opéra-Comique in 1869. The most important of their composers during this period was Ambroise Thomas, who, after two minor and unsuccessful works at the Opéra, went to the Opéra-Comique to dominate its repertoire with *La Caïd* (1849), *Le Songe d'une nuit d'été* (1850), *Psyché* (1857), and finally *Mignon* (1866). His major interpreters were the baritone Faure, Mme Cabal, and after 1863 the tenor Capoul. After the success of *Mignon*, both Faure and Thomas went to the Opéra, where the summit of both their careers was reached with *Hamlet* (1867). Mlle Nilsson came from the Lyrique to sing the part of Ophelia.

The Opéra's major advantage over the Lyrique was in the ballet, but the losses of Emma Livry, Rosati, and Ferraris proved nearly fatal to this genre. More than ever, the ballet of the 1860s relied on the technical effects of Desplé-chin, Cambon, Thierry, and Sacré, who redesigned *Giselle* with sliding traps and a system of enormous mirrors to simulate the forest pool. At last Saint-Léon felt he had developed a new first ballerina in Adèle Grantzow. Custom dictated that she appear in a romantic vehicle such as *La Sylphide* or *Giselle* which could henceforth be associated with her; the result was *La Source* (1866), the first major new ballet in five years. As usual, Mlle Grantzow had to share the honors with Despléchin and Sacré, who created a practical mountain and a spring of real water, but her success was indisputable. Unfortunately, she then found offers to play in Russia too attractive to resist, and her talent was scarcely demonstrated before it was lost to the Opéra. The decline of ballet continued, with 43 performances in 1866, 32 in 1867, 28 in 1868, and only six in 1869. The dance had sunk so low by 1869 that the major interest that year in a revival of *Le Prophète* was in two English roller-skating artists in the *quadrille des patineurs*. Perrin made one final attempt to revivify the ballet with a new discovery, Guiseppina Bozzachi. Saint-Léon and the composer Léo Delibes created for her debut *Coppélia* (1870), the last and one of the greatest of the romantic ballets, a triumph for all concerned. But Saint-Léon, who had been ill for many years, did not long survive the triumph, and Mlle Bozzachi was struck down by smallpox barely two months later. With them died the last traces of the romantic ballet.

After the war of 1870 the Opéra-Comique, under a new director, Du Locle, moved into the commanding position among Paris' lyric theatres. The Théâtre Italien was still officially in existence, but with no government subsidy and little public interest its theatre, the Ventadour, was now more often closed than open. In 1873, when the home of the Opéra on the rue Le Peletier burned, that company moved into the Ventadour, forcing the Italians to play wherever they could find a vacant theatre. The Théâtre Lyrique, closed before the war began and its home having been burnt during the Paris fighting, existed now only in its repertoire, most of which Du Locle inherited, along with many of the Lyrique's best singers. Halanzier, the new director of the Opéra, offered a conservative repertoire of largely undistinguished revivals. For several years, then, the Opéra-Comique's activity was prodigious; 1872 alone saw premieres by Bizet (Djamileh), Saint-Saëns (La Princesse Jaune), and Massenet (Don César de Bazan).

After 1875 Du Locle had much more competition, most notably from the Gaîté, the Opéra, and a temporarily revived Théâtre Italien. The Gaîté, converted into the Théâtre National Lyrique by Albert Vizentini in 1876, was the least significant, since its director discovered after two years of operation that the expenses of lyric production were beyond his resources and returned to regular drama. Far more serious competition came with the opening of the new Opéra in 1875, fifteen years after Napoleon III had called for its construction. This outstanding product of Second Empire architecture was thus not completed until after both Empire and Emperor had passed into oblivion, but in its eclecticism, its bravado, even its ponderous bulk, the architect Charles Garnier's creation well summed up the artistic inclinations of that period. It was also the most ambitious manifestation of a general approach to opera-house design found all over Europe during the nineteenth century. The key to understanding such design is remembering that an opera-house contained two spectacles, the play and the audience (the latter if anything more important) and ample provision had to be made for the display of both--hence the sweeping grand staircase, and hence also the vast galleries and seemingly endless antechambers that surround the theatre on all sides. Few other theatres could hope to offer such a richness of interior space; after all, the Opéra contained more than three times the cubic volume of the next two largest theatres in Europe, the Alexandra in St. Petersburg and the Munich Opera. Imitation of the Garnier Opéra, therefore, could generally be seen in decoration rather than size, and particularly in elaborate façades. The Opéra marks the shift from the modified classicism which had characterized theatre façades throughout the century to a kind of elaborate neo-baroque. This can be seen in Paris as early as Charlu's Théâtre de la Renaissance, built in 1872 when the exterior of the Opéra at least was available as a model. The same style spread into the provinces with such Garnier students as Cassin-Bernard, who designed the new theatre at Montpellier in 1884.

Halanzier, who remained at the Opéra until 1879, seemed content to let the new building alone attract audiences, which it did quite well. No new dancers appeared. The unimaginative revivals continued. Mme Carvalho came in 1875 from the Opéra-Comique, but Faure left the same year and Halanzier made no effort to replace him. Of the few new works, only Massenet's Le Roi de Lahore (1877) attracted any attention. Settings and costumes, while spectacular, were little different from those of the Second Empire, indeed were largely the work of designers whose styles had been established then: Rubé, Chaperon, Cambon, Lavastre, Desplechin, Daran, and Lacoste. Moreover, the new building itself seems to have had an unfortunate effect upon the company. The larger hall encouraged shouting rather than singing, larger and less subtle gesture and movements, and until the artists learned to adjust, the quality of their interpretation clearly suffered.

When the opening of the new Opéra permitted that company to leave the Ventadour, the Italians returned to the latter house and for several years recaptured something of their old popularity. The company was now headed by a popular new singer, Mlle Albani, who despite her obligatory Italian stage name was born Mlle Lajeunesse of French parents in Albany, New York. The Italien's premiere of Verdi's Aïda (1876) was one of the great productions of this period, and the Ventadour continued also to offer touring productions of major Italian actors, such as Rossi and Salvini. This brief renaissance ended in 1879 when the Ventadour was closed and converted into a bank. Despite the Italien's success during the previous few years, neither the public nor the government was sufficiently interested in this venture to enable it to find a new permanent home. Thus, after 1879, Italian singers appeared in Paris only as occasional guests at other theatres, the Gaîté, the Nations, even the Opéra, where as late as 1897 Verdi's Otello was presented with a French chorus and Italian leads. Their repertoire either disappeared from the Paris stage or was absorbed by other theatres in French translation.

5. Minor Theatres, 1850-1880

Though permits still had to be obtained for the opening of new theatres, the government made little attempt after 1850 to control either their number or their repertoire. Due to the pressures of competition, however, the total number of houses open at any one time in the city did not fluctuate greatly during this period, even though smaller theatres frequently opened and closed. These most ephemeral ventures were also the most eclectic in genres offered, since a longer-established and larger theatre tended to favor certain types of plays congenial to its company, its regular audience, and its facilities. Rarely did any larger theatre attempt regularly to present more than two of the period's five major genres--drama, comedy, _vaudeville,_ spectacle drama, and operetta--and many were content with one.

Pure comedy survived only with difficulty in this period when the operetta and related forms were enjoying an enormous success, and only three theatres regularly presented comedies and the comedies mixed with song called _vaudevilles._ At two of these, the Gymnase and Vaudeville, as we have seen, comedy tended to be subordinated to drama, so that the Palais-Royal was in fact the only comedy theatre in Paris during much of this period. The favored author was Labiche, who during most of the Empire brought his major works to this theatre, as he had done since 1838. With Marc Michel he wrote the great success of 1850, _La Fille bien gardée,_ starring a six-year-old prodigy, Céline Montaland. The next year the same authors produced their most popular and lasting work, _Le Chapeau de paille d'Italie._ Jules Brasseur, who became one of the theatre's most popular actors and eventually its director, made his debut in Labiche, Lubize, and Siraudin's _Le Misanthrope et l'Auvergnat_ in 1852. Almost every year saw a new triumph by Labiche and his collaborators until 1864, when _Le Pont de Mire_ and _La Cagnotte_ terminated this impressive series. The extent of the Palais-Royal dependence on Labiche is revelaed by the fact that in the six years after the production of _La Cagnotte_ the only important success here was Labiche's single new work, _La Grammaire_ (1867).

Despite their dominance, however, Labiche and his collaborators were not the only successful Palais-Royal authors during most of this period. Clairville worked in the early 1850s with Dumanoir, and later with Siraudin and Frascati on popular comedies such as *Ma Nièce et mon ours* (1859). Lambert Thiboust, already mentioned as an author of social dramas, produced a series of attractive works for Hortense Schneider, who built a sizeable reputation here in comedy before going on in 1864 to specialize in Offenbach operetta at the Variétés. Her first Palais-Royal production was Thiboust's *Les Mémoires de Mimi-Bamboche* (1860), her most popular later creations Thiboust and Grange's *La Mariée du Mardi Gras* (1861) and Thiboust and Barrière's *Une Corneille qui abat des noix* (1862). An outstanding company supported Brasseur and Schneider in such light works. The theatre in 1847 gained the popular author and comedian Louis Hyacinthe Duflos, in 1853 Geoffrey, one of the best actors of the Gymnase, in 1854 Gil Perez, in 1858 Lassouche and Delaunay, who in later years became one of the most popular actors of the Comédie.

When the war of 1870 broke out, the Palais-Royal had just opened with Labiche and Gondinet's *Le plus heureux des trois* with Brasseur, Geoffrey, and Gil Perez, but it was quickly replaced with more patriotic fare, such as *Les Tribulations Prussiennes du Palais-Royal*, which was offered until the general closing of the theatres. When the theatre reopened under more normal conditions in 1871, it was with *Le plus heureux des trois*. Labiche's *Doit-on le dire?* (1872) and Gondinet's *Le Panache* (1875) brightened subsequent seasons.

The major Palais-Royal authors of the 1870s were Offenbach's librettists Meilhac and Halévy. They adroitly combined the farce spirit of earlier comedy and *vaudeville* writers such as Labiche with more realistic pictures of contemporary life, producing a series of great successes from *Tricoche et Cacolet* (1871) to *Le Prince* (1876). The Palais-Royal director who encouraged this profitable collaboration, Choler, retired in 1877, and Meilhac and Halévy took their last major work, *La Cigale*, to the Variétés, where it enjoyed a great success with the interpretations of Adolphe Dupuis and Céline Chaumont.

Melodrama remained the major offering during the Second Empire at its traditional homes--the Ambigu, the Gaîté, and the Porte-Saint-Martin--as well as at several smaller houses, but various influences took the genre in different directions. Some houses emphasized spectacle, and were thus led from the melodrama to other spectacle genres, such as the fairy play. Others showed influence from Scribe in emphasizing tightly-knit plots or Scribean historical studies. The success of Augier and Dumas _fils_ encouraged some writers of melodrama to attempt the more subtle effects of the realistic drama.

The influence of such writers as Scribe, Augier, and Dumas _fils_ could be most clearly seen in the plays of the popular and prolific Anicet Bourgeois and Adolphe Dennery, the major authors of the Ambigu and Gaîté. Like Scribe, they produced almost all their works in collaboration. The Ambigu's major offering in 1851 was Bourgeois and Dennery's _Marthe et Marie_. The Gaîté that year gave the same authors' _Le Muet_ and Dennery and Fourier's _Paillaise_, in which Frédérick Lemaître achieved great success as a broken-hearted clown.

Lemaître's dominance at the Gaîté was sharply challenged by a young actor, Paulin Ménier, who was discovered in 1850 as Choppard in Siraudin's _Le Courrier de Lyon_, a popular melodrama which Ménier revived to continual public acclaim until his death in 1898. Less durable, but equally popular in its own time, was his leading role in Adolph Arnault and Louis Judicis' _Les Cosaques_ (1853). Lemaître attempted, unsuccessfully, to surpass this new rival in an adaptation of Eugène Sue's _La Bonne Aventure_ (1854). When this failed, he attempted no more original works, and soon left the Gaîté altogether to present a series of revivals of proven successes at the Ambigu.

While Dennery served most of the boulevard theatres of the period, his collaborator Bourgeois after 1853 became closely associated with the Gaîté. He and other collaborators wrote several plays specifically for the actor Laferrière of that theatre, most notably _Le Médecin des enfants_ (1857). The Ambigu during the same years had a sort of playwright-in-residence in Brisebarre, who gave this theatre such popular works as _Les Pauvres de Paris_ (1856). While most of his works placed their emphasis either on emotional situations or exciting plots, the Ambigu and Gaîté did not neglect the melodrama of spectacle. Ferdinand Dugué seems to have specialized in this sort of production, collaborating during the 1850s with both Bourgeois and Dennery in a series of picturesque and exotic pieces such as _La Case de l'Oncle Tom_ (1852) at the Ambigu and _La Bergère des Alpes_ (1852) at the Gaîté.

Though the play of pure spectacle existed as a distinct genre during the latter part of the nineteenth century, a certain interest in scenic display could of course be found in much of the popular theatre. Before speaking of the houses devoted primarily to spectacle, therefore, we should note that even the smallest boulevard houses tended to rely to some extent on such effects to attract audiences. The plays of Charles Charton at the Funambules, certainly one of Paris' most modest theatres, provide a good example of this. Not at all uncommon was the sort of decor required for a scene in Les Pêcheurs napolitaines (1854): "In Naples. In the distance Venice is seen, and beyond, the Danube." The play Arcadius ou Pierrot chez les Indiens (1852), though "set in America at the time of Christopher Columbus," opened with a scene "in the dwelling of the Great Spirit of the Indians, a gilded gothic hall in the German fashion, closed at the rear with a silk curtain." Later scenes included "an Indian palace, with arcades opening onto Oriental gardens," "an African site with steep cliffs," "a lugubrious and dimly lighted cavern," "a gothic palace with fanlights," and even "a chain of mountains bathed by the Caspian sea."[28]

The theatres during the 1850s which were most noted for such productions, and best equipped for it, were the Porte-Saint-Martin and the Cirque Olympique. The Porte-Saint-Martin before 1853 tended to emphasize drama and comedy, but then resumed its position as Paris' leading theatre of spectacle under a new director, Marc Fournier. Such strange works as Les Sept Merveilles and Les Cinq Cents Diables filled the theatre until Fournier's retirement in 1868. Rachel's brother, Raphaël Félix, then attempted to bring the theatre back to a more traditional drama, but failed so decisively that by 1870 he was forced to close. The single significant production of his administration was Sardou's Patrie (1869), an historical drama set in the Netherlands during the war for independence. It was Sardou's first history play, and one of his best. The Cirque Olympique occasionally entered the domain of the Porte-Saint-Martin with such fairy plays as Les Pilules du diable, but its major emphasis was on military display, reflected in its change of title in 1848 to the Théâtre National. The theatrical myths of Napoleon were revived here once again in such works as Dennery's L'Histoire d'un drapeau (1860), which recapitulated the Emperor's entire career with some 400 extras and horses for the huge battle scenes.

Despite its prosperity, the old boulevard, center of

the capital's secondary theatre for over a century, came to an end during the Second Empire. The great new system of boulevards planned by Napoleon III and his Prefect of the Seine, Georges Haussmann, called for three major new streets in the east end of Paris to intersect at a new square, the Place du Château d'Eau (now the Place de la République). This was located just on the site of the old boulevard theatres, and all seven of those remaining in the area were marked for destruction in 1862. The two least prosperous minor houses, the Funambules and Petit-Lazzari, closed permanently when the demolition began. The Délassements resettled briefly but soon followed them into oblivion. The four larger houses survived. The Folies-Dramatiques, under the prosperous but undistinguished direction of Thomas Harel, a nephew of Mlle George, moved not far from its boulevard site to a new home on the rue de Bondy. The Théâtre-Lyrique and the Théâtre National aided Haussmann's plans for a new Paris by raising impressive structures opposite each other on his new Place du Châtelet. The Gaîté built a less ambitious home on the Square des Arts et Métiers. This, the oldest of the boulevard houses and only two years away from its centenary, was allowed a special dispensation to be the last to close. When it gave its final production on August 3, 1862, demolition of neighboring buildings was already under way.

The construction of three major new theatres in 1860-62, along with the competition in those years for plans for the new Opéra, stimulated great interest in theatre architecture. A large number of pamphlets on the subject appeared, the most influential of which was Émile Trélat's *L'Architecture et le théâtre*, in which the author argued against several early nineteenth century practices, particularly that of lighting the house by a huge central chandelier with a chimney above to draw off the heat. The architect Davioud, who designed both of the Châtelet houses, therefore replaced the usual chandeliers with indirect lighting around the cupolas, diffused by means of frosted glass. This improved sight lines and reduced the heat in the upper galleries, but made the whole theatre colder and more gloomy. The experiment was not widely copied, but certain of Trélat's other suggestions--a system of hydraulic lifts for sections of the stage floor, and an improved ventilation system with outlets in each gallery--exerted a continuing influence on subsequent theatre design.

In size and in facilities the two new stages rivalled

the Opéra and the Porte-Saint-Martin, hitherto the best equipped theatres for spectacle in Paris. The National, in addition to immense decors, could accomodate casts of up to 400 persons with twenty to thirty horses. The military pageants for which the old Cirque Olympique had been noted could have been presented more elaborately than ever here, but public interest in them had diminished, and after the apathetic response given to Dennery's Marengo (1863), the director, Hostein, turned instead to fairy plays and spectacular melodramas. The great majority of the offerings of the following years were revivals of the classics in these two genres--melodramas such as Le Case de l'Oncle Tom, and fairy plays such as Les Sept Châteaux du diable. The few new works offered were almost without exception historical dramas offering opportunity for scenic display: Dennery and Dugué's Les Mystères du vieux Paris (1866), Eugène Nus' La Camorra (1873), Victor Séjour and Maurice Drack's Cromwell (1875). The contribution of the actor to such works was so little that François-Louis Lesueur was strongly criticised in 1868 for debasing himself and his art by coming to this theatre from the Gymnase. The other Châtelet theatre, the Lyrique, reorganized after the war of 1870 and renamed the Historique, presented a very similar program during the 1870s. Indeed, in the latter part of the decade a single director, Castellano, managed both houses. Among the major new works at the Historique were Dugué's Drame au fond de la mer (1876), and Bourgeois and Masson's Marceau (1878).

The Porte-Saint-Martin, traditional home of spectacle drama, did not seem to suffer from this sharply increased competition. Overrun by troops during the suppression of the Commune in 1871 and completely burned, the theatre was rebuilt in 1873 by Jean Ritt, a former director of the Opéra-Comique, and Larochelle, organizer of the first chain of suburban theatres in Paris. They opened with a revival of Marie Tudor, chiefly remembered for the last appearance of Frédérick Lemaître, but their first real success came in 1874 with Dennery and Corman's Les Deux Orphelines. This unbeatable combination of scenic spectacle and sentimental melodrama, with Taillade as its hero and Angèle Moreau as the persecuted heroine, proved one of the most popular works of the century, presented 200 times during its initial run and revived for half a century after on popular stages all over France. Such a success was naturally gratifying to its authors, but their popularity was assured without it; the prolific Dennery could already claim over 200 works produced in Paris, and Corman, who had started somewhat later, already had 170.

The public demand for Les Deux Orphelines prevented for a time the opening of the Porte-Saint-Martin's next production, a new adaptation by Dennery from Jules Verne's novel, Le Tour du Monde en quatre-vingts jours, and the former work eventually had to be moved to the Théâtre-National on the place du Châtelet to make room for the new offering. Its success was if anything even greater. Dennery naturally stressed the spectacle of the work and adapted with considerable freedom, adding new characters, most notably the American Archibald Corsican for the actor Dumaine, and whole new melodramatic scenes, such as a suspenseful encounter between Phileas Fogg and the chief of the Pawnees. This success called attention to the novels of Verne as ideal vehicles for spectacular theatrical presentation and so inflated the prestige of Dennery that he henceforth changed his name to the more aristocratic D'Ennery. In 1877 the two prosperous directors of the Porte-Saint-Martin took over the declining Ambigu, bringing the best actors of both companies to the larger theatre. Their contribution to the "Russian season," which saw Les Danitchev at the Odéon, was Eugène Nus' Exilés, featuring Russian costumes and settings, sleigh rides, conflagrations, even Eskimo dogs. For the Exposition of 1878, D'Ennery produced a popular new Verne adaptation, Les Enfants du Capitaine Grant, with shipwrecks, whales, and scenes on exotic islands.

In 1879 Edmond de Goncourt wrote a new preface for Henriette Maréchal which called for new life and freedom in the theatre, but expressed at the same time a fear, shared by many contemporary critics, that the serious theatre was dying out altogether:

> With the evolution of genres the centuries have brought and as the novel, either realistic or fanciful, has moved into first place, with the imminent departure from the French stage of the irreplaceable Hugo... with the minor influence of the present European theatre, with the retreat of dramatists into worn-out formulas while all other branches of literature are advancing, with the dramatists of the present generation all being distinctly second rate in creative faculties, with the obstacles placed in the path of drama by men of letters... and with other withs that could stretch on forever--the great French art of the past, the theatrical art, the art

> of Corneille, Racine, Molière, and Beaumarchais, is destined within fifty years at most to become only a crude distraction, having nothing more in common with literature, style, or wit, something worthy to be ranked with marionettes and performing dogs.[29]

The offerings of the 1870s strongly supported this pessimistic prophecy. The place of comedy and drama had been usurped by the operetta and the spectacle play; the literary side of theatre did indeed seem to be disappearing entirely. The major serious dramatists discovered during the Second Empire, Augier and Dumas *fils*, were now well past their prime, and no important new figures had appeared to replace them. Several interesting experiments were undertaken by the major novelists of the period, but with universal lack of success. Villiers de l'Isle-Adam's *La Révolte* (1870), an imaginative but now almost forgotten work, was banned at the Vaudeville after five performances. It showed a wife with a poetic soul deciding at last to desert her selfish materialistic husband, even if this meant losing her child. Though the play ends with a reconciliation, it raises many of the same questions as Ibsen's *A Doll's House*, which it anticipated by nine years. Flaubert's *Le Candidat* (1873), a political satire, and Daudet's *L'Arlésienne* (1873), offering a new realism in local color, were both failures, though the latter, at the Odéon, had the extra support of a talented debutante, Julia Bartet, and music by the young Bizet.

The most significant of the frustrated reformers of the 1870s was unquestionably Emile Zola. The publication of *Ventre de Paris*, third in his huge cycle of scientific or "experimental" novels, established him as an important new force in French literature, and having begun to achieve his goals in the novel, he turned his attention to the theatre, which, he observed, was "dying of inanity." He felt that the salvation of the theatre, as of the novel, was the introduction of the "scientific and experimental spirit of the century."[30] In practice this meant a greater attention to detail, especially that of everyday life, a concern with the effects of milieu on character, an interest in the pathological, and a disinterested, even ironic stance on the part of the author.

Zola's first attempt at applying this experimental spirit, which he called naturalism, to dramatic practice was *Thérèse Raquin*, adapted from his novel and presented in 1873 at the Renaissance, the little operetta house which had just opened on the boulevard Saint-Martin. The play was hissed by its audiences and condemned by such influential critics as Paul de Saint-Victor and Francisque Sarcey, who wrote: "These brutal incongruities, which I found displeasing enough in the novel, are insupportable on the stage."[31] The production closed in five days and was the Renaissance's last venture outside the genre of light musical comedy for several years. This same obscure theatre, however, was destined to make another contribution to the new drama, by presenting Henry Becque's La Parisienne in 1885 after its rejection by the Comédie.

Zola's second play, Les Héritiers Rabourdin (1874), fared little better. The only director Zola could find who was willing to risk the production was Camille Weinshenk of the Cluny in the Latin Quarter, a theatre even less significant than the Renaissance. Again critical reception was severe, Sarcey in the Temps calling the work "dull, repulsive, and immoral," and the production closed after seventeen performances.[32] Zola now shifted from prosecuted to prosecutor by taking a position as dramatic critic on Le Bien Publique, where he fulminated against the authors he could not displace, particularly Scribe, Sardou, and Dumas fils.

The unprecedented success of his new novel, L'Assommoir, in 1877, encouraged Zola to attempt once again to conquer the stage. The popularity of the novel assured an audience for an adaptation, but even so, Zola took the extra precaution of calling in William Busnach, a veteran writer of melodramas, to convert it into dramatic form. In the meantime Zola attempted another work on his own, a little farce called Bouton de Rose. Though presented by the excellent comedy company of the Palais-Royal in 1878, it was a disaster which the audience did not even allow to finish. Busnach's adaptation, on the other hand, ran most of the following year at the Ambigu. Zola bowed to this evidence and henceforth relied on adapters to bring his ideas to the stage. The results were a popular Nana (1881) at the Ambigu, and a less popular, but passable Pot-Bouille (1883), both the work of Busnach. As illustrations of Zola's ideas, however, these were even less satisfactory than his own first attempts, and for the next generation of dramatists, Zola was much less influential as a playwright than as a critic. The preface to Thérèse Raquin and the later essays, Le Naturalisme au théâtre and Nos Auteurs dramatiques, formed the bedrock of naturalist critical theory and a point of reference for a fresh start in the theatre.

Notes to Part III

1. E. Augier, Théâtre complet (Paris, 1890), p. 203.

2. A. Dumas fils, "Notes" on La Dame aux camélias, Théâtre (Paris, 1898), VIII, 8.

3. J. Weiss, Le Drame historique et le drame passionnel (Paris, 1894), p. 203.

4. Revue française, May, 1880, from the Montigny dossier, Bibliothèque de l'Arsenal.

5. A. Dumas fils, Nouveaux Entr'actes (Paris, 1890), pp. 214-15.

6. G. Bapst, Essai sur l'histoire du théâtre (Paris, 1893), pp. 383-85.

7. F. Febvre, Journal d'un comédien (Paris, 1896), I, 141.

8. S. Kracauer, Orpheus in Paris (trans. David and Mosbacher, New York, 1938), p. 155.

9. Kracauer, Orpheus, p. 176.

10. Quoted in Kracauer, Orpheus, p. 186.

11. Quoted in R. Williams, The World of Napoleon III (New York, 1957), p. 111.

12. A. Houssaye, Behind the Scenes of the Comédie Française (trans. A. D. Vandam, London, 1889), p. 264.

13. Quoted in H. Kindermann, Theatergeschichte Europas, VII (Salzburg, 1964-65), 49.

14. A. Ristori, Memoires and Artistic Studies (trans. G. Mantelli, New York, 1907), pp. 191-92.

15. G. d'Heilly, Journal intime de la Comédie-Française (Paris, 1872), p. 271n.

16. A. Daudet, Oeuvres complètes (Paris, 1930), XVIII, 105.

17. d'Heilly, Journal intime, p. 17n.

18. E. and J. de Goncourt, Préfaces et manifestes littéraires (Paris, 1888), p. 104.

19. F. Coppée, Journal, January 23, 1896, quoted in R. Baldick, The Life and Times of Frédérick Lemaître (London, 1959), pp. 225-26.

20. F. Coppée, Souvenirs d'un Parisien (Paris, 1910), pp. 95-96.

21. F. Sarcey, Comédiens et Comédiennes (Paris, 1876-84), I, pp. 6-7.

22. Sarcey, Comédiens, I, pp. 14-15.

23. T. de Banville, Critiques (Paris, 1917), pp. 370-72.

24. Sarcey, Comédiens, p. 188.

25. F. Febvre, Journal, II, 42.

26. G. Servières, Richard Wagner jugé en France (Paris, 1887), pp. 25-29.

27. Quoted in I. Guest, The Ballet of the Second Empire (London, 1953), p. 14.

28. L. Pericaud, Le Théâtre des Funambules (Paris, 1897), pp. 359-60.

29. Goncourt, Préfaces, pp. 40-41.

30. E. Zola, Théâtre (Paris, 1923), p. 8.

31. F. Sarcey, Quarante Ans de Théâtre (Paris, 1902), VII, 26.

32. E. A. Vizotty, Emile Zola (London, 1904), p. 149.

IV. REALISM AND SYMBOLISM
1870-1900

In France, as elsewhere in Europe, the final decades of the nineteenth century provide the richest variety of theatre. Identifying the period with a single movement is therefore even more misleading here than identifying the 1830s and 1840s with the then-dominant romantic school. Nevertheless, there is considerable justice in the common association of the end of the century with realism. Realism, like romanticism, is subject to a wide range of interpretation, even if we restrict ourselves only to its manifestations in the theatre. It may suggest the literal reproduction of everyday life, a trend already present to some extent in such reformers as Montigny but carried much further in this period by Antoine. It may refer only to the use of contemporary as contrasted with classical or mythological subjects. Since Scribe and Augier had already studied the monied classes, this usually meant that the contemporary subjects of later realists were drawn from the lower classes. Realism may also involve a concern with historical accuracy (a concern it shares with romanticism). This may lead on the one hand to attempts to recreate the period of the play's action in the manner of Pixérécourt, Charles Kean, the Meininger, or the spectacles of Bernhardt and Sardou, or on the other to attempts to recreate the original conditions of production, as in the Poel Shakespearian stages or the Greek revivals done late in the century at the Odéon and Comédie. Each of these aspects of realism was involved in the experimentation undertaken by the Parisian theatre of this period.

This experimentation took many other forms as well, some rivaling realism in significance for the coming century, but in at least two respects realism's significance was unique. First, it was the realists who eventually achieved the shattering of the established and sterile forms that Zola so deplored, thereby opening the way to other experiments. Second, in this period so dominated socially and intellectually by the forces of positivist philosophy, materialism and scientism, the works of the realists struck a more responsive chord and thus won a wider and more lasting support than any of the subsequent movements the theatre offered.

The most important of these later alternatives to realism was the symbolist movement, appearing in the 1890s. It was in many respects a return to romanticism after the harsh and sometimes banal offerings of the realists. It emphasized the vague and the universal over the specific, emotion over reason, and, doubtless due to the influence of Wagner, a harmony of all elements in the work of art. The tradition of experimentation outside the established theatre was developed further by both realists and symbolists. The Porte-Saint-Martin, the Gymnase, and the Vaudeville had proven earlier in the century that established minor houses could challenge the national theatres. Antoine's Théatre-Libre and Lugné-Poe's Théâtre de l'Oeuvre carried the process a step further, by mounting their challenge from entirely outside the existing theatre system. They thus established the pattern the avant-garde in the theatre has followed since. The Comédie eventually assimilated these new schools, or at least their most important products, but its major role had become that of repository of the established classics.

1. Henry Becque and André Antoine, 1881-1894

During the 1870s and early 1880s the French theatre experienced a rising sense of dissatisfaction, a growing suspicion that a plateau had been reached and that the existing system had become too rigid to allow new directors, new actors and, especially, new playwrights an opportunity to add vitality to the art. Young authors were discouraged by the preference of major theatres for Augier, Sardou, and the proven dramatists of the Second Empire. Censorship was reintroduced in 1874, but when Zola mounted a campaign against it in 1885 after the banning of *Germinal* he found most of the established dramatists in Paris united against him. He joined with other novelists such as Flaubert and Daudet to challenge the hold of these established authors on the theatre, but either their dramatic imagination or their determination proved insufficient, since all ended by allowing their works at last to be adapted by popular hacks such as Busnach or Belot, who had little concern for either experimentation or originality.

The major victim of this situation was Henry Becque, who complained frequently and bitterly of the commercialism and exclusiveness of the system which indeed denied him his rightful position as the major serious dramatist of France during this period. "About twenty-five authors," he observed, "share the theatres. The vogue of their works, almost always legitimate, but frequently somewhat excessive, and furthermore aided by outstanding interpretation, leads to runs of 200, 300, and even 500 nights. When these authors compete with each other and are often obliged to wait their turn even for guaranteed productions, how can unknowns hope to gain a turn?"[1] Becque, of course, persevered and triumphed, but his assertion that many other potential playwrights of his generation were stifled, while impossible to prove, seems unfortunately likely.

There was admittedly little in Becque's early work to indicate the development of a major talent. All of his first four plays were clear failures except a drama, _Michel Pauper_ (1870), which Becque mounted at his own expense at the Porte-Saint-Martin. Thanks largely to the interpretation of Taillade, it achieved a favorable, if not enthusiastic, response. This was hardly enough to interest Parisian directors of the 1870s in a new author, and Becque tried in vain for five years to find a theatre to present his major work, _Les Corbeaux._ Neither Montigny nor his successor Koning was interested, neither Duquesnel nor his successor La Rounat at the Odéon, not Deslandes at the Vaudeville nor Ritt at the Porte-Saint-Martin. Even the less popular Gaîté, Ambigu, and Cluny refused him. At last, in 1881, despairing of ever seeing the play performed, Becque arranged for its publication. Then remarkably his publisher, Stock, praised the work to his friend Thierry, the former director of the Comédie, who arranged for a reading at the national theatre. Even more remarkable, the widely refused play was accepted by the Comédie for presentation by a vote of six to two.

All too soon, Becque found that this apparent triumph merely opened to him a new set of agonies. The actors of the Comédie, accustomed to the "realism" of Augier, Dumas _fils_, Feuillet, and Erckmann-Chatrian, were confused and irritated by this harsh and savage study of the destruction of a family by the former friends of its dead father. Like Hugo fifty years before, Becque found himself in constant quarrels with conservative actors over interpretation, indeed even over the language of his work. Just as Mlle Mars had refused to say Hugo's "_lion superbe et généreux_," Coquelin now demanded that Becque's "_boustiffouller_" be replaced by "_se_ mettre à table."[2] Got was clearly relieved to be withdrawn from the central role of Teissier in order to appear in a revival of Le Roi s'amuse. The opening was rather stormy, but far from another "battle of Hernani." Les Corbeaux was generally associated in the public mind with Zola's new "naturalist" movement, but though opinion on the movement was sharply divided, little of the explosiveness of the early romantic period was now present. Reviews of the play were generally re-statements of the reviewers' previously expressed opinions on naturalism in general, so that conservatives spoke disparagingly of the "cynicism and salaciousness" of the work, while Zola's partisans praised its "realism and tough-mindedness."[3] Neither the criticism nor the generally indifferent interpretation engaged the attention of the general public, and the run was a short one.

How far the battle for "naturalism in the theatre" was from being won by this single skirmish was made clear later, in 1882, when the Comédie refused by a vote of six to three to produce Becque's second major work, La Parisienne. Once again Becque made the rounds of Parisian theatres and once again found his work rejected in favor of such established figures as Sardou, Labiche, or Gondinet. In 1885 Becque wrote to Thierry, who had continued to give him encouragement, that he had been forced to entrust his work to the "inadequate artists and poverty-striken director" of the Renaissance.

Certainly, after acceptance at the Comédie, Becque had reason to complain of his fall to one of the capital's more obscure houses, but the little organization which presented his second work was not simply one among many indistinguishable ventures, and deserves more attention than theatre historians have given it. The director, Fernand Louveau (whose professional name was Samuel), began as the leader of an amateur dramatic society, the Cercle des Arts Intimes, which gave unproduced works by known authors. Louveau moved on to direct the Renaissance in 1884, but retained for several years his interest in experimentation, even in this commercial situation. Though La Parisienne was his only significant production, Louveau should be remembered as one who provided a model for the more influential André Antoine a few years later. The actors at the Renaissance had little training, of course, but for that very reason, as Antoine also later discovered, were in some ways better suited to the new approach in drama than the traditionally trained actors of the major houses. Mlle Antonine in particular, who played the original Clotilde, was generally considered superior to Suzanne Reichenberg in the 1890 revival at the Comédie. La Parisienne was a far more successful work than the more bitter Corbeaux, and Becque had no difficulty in finding theatres willing to present the five lesser plays he wrote before his death in 1899. After 1885 he busied himself also with reviewing for several journals, defending his two major works, and organizing their revivals. The 1890 revival of La Parisienne at the Comédie was a failure, but Réjane at the Vaudeville gave the piece a triumphant vindication in 1893.

Despite Becque's eventual success, the difficulties he had in attaining it guaranteed that few of his contemporaries would follow his example. Slowly, the Parisian theatre began to evolve less difficult procedures for the discovery and encouragement of new talent. Louveau's productions made an important but limited contribution, since his authors were established even though the plays were unfamiliar. Another step was taken by a more prominent figure in the theatre world, Hilarion Ballande. In 1867 Ballande formed a Société de patronage des auteurs dramatiques inconnus which supported matinee performances of new playwrights. Unable to engage the interest of the public, Ballande changed two years later to "classic matinees" at the Gaîté and later at the Porte-Saint-Martin. These productions, like Louveau's, were of unusual works by known authors, though the Ballande matinees gained a far greater reputation because of his ability to attract to them most of the great names among established actors as well as the most promising new talents--Mélingue, Laferrière, Coquelin, Bernhardt, Desclée, Mounet-Sully, Taillade, Montaland, Reichenberg all were seen in Ballande productions. The matinees proved so successful that by 1880 almost every major theatre in Paris had established an experimental matinee program. Most followed Ballande's example in reviving minor classics, but some, most notably the Gymnase, produced even the more ephemeral comedies and vaudevilles of the early part of the century. In 1876 Ballande purchased the Déjazet, which he renamed the Troisième Théâtre-Français. Here again he attempted to introduce young authors, but his most important discovery was the distinctly minor Ernest Calonne, and his greatest successes continued to be revivals. Far more productive were the "matinées inédites" which Tallien began giving at the Cluny in 1879 and which introduced Hennique, Brieux, and Salandri to the stage.

The tentative and often unsuccessful experiments of

Louveau, Ballande, and Tallien prepared the way for the venture which truly opened the French theatre to the young, André Antoine's Théâtre-Libre. Though Antoine in later years attempted to present this venture as the product of chance and circumstance, playing down his own interest in theatre and avoiding mention of his predecessors, the illuminating research of Pruner has recently given us a more reasonable account of the founding of the Théâtre-Libre. Antoine, it now appears, was from the outset acutely aware of his aims and the methods necessary to achieve them. Refused by the Conservatoire in 1878 and shortly after called to the army, he allied himself upon his return to Paris in 1884 with one of the city's many amateur dramatic societies, the *Cercle Gaulois.*

Until 1887 the standard fare of this venture was revivals of popular successes from the large theatres with an occasional original review. Then Antoine convinced his fellow actors to attempt a program of original works. The experiments of Ballande and others had demonstrated the difficulty of attracting the public to such offerings, but Antoine had a new idea--the presentation of works by known authors which for some reason had not been accepted elsewhere, along with works by unknown authors on the same bill. At this period, and with this goal, it was not surprising that Antoine should become closely associated with Zola, whose presence dominated the first year of the enterprise. Though the generation of 1870 was united in its rejection of the Second Empire writers, it had internal factions, the strongest of which were those grouped around the Goncourts and including Daudet, and those grouped around Zola and including Paul Alexis and Henry Céard. Daudet had achieved the most success in the theatre of any of these authors, though with the aid of collaborators--Belot on *Fromont jeune et Risier aîné* (Vaudeville, 1876) and Lafontaine on *Jack* (Odéon, 1883). The first success of the new Porel administration at the Odéon in 1884 was Daudet's first play, *L'Arlésienne,* which had failed at the Vaudeville twelve years before. The Goncourts' *Henriette Maréchal* was revived in 1885, with a similar improvement over its first reception. No such successes came from Zola or his party; indeed, Céard's adaptation of the Goncourts' *Renée Mauperin* (1886) was so great a failure that Porel not only refused to consider further works from Céard, but even cancelled a pending production of a play by Céard's colleague, Alexis.

Antoine was quick to seize this opportunity to produce

the writers rejected by the Odéon, and the major offerings of his first bill on March 29, 1887, were Alexis' Mademoiselle Pomme and an adaptation by Léon Hennique of Zola's Jacques Damour. To keep himself outside the world of the public theatres, Antoine organized the evening as a subscription performance, and distributed announcements in the form of invitations to a private event, a practice which he continued for later productions. Most Parisian critics ignored this opening production, but a few influential ones were present--Fouquier, La Pommeraye, and Henry de Pène--as well as many literary figures such as Mallarmé, attracted by the Zola offering. Jacques Damour was a great success, drawing a favorable review on the front page of the Figaro and an offer from Porel of production at the Odéon. By the end of the next month Antoine had prepared a second bill, a short realistic work by a new dramatist, Oscar Méténier, called En Famille, and a full-length verse drama by the already established Emile Bergerat called La Nuit Bergamasque. Most of the major critics of Paris were in the audience for Antoine's second offering, and while not all applauded the plays, praise for the acting, directing, and design were almost universal. The productions were simply done, but with an honesty and vitality which set them clearly apart from anything else than being done in Paris. Inspired by an article in the Revue Wagnérienne, Antoine darkened his auditorium for the first time for this production.

The interest stimulated by his first two offerings allowed Antoine to announce a full season, and the Paris summer papers of 1887 were enlivened by plans and promises concerning the new experiment. Antoine wished to keep the balance between poets and realists shown in his opening programs, and announced proudly that the flamboyant Parnassian Catulle Mendès and the witty and fanciful Théodore de Banville had both promised him plays. Significant new foreign dramatists were also sought, and in July Alexis announced in Le Cri Antoine's plans to present Ghosts and The Power of Darkness. The realists, of course, were not forgotten; Antoine opened his 1887-88 season with Villiers de L'Isle-Adam's L'Evasion and an adaptation by Arthur Byl and Jules Vidal of the Goncourts' Soeur Philomène. In the latter production Antoine for the first time developed his action on stage as if the proscenium opening were an invisible fourth wall of the room on stage. This convention, which became a standard one at the Théâtre-Libre, grew naturally out of Antoine's interest in authenticity in acting, but was nevertheless a radical departure from the audience-oriented interpretations of the past. Jean Jullien, who became the critical spokesman for the theatre, considered this apparent obliviousness of the audience an essential part of Antoine's new style:

> Although the actor must always be mentally aware of the impression on the audience, he should show nothing of this. He should play as if he were at home, unconscious of the emotion he is arousing, of cheers or hisses. The curtain line must be a fourth wall--transparent for the audience, opaque for the actor.[4]

The result was a realism which was both powerful and evocative, as Sarcey observed in his review of this production:

> We enjoy these accurate settings; we delight in the reality of the picturesque detail. That is the basis of this production. Sister Philomène kneels at the back of the stage, murmuring a sacred _oremus_ in a cool, soft voice. Around her, the rows of sick persons answer, as if they were hurrying through a daily task, and one hears above the confused murmur only a few Latin words, which seem to float on the surface. All this seems quite real and excites the imagination.[5]

Soeur Philomène was Antoine's last offering in the little hall in Montmartre which had been fitted out for the _Cercle Gaulois_, and both he and the _Cercle_ were apparently relieved when his burgeoning venture moved in November to the larger and better equipped, if more remote, Théâtre Montparnasse. There, in the remaining months of 1887, Antoine indisputably established the Théâtre-Libre as Paris' major experimental theatre. Both his poetic offerings--Mendès' _La Femme de Tabarin_ and Banville's _Le Baiser_--were accepted by the Comédie. Hennique's _Esther Brandès_, a character study in the realist manner, provided Antoine with one of his first opportunities to demonstrate his excellence as an actor. Céard brought Zola another stage success with an adaptation of _Le Capitaine Burle_ called _Tout pour l'honneur_. Finally, Jean Jullien's first play, _La Sérénade_, introduced the note of harsh, cynical realism called _rosserie_ which came to be one of the dominant aspects of Théâtre-Libre works.

Clearly the most important production during the

spring of 1888 was Tolstoi's The Power of Darkness, the first in a series of foreign presentations that were among Antoine's most significant contributions to the French stage. The production was a bold step, despite Tolstoi's popularity as a novelist in France and a general vogue in the 1880s for things Russian. The French stage had traditionally accepted foreign dramatists only with great caution, and The Power of Darkness was an untried work, banned in Russia and never yet produced anywhere. Antoine further insisted on an accurate translation, when even Mounet-Sully's noted Oedipe and Hamlet at the Comédie were adaptations, based on the assumption that the French public would not accept foreign works on any but French terms. While the merits of the play were hotly debated, all critics agreed on the excellence of the interpretation and the power of the realistic settings and costumes. One review concluded: "Let us add that the Russian costumes were perfectly accurate and that everything was artistic in this curious and moving presentation."[6]

So much general interest was aroused that Antoine consented to a public performance. The praise given to his actors as individuals and as an ensemble was particularly gratifying to Antoine since they were all, like himself, persons with almost no professional theatre training or background:

> Cernay, who plays Piotr, is a cane merchant; Pinsard is not only an architect, but even has a shop with a rather large clientele; Tinbot works at Firmin Didot's establishment; Mlle Barny is a seamstress; the young actress who plays Marina works at the telegraph office. Among the others there is a wine merchant and a head book-keeper at the bank.[7]

Gradually Antoine became convinced that such amateurs were in fact preferable for his theatre to professionally trained actors who had to laboriously unlearn all the artificial tricks of delivery they had spent so much time in developing.

In the other spring offerings of 1888, Antoine sought variety with some rather unsuccessful poetic dramas and an evening devoted to works by the "Five"--a group of young authors who had recently stirred the literary world by a public split with Zola. The final program introduced a bright new comic writer in Georges Ancey, though his M. Lamblin was quite eclipsed by the scandal of Alexis' La Fin de Lucie

Pellegrin, which dealt with the forbidden subject of lesbianism. This controversial though dramatically undistinguished work caused division not only among Antoine's supporters, but in the theatre itself, for Alexis wanted to capitalize on the controversy with a public performance, Antoine refused, and at last only the intervention of Zola was able to resolve the quarrel.

In July of 1888 the famous Meininger troupe from Germany played in Brussels and many persons from the Paris theatres went to see them, including Antoine, Claretie, and Porel. Antoine recorded his observations in a long, often-reproduced letter to the critic Sarcey which spoke particularly enthusiastically of the Meininger use of crowds, and promised similar experiments in the coming season at the Théâtre-Libre. Before fulfilling his promise, Antoine presented two programs in his new home in the Menus-Plaisirs--Louis de Gramont's grim naturalist tragedy Rolande and an evening of one-acts chiefly remembered for the realism of their settings; a practical fountain in Giovanni Verga's Chevalerie rustique and real sides of meat in the shop of Fernand Icres' Les Bouchers. Hennique's La Mort du duc d'Enghien, a sprawling historical drama, gave Antoine his first opportunity to try out the mass movements of the Meininger and thus served as a kind of trial run for the more ambitious but less successful La Patrie en danger, written by the Goncourts in 1873 but never before produced. A high point of Hennique's play was a council of war in the third act, illuminated only by lanterns which achieved a chiaroscuro effect unanimously praised by the critics: "the theatre in darkness, as at Bayreuth, and the stage lit dimly by the few lanterns placed on the table of the military leaders."[8]

For La Patrie en danger Antoine combined this effect with a huge crowd to produce a spectacular scene:

> I had nearly five hundred supernumeraries flow into a rather small setting through a single door. They slowly filtered in, like a subtle tide, at last inundating everything, from the furniture to the characters, and in this semi-darkness with light falling here and there on a teeming mass, the effect was extraordinary.[9]

Unfortunately, the script itself offered little to supplement Antoine's careful attention to crowd movement and lighting for special effects, and the general critical reaction was summed up in Emile Faguet's phrase: "a memorable evening in the annals of public boredom."

The same program, however, offered Antoine compensation in the success of *La Chance de Françoise,* a charming trifle by Georges de Porto-Riche, one of the Théâtre-Libre's most talented discoveries. In the next program, Ancey's *Les Inséperables* proved even more successful than *M. Lamblin.* New acting talents were appearing at the theatre too--Aurélien Lugné-Poe in *Les Inséperables,* and Gabrielle Fleury and Eugenie Nau in another "shocking" work, Méténier's *La Casserole,* which ended the season. Antoine's repertoire and his actors were now being sought by commercial managers. His old companion Mévisto left at the end of this season for the Odéon. Koning at the Gymnase presented *La Chance de Françoise,* and Carré at the Vaudeville even anticipated Antoine's planned production of an adaptation of Paul Bourget's novel, *Mensonges.* The influence of Antoine could now also be seen in the presentation by many theatres of plays hitherto considered too daring for Parisian audiences--Sardou's *Marquise* at the Vaudeville, Meilhac and Halévy's *Fanny Lear* at the Odéon, Dumas *fils*' *M. Alphonse* at the Gymnase. The Comédie revived Augier's *Maître Guérin* for the first time with the original ending, where the old notary does not remain with his family but deserts with his gold-digging servant. Theatres founded in imitation of Antoine now began to appear too: the Théâtre Moderne and Théâtre Indépendent, which like Antoine sought new authors; the Théâtre-Libre Ancien, devoted to forgotten classics; and the Théâtre d'Application, dedicated to training young actors.

Antoine's third season, 1889-90, was in many ways his most significant. The influence of the Théâtre-Libre was beginning to spread; this season saw Ancey's *Grand-mère* and Hennique's *Amour* presented by the Odéon, Alexis and Méténier's *M. Betsy* by the Variétés, and Lavedan's *Une Famille* by the Comédie itself. Jean Jullien provided a major critical outlet for the ideas of the new school by founding a review called *Art et Critique.* His new phrases--"the fourth wall," "a slice of life"--became a part of every critic's vocabulary. In the meantime, Antoine himself did not stand still. His introduction of foreign authors continued with Turgenev's *Le Pain d'autrui* and, far more significant, Ibsen's *Ghosts,* the play which became the symbol of the new drama for theatres like Antoine's all over Europe. With the possible exception of Antoine, who played Oswald, the Théâtre-Libre actors found the interpretation of this play unusually difficult. They had begun to evolve a style of their own, and the realism of Jullien, Alexis, and Méténier was quite different from that of Ibsen. The former required a dry, even ironic playing of moment to moment situations, even when those situations were ones of considerable psychological complexity. Ibsen demanded a more evocative approach with clear references to deeds and relationships mentioned but not shown. This called for a command of language still lacking in many of Antoine's actors. Whether this insecurity was conveyed to the audience or whether the public found the play confused and unclear because they found most non-French works confused and unclear is impossible now to determine. In any case, the production was a failure, but an influential one, since even among the severest critics there were those who admitted the power of the work.

In March, Antoine presented Ménages d'Artistes, the first play by Eugène Brieux, who gradually surpassed Jullien and Ancey to become the major dramatist of the Théâtre-Libre. Antoine concluded this productive spring by publishing a brochure of about 200 pages outlining for the first time in detail his plans for a new theatre. Very little in the program was original, but Antoine combined ideas from Zola, Wagner, Becque, Strindberg, and the Meininger to produce one of the most detailed statements of his time on the direction the new theatre of the 1880s was taking. Among his suggestions were replacement of the star system by a well-trained ensemble, making the theatre financially accessible to the general public, more experimentation in all phases of production, encouragement of young authors, better seating with improved hearing and visibility, more honesty and less decorative detail in settings, costumes, and acting style. The Théâtre-Libre never accomplished most of these impressive goals, but they continued to form the basis of Antoine's later directorships of the Théâtre Antoine and Odéon, and remain valid recommendations for progressive theatres still.

This same spring also saw the beginnings of a reaction to the Théâtre-Libre. Despite Antoine's continuing struggle to keep his theatre open to all schools, the public, the critics and many authors persisted in equating him with Zola, and thereby with naturalism. The Théâtre-Libre thus suffered from the reaction to this movement which by 1890 was already well under way, though specific rival schools had not yet clearly formed. The most distinct manifestation of this reaction in the theatre was the formation of the Théâtre Idéaliste in 1890 by Louis Germain. This venture was inspired by the cluster of sentiments that were growing up around the works of Wagner during this period--concerns with the mystic, the universal, the evocative, which Mallarmé and others had found in the German composer and were now introducing to French letters. The Théâtre Idéaliste never opened, but its ideas were adopted by the Théâtre Mixte, which opened in June, and which led in turn to Paul Fort's Théâtre d'Art in November. Each organization stated clearly that it wished to complement Antoine, not replace him, and indeed none of these theatres gave him serious competition. Yet by taking leadership of the young from him, as he had taken it from Porel, they began the process of erosion which led in 1894 to his abandonment of the Théâtre-Libre.

The season of 1890-91 already showed some falling-off. Such brutal and shocking works as Henry Fèvre's L'Honneur, Maurice Biollay's M. Bute, and Jean Ajalbert's adaptation of the Goncourts' La Fille Elisa confirmed the general feeling that Antoine was favoring the naturalists, and indeed the most abandoned among them. The critics who had at first praised Antoine's realism in setting and acting were becoming increasingly conscious of certain flaws in the new style. A note of amused condescension crept into some reviews: "The second act is set in a hotel room which we all recognize and which is rendered with rigorous exactitude. There is lacking, however, near the wash-basin and the lavatory, a small article of furnishing whose omission, under the circumstances, is quite incomprehensible."[10] Sarcey now regularly expressed an irritation with Antoine's methods:

> When the author has taken the trouble to inform me in a monologue of the social position of the mistress of the house, of the lovers she has had, of the affairs she has had with them, of the name of her latest, it is presumably because the knowledge is helpful to the understanding of the future action; it is so that I will know these details. Well, the staging is planned so that not a word, not a single word of this monologue reaches the ears of the audience. Mme Luce Collas, from the beginning of the scene to the end, dusting the furniture, turns her back to the audience and speaks between her teeth. 'This is more natural,' M. Antoine tells me. And I always come back to my objection--why is it more natural to dust facing away from the audience than facing toward them? Why is it more natural to swallow syllables than to articulate

> them?[11]

Antoine's reputation as a producer of sensational material attracted to his theatre audiences more interested in such sensation than in theatrical experimentation. A new attempt at crowd spectacle set off an unfortunate reaction in this rude and boisterous assembly which Antoine reports in his Souvenirs:

> In the third act, for a meeting in a London square, I brought together almost five hundred supernumeraries with their banners and three bands. For some inexplicable reason this enormous display on stage put the audience into an uproar, and, since the noise on stage was great and the spectators felt that their jokes and gibes would not even be able to reach us in the hullabaloo, for lack of anything better to do, they struck up in chorus the refrain of the Salvation Army song. Lost in the midst of the supernumeraries, I was put into such a rage that I gave a signal by whistle and three hundred extras unloosed on a stage a storm so violent and prolonged that the stunned and exhausted spectators were reduced to silence.[12]

The reputation of the Théâtre-Libre suffered so that a measure was even introduced in the Senate which sought, unsuccessfully, to condemn the Ministry of Education for making a modest grant to this "immoral and unpatriotic" venture.

Antoine sought to give his work a new image by presenting Ibsen's The Wild Duck, for despite the failure of Ghosts, it was already clear that the young dramatists of Europe were looking to Ibsen and not to Zola for their inspiration. "Just as I was the first to open my doors to the naturalist drama," Antoine proclaimed, "so shall I open them to the symbolist drama."[13] The critical reception of The Wild Duck, however, was even more uncomprehending and unfavorable than that of Ghosts, and despite his protestations, Antoine henceforth left Ibsen and the "symbolist" drama to other directors.

The offerings of 1891-92, therefore, continued to favor the naturalists, and with only a few plays of particular significance. The most important work was surely Brieux' first undisputed triumph, Blanchette, a domestic tragedy of a country girl whose taste of a possibly better life serves only to increase her misery. On the same bill was the first play by François de Curel, probably the second most noted of the Théâtre-Libre playwrights. L'Envers d'une sainte attracted little attention, but Les Fossiles, given the following fall, established Curel and was ultimately accepted by the Comédie. Though written in prose, this sympathetic study of the final agonies of a dying aristocracy achieved a real poetic power uncommon in Théâtre-Libre plays.

Antoine's penultimate season, 1892-93, reversed the decline of the two before to rival the triumphs of 1889-90. After the great success of Curel, another young dramatist, Courteline, won high praise for his Boubouroche. This more typical Théâtre-Libre offering derived cynical amusement from a café loafer who decides that it is easier to pretend his mistress is faithful in the face of all contrary evidence than to concern himself over her infidelity. The introduction of major foreign dramatists continued with Strindberg's Miss Julie in January and Hauptmann's The Weavers in May. The latter production was particularly gratifying to Antoine for two reasons: it allowed him to continue with great success his experimentation with crowd scenes, and it introduced to Paris the major dramatist of the German Freie Bühne, one of the most distinguished of the many European theatres founded under the inspiration of his own work.

The Weavers was surely one of Antoine's most impressive productions, but also one of his most expensive, and financial problems, which had always plagued his theatre, now became so great that he began seriously to consider closing. He even derived some grim humor from his selection to open his final season, A Bankruptcy, by Ibsen's countryman Björnsterne Björnson. Little else in the 1893-94 season was of great interest, except perhaps Antoine's last foray into quasi-symbolic drama with a second offering by Hauptmann, L'Assomption de Hannele Mattern. In June, 1894, Antoine turned the theatre over to Larochelle, who continued on for two more seasons with pale imitations of his predecessor's work.

Antoine himself remained a dominant figure in the French theatre for another half-century, but it is for his seven years at the Théâtre-Libre that he is most remembered, and rightly so, for hardly any aspect of the theatre escaped influence from his productions during these years. He discovered a whole generation of playwrights and actors; a generation of directors found his influence inescapable, even when they rebelled against it; stage lighting, design, and composition all were affected by his experiments. The wit, Désiré Luc, recalling Antoine's humble beginning as a clerk in the Paris Gas Company, summed him up as well as anyone: "It is from the gas that we get our light today."[14]

2. Sardou and Sarah, 1880-1907

Daniel Rochat (1880) was Victorien Sardou's first Comédie presentation since the unsuccessful Papillonne eighteen years before. It clearly attempted to capitalize on the political and social controversies of the day by bringing together two of the most hotly debated topics of the period, the divorce question, stimulated by Parliamentary debate over the new Naquet divorce law, and the conflict between free thought and traditional religion, represented in the play by a radical young orator and the girl who loves him but cannot accept marriage without a religious ceremony. Three years before, on the occasion of Sardou's acceptance into the Academy, Charles Blanc had admonished him: "Permit me to tell you that your occasional incursions into the domain of politics have not always been happy, and that they have added nothing either to your talents or to your reputation."[15] Daniel Rochat substantiated this judgment, for its controversial themes bitterly divided its audiences and insured the failure of the play. Few critics had kind words for Sardou, though they warmly praised the interpretation of Delaunay as the young orator and Julia Bartet, who made an impressive Comédie debut in the role of Léa Henderson, Rochat's wife. Sardou's disappointment over this failure was softened by the great success the same year of his comic treatment of divorce, Divorçons, at the Palais-Royal. The Naquet debates stimulated a whole series of plays in addition to Sardou's during the 1880s--Augier's Madame Caverlet (1882), Emile Moreau and George André's Divorçons (1884), and Bisson and Mars' Les Surprises du divorce (1888)--but Sardou's farce proved not only the most popular of these, but also the only one amusing enough to bear revivals when the popular interest in the theme had diminished.

With Odette (1881), Sardou returned to the Vaudeville and to contemporary domestic tragedy in the style of Dumas and Augier. Marie Legault, who had replaced Julia Bartet as the Vaudeville's leading lady, proved excellent in the new offering, but her association with Sardou was not continued.

Just at this time the Vaudeville was able to offer him a far more attractive star, the brilliant if erratic Sarah Bernhardt, who was to become Sardou's greatest interpreter. Bernhardt, whose financial stability was never great, was in particular difficulty in 1882, owing to the loss of a breach-of-contract suit brought against her by the Comédie and to the demands of her son Maurice, who was in the process of purchasing the Ambigu. She therefore signed a contract with Bertrand and Deslandes of the Vaudeville on the express condition that they commission Sardou to create a play for her and her new husband, the Greek actor Damala. The result was the extremely popular *Fédora* (1882), which became part of Sarah's permanent repertoire. Damala, unfortunately, proved unacceptable to Sardou, and had to be replaced by Pierre Berton, who had played leading man to Sarah in earlier productions. For her disappointed husband, Sarah obtained a play from Catulle Mendès, *Les Mères ennemies*, which proved the first success of Maurice's management at the Ambigu. Its popularity was so much eclipsed by that of *Fédora*, however, that Damala left Paris, and Sarah, appparently for good.

The Ambigu management of Maurice lasted only one year more, its only other success being *La Glu* (1883), a poetic tragedy of Breton peasant life which launched Jean Richepin as a dramatist. During the next two years, when both Sarah and Maurice were at the Porte-Saint-Martin, Richepin worked closely with them, creating for Sarah a poetic Indian extravaganza, *Nina Sahib* (1883) and a mutilated adaptation of *Macbeth* (1884) which were presented there along with revivals of *La Dame aux camélias*.

In 1884 Sarah turned again to Sardou to create a historical spectacle suitable for her talents and for the elaborate facilities of the Porte-Saint-Martin. The Byzantine *Théodora* was the result, the greatest triumph of the Sardou-Bernhardt collaboration, though it must be admitted that the play was at least as much celebrated for its costumes and settings as for its script or its interpretation. The old master of spectacle, Duquesnel, was recalled from retirement at Sardou's request to produce the work, and he in turn commissioned Massenet to write incidental music. The *mise-en-scène* was one of the most elaborate and talked-about of the century. Some critics wrote almost exclusively about the costumes, noting in awe that over 42,000 francs (about $3000) had been spent just on gems to decorate the dresses, there being no less than 4,500 such gems on Mme Bernhardt's mantle alone. The scholarly world was so challenged by the enormous detail of the setting that, for months after, Sardou carried on a lively debate in the journals with historians over such questions as whether forks were known in Byzantium and if Justinian's cabinet could contain blue glass. But like Pixérécourt at the beginning of the century, Sardou had based his play on the most painstaking research, and he was rarely, if ever, caught in error.

Sarah spent most of 1886 and 1887 on tour, first to South America, then to England. In the meantime, Sardou collaborated again with Massenet on Le Crocodile (1886), a shipwreck extravaganza at the Porte-Saint-Martin which proved too insubstantial even for Sardou's most dedicated partisans. Happily he was able to work with Sarah again on his next play La Tosca (1887), which gained its greatest fame in Puccini's 1900 operatic adaptation. The critics united in praise of the actress, but many, led by Sarcey, found little merit in the script. Sardou published a bitter letter in response to Sarcey, swearing that Nature had denied the critic "any sense of the artistic." "It is not therefore surprising," he continued, "that he should be not only indifferent, but even hostile to any attempt to reproduce the scenes, costumes, or customs of the past."[16] It is both striking and significant that Sardou's interpretation of the "artistic" deals with historical rather than literary or theatrical concerns.

In 1888 Sarah turned authoress, and gave to the Odéon a grim study of the mother of a dying child, L'Aveu, attractive only because of the Bernhardt name. She then fell back on the indestructable Dame aux camélias, now presented with her estranged husband Damala, whom Sarah had discovered near death in Paris and nursed back to sufficient health to spend his final few months on the stage. Sardou in the meantime was faring no better without his famous actress than she without him; his Marquise (1889) at the Vaudeville failed even with Réjane, who was now generally considered the rival of Mlle Bartet of the Comédie as the outstanding comedienne of the period. None the less, Sardou hesitated to fulfill Sarah's next request, for a Cleopatra play, for he feared comparison with Shakespeare. He need not have worried, for the critics all frankly accepted the Porte-Saint-Martin production of Cléopâtre (1890) as little more than a vehicle for Sarah, and spent all their efforts praising her. After this new triumph, the actress departed on her longest tour, which took her completely around the world and lasted until 1893.

Sardou, for his next play, turned again to politics and to the period of the French Revolution, choosing as his central character Labussière, the clerk in the Committee of Public Safety who saved many, including the actors of the Comédie, from the guillotine. Thermidor (1891) was planned for the Porte-Saint-Martin and its central role for Coquelin, who had come to that theatre from the Comédie in 1889. But Claretie, the Comédie director, was anxious to regain his departed actor, and negotiated for Thermidor to be given with Coquelin at the Comédie. Remembering her contribution to Daniel Rochat, Sardou requested Mlle Bartet for his heroine, and the third major role was filled by a promising debutant, Marais. The play had a tranquil opening, but its condemnation of the Terror aroused the anger of pro-Revolutionary groups. On the second night of the production students from the Latin Quarter initiated one of the most serious theatre riots of the period. Constans, the Minister of the Interior, was sufficiently alarmed to ban the play from any government theatre. More moderate members of the Cabinet protested that the play only condemned the extremes of the Revolution, but they were silenced by a stirring speech from Clemenceau, who argued that an attack on any part of the Revolution was an attack on the whole. Thus the ban remained in effect, insuring Thermidor a notoriety among Sardou's works which it scarcely deserved. After this third failure, the dramatist did not again attempt to conquer the Comédie.

The most influential part of the short-lived production was probably the settings, which reflected Sardou's own interests and were among the most scrupulously detailed and historically exact the Comédie had yet seen. The names of the production's designers were virtually a roster of the champions of the new realism. The first act was by the rather conservative Lemeunier. The second and third were by Chaperon, who had made his reputation with Montigny at the Gymnase (where he had designed Sardou's own Pattes de mouche), and by Rubé, who had been responsible for the noted settings of Le Sphinx. The fourth was the work of Cambon's pupils, Carpezat and Lavastre, who in turn trained a whole new generation of designers. The rich and authentic costumes were the creations of Bianchini. Predictably, with all this attention to production, the script itself was rather weak. Yet when Coquelin returned to the Porte-Saint-Martin in 1895, one of his first productions there was a revival of

Thermidor, and the publicity the play had previously received guaranteed its success.

Undaunted by the fate of Thermidor at the Comédie, Sardou turned again to the Revolutionary period to produce a much richer piece, Madame Sans-Gêne (1893). This time history worked in his favor. Napoleon and the Empire were now much in fashion, and Madame Sans-Gêne became the most popular of many plays catering to this interest. The play was presented at the Vaudeville, with Réjane in the title role of a witty laundress whose fortunes become entangled with the Emperor's, a role ideally suited to her and quite different from the suffering queens Sardou was accustomed to creating for Sarah. Even so, emphasis remained on the physical surroundings, so that Sarcey and other critics called the play a triumph for the designers and costumer rather than for the actors or playwright.

When Sarah Bernhardt returned to Paris in 1893, it was again as directress of a theatre; this time the Renaissance, which she managed until 1898. During these years she produced few important plays, but launched three popular young actors whom she personally selected to lead her company: Abel Deval, Lucien Guitry, and Edouard de Max. Sardou furnished her with a new spectacle, Gismonda (1894), set in fifteenth century Athens. This play proved the most popular in which Sarah appeared at the Renaissance, but Sardou's hold on the public was loosening. The play was all too clearly written according to a formula, which included even the exotic setting. In England, William Archer pointed out that although Gismonda married her lover at the end instead of dying in some spectacular way, she was otherwise almost indistinguishable from Fédora, Théodora, or La Tosca; and Shaw, never a friend of Sardou, was even more sardonic than usual: "I had seen Diplomacy Dora, and Théodora, and La Toscadora, and other machine dolls from the same firm. And yet the thing took me aback."[17]

Rostand's La Princesse Lointaine (1895) proved too delicate and sentimental to endure, despite the talents of Bernhardt, Ernest Coquelin, Guitry, and de Max. Indeed, Sarah's administration at the Renaissance was blessed with only two successful productions. One was surely her boldest offering--Musset's Lorenzaccio, written in 1834 and never yet produced. The play consisted of twenty-nine scenes, each calling for a different setting, and was built around a neurotic and mercurial hero that French critics found as elusive and difficult as Hamlet himself. Finally, in the 1890s, Armand d'Artois solved the first difficulty by reducing the settings to five, one for each act, with only minor adaptation. The adaptor then undertook the difficult search for an actor to play the leading role. Dumas fils advised him: "You need Frédérick Lemaître at twenty. Mounet-Sully is now too old. Some woman perhaps? But a travesty role would be risky." But when d'Artois mentioned Sarah, Dumas agreed at once. "She is surely capable of it. She can do anything."[18] The play was a great success, given 85 times at the Renaissance, and Bernhardt, now 52, played the young hero with a spirit and intensity which won her universal praise. Ironically, the only other clear success of her administration was Maurice Donnay's Amants (1895) in which Claudine, the charming liberated woman who plays the central role, was created not by Sarah, but by Jeanne Granier. Sardou's Spiritisme (1897), on the other hand, a weak exploration of a supernatural theme, was the first distinct failure Sarah had experienced with her favorite dramatist.

Deciding that the Renaissance was bringing her ill luck, Sarah signed a twenty-five year lease on the huge Théâtre des Nations, which she renamed the Théâtre Sarah-Bernhardt. During this spring, while Sarah was on tour in England, the great Italian actress Eleonora Duse announced her plans to visit Paris, and Sarah immediately offered her the hospitality of her new theatre. Her motives do not seem to have been entirely disinterested, for in addition to seeing that proper publicity was given to this "hospitality," she talked Duse into opening in June, not with Magda, which was one of Duse's best roles and Sarah's worst, but with La Dame aux camélias, wherein the inevitable comparisons would be more likely to favor Sarah. The result was that the major artists and critics assembled at Duse's opening considered it rather a disappointment. The Italian artist's style was new and alien, a subtler style than Bernhardt's and one which required time to be accepted. The association of Sarah's interpretation with the particular role naturally added to the difficulty. Félix Duquesnel, writing in Le Théâtre years later, recalled the confused impression made by Duse's first Parisian appearance: "The first impression was complex, strange I might almost say, a defeat of all the customary conventions. One looked in vain for the traditional ideas... One had to grow accustomed to it. One had to overcome prejudice and submit to an initiation."[19]

Magda, the next week, was more successful, but did

not erase this initial unfavorable reaction. In subsequent offerings, Duse was careful in her selections. She refused an offer from Sarah which would have resulted in the two stars performing alternate acts from La Dame aux camélias to benefit a fund then being raised for a memorial to Dumas fils in Paris, and gave an act of La Femme de Claude instead. Yet when fall came and her engagement was completed, Duse prepared to leave Paris in the midst of what seemed to be general indifference. Then an open letter in Le Temps, signed Sganarelle but actually by Sarcey, begged her to give a final matinee for all the artists of Paris who had been inspired by her visit. Suddenly the tide turned. Duse's unfamiliar style had won its public and warm testimonials began to appear, headed by a major article by Gustave Larroument in the Figaro. Once again Sarah attempted to turn the situation to her own advantage by suggesting that the proposed matinee be by invitation signed jointly by her and Duse, but the Italian actress declined, and made arrangements to appear at the Renaissance in her own program. When the demand for tickets continued to grow she moved to the larger Porte-Saint-Martin. Even so, she received over 15,000 requests for the 1,500 available seats. She presented Verga's Cavalieria Rusticana and single acts of La Dame aux camélias and La Femme de Claude to the most unreserved admiration. It was one of the great theatre events of the century and of the career of Duse, who returned to Italy unreservedly accepted by the French as one of the great serious actresses of the era.

The always unpredicatable Sarah returned to triumph in two male roles, Hamlet (1899) and Rostand's L'Aiglon (1900). Her successes at her own theatre, and her exhausting tours, continued almost until her death in 1923. It is pleasant to report that among the successes was her last collaboration with Sardou; that after the disappointment of Spiritisme, the old partners triumphed a final time with La Sorcière (1903). Sardou's popularity continued, despite the scorn of many of the young, until his death in 1908. At the age of 76 he gained his last success with L'Affaire des poisons (1907) at the Porte-Saint-Martin. The plot, dealing with the famous scandal of Louis XIV's court, showed all Sardou's old skill in historical re-creation, supported as always by a lavish setting. One scene, showing the grotto of Thetis at Versailles, was a totally exact copy of the original, and was credited as the most elaborate setting ever placed on the Paris stage. The same year Sardou was awarded the Cross of the Legion of Honor, and it must have given the old playwright particular satisfaction to receive the award from his opponent of the Thermidor controversy, Clemenceau.

3. Minor Theatres, 1880-1900

The trends among Paris' lesser theatres already apparent during the Second Empire resulted during the last twenty years of the nineteenth century in a theatrical situation almost as confused and complicated as that resulting from the Revolution. Many ephemeral ventures were launched, particularly in the 1890s, after the great impact of Antoine's Théâtre-Libre, their numbers and offerings subject only to the pressures of competition. The old pattern of a theatre presenting a single genre with a moderately stable company now almost totally disappeared. A popular actress such as Réjane could be found almost every year at a different theatre, while even the Comédie was not able to prevent such important members of its troupe as Bernhardt or Coquelin from leaving to try their fortunes at other Parisian houses.

In these rapidly changing times, the Gymnase remained the most stable of the boulevard theatres in management, company, and repertoire. Koning, the director from 1880 until 1893, was less innovative than his predecessor Montigny, but he did encourage a new generation of social dramatists, headed by Georges Ohnet. Ohnet was a popular novelist who, unlike Zola, had little difficulty in adapting his novels to the stage. Both Serge Panine (1882) and Le Maître de forges (1883) were great successes. The latter was widely regarded as the most powerful social drama of the post-Augier generation and was praised for its originality in avoiding the theme of marital infidelity so central to Dumas fils and Augier. Neither power nor originality are so apparent today, for the problem of infidelity remains, though no sin is actually committed, and the other concerns of the play are hardly original--the money theme so widely found in serious drama of the century, the common agonies of aristocrats married into the merchant class and vice versa, even the tedious gaucheries of the nouveau riche, exploited by French comic dramatists ever since Molière. Dialogue and characters are weaker than the better work of Augier; the plot, culminating in a melodramatic duel, more contrived than most of Dumas fils'. Even so, Ohnet's work was superior to that of most of his competitors, even if we include the last plays of Dumas and Augier, and his popularity was to that extent deserved. He also had the advantage of excellent interpreters in these plays and in the later Comtesse Sarah (1887). Jane Hading, after gaining a modest success in operettas at the Renaissance, surprised her public by joining the Gymnase in 1883 and turning to drama. The wisdom of her change was demonstrated by her brilliant interpretation of Claire de Beaulieu in Le Maître de forges. The creation, said Sarcey, was "stunning and unbelievable":

> It is not enough to say that Mme Jane Hading was good; she showed herself to be a remarkable actress. She, whom we have seen so gauche, so stiff in the eccentricities of operetta, in the drama she has a harmony of movement which is full of grace. Her features are serious and even sad, her voice pathetic; perhaps a trifle weak, but she speaks perfectly and her words melt into tears. In short, we were enchanted by her. Koning is truly a lucky devil! Who would have suspected such a metamorphosis![20]

Hading married the Gymnase director Koning in 1884, and for the next decade remained at that theatre, adding to her reputation as an interpreter of social drama. Her usual leading man was Lafontaine, a less brilliant but quite popular actor.

Most of the period's important writers of social drama and of social and political comedy were presented by the Gymnase. Octave Feuillet, after the success of Le Sphinx at the Comédie, offered the Gymnase his Un Roman parisien (1882). Jules Claretie gave the theatre political comedy in the manner of Augier with Monsieur le Ministre (1883). One of Mme Hading's greatest roles was Daudet's Sapho (1885), as adapted by Belot, a success which encouraged later Daudet adaptations. Koning was the first of the boulevard directors to acknowledge the work of the Théâtre-Libre, reviving Porto-Riche's La Chance de Françoise in 1889, the first public presentation of one of Antoine's discoveries. Jacques Normand's adaptation of Maupassant's Musotte (1891) was developed in a bitter tone clearly influenced by Théâtre-Libre offerings, and 1892, the final year of Koning's administration, saw more works by Antoine's dramatists--Pierre Wolff's Leurs filles and Celles qu'on respecte, and Alexis and Méténier's adaptation of the Goncourt novel, Charles Demailly.

The administration of Albert Carré and Paul Porel,

which continued until the end of the century, maintained the general emphases of Koning, though toward the end of Porel's direction a new note was introduced by the broad comedies of Alexandre Bisson and his collaborators, beginning with *Disparu* (1896). Contemporary social concerns remained the theatre's major subject matter, sometimes treated seriously, sometimes comically. Marcel Prévost's *Les Demi-vierges* (1895) and Brieux' *Les Trois Filles de Monsieur Dupont* (1897) were the outstanding serious studies, typical in their treatment of such contemporary social problems as the financially arranged marriage. Among the lighter works on similar themes were Alfred Capus' *Le Mariage bourgeois* (1898) and Jules Lemaître's *L'Age difficile* (1895). Lemaître's play achieved a great success with an unlikely combination of stars: Mme Judic, who had made her reputation in *vaudeville* and operetta, and Antoine, recently departed from the Théâtre-Libre.

Popular melodramas stressing action, spectacle, and sentiment were the preferred fare at the Ambigu, Busnach's adaptations of Zola such as *Nana* (1881) being no exception. For the gentlemen there were cape and sword plays such as Émile Blavet's *Fils de Porthos* (1886), and for the ladies such stimulants to the emotions as d'Ennery and Edmond Tarbé's *Martyre* (1886) which, it was said, wetted more handkerchiefs than any melodrama since *Les Deux Orphelins*. Later successes followed these models: Jules Mary and Georges Grisier's *Roger la Honte* (1888), with a notable interpretation by Pauline Breton; Xavier de Montépin and Jules Dorney's *La Porteuse de pain* (1889); and Mary and Grisier's *Régiment* (1890). A change in director from Rochard to Mme Zulma Bouffar in 1891 did not interrupt this successful series, but somewhat altered its focus, since Mme Bouffar tended to follow the increasingly more common boulevard tendency to emphasize production over plays. Such works as Jules Dorney's *Les Cadets de la reine* (1892) were billed as historical dramas, but actually consisted of little more than elaborate scenery. This emphasis continued until 1898, when new directors, Holacher and Pontet, converted the theatre to comic opera.

Scenic spectacle was in general even more elaborate and widely employed in minor theatres in the 1880s and 1890s than it had been in the 1870s, but only one theatre, the Châtelet, placed its emphasis primarily on spectacle throughout this period. Other houses either mixed plays of pure spectacle with offerings in other genres, as at the Porte-

Saint-Martin or the Nations, or used spectacle to reinforce the effectiveness of a preferred genre; melodrama at the Ambigu, operetta at the Bouffés. Emile Rochard, who followed Castellano as director of the Châtelet in 1880, relied almost entirely on revivals of such classic spectacle and fairy plays as Pilules du diable, more elaborately mounted than ever. Duquesnel produced the d'Ennery and Verne adaptation of Michel Strogoff in 1880, and although he made the surprisingly conservative decision to omit the wolves which had appeared in the earlier Odéon version, little other restraint was observed. Eight designers created the complex settings, and Thomas designed over 1, 200 costumes for the production. Rochard's successor in 1882, Floury, fittingly a painter, offered more original but no less spectacular displays: d'Ennery and Clairville's Poule aux oeufs d'or (1884), Ernest Blum and Raoul Touché's Les Aventures de Monsieur de Crac (1886), d'Ennery and Paul Férier's Trésor des radjahs (1894). Floury presented fewer new spectacles in the 1890s, not because the appeal of the genre had diminished, but because he found it less exhausting to go back to Rochard's policy of relying on a few invariably profitable revivals.

The Châtelet's neighbor theatre, the Nations, enjoyed no such stability. Ballande, director from 1880 to 1883, presented spectacular melodrama such as Les Nuits du boulevard (1880). Next came an Italian opera company, headed by the Corti brothers from La Scala. A variety of other directors and genres followed, but none made any real impact on the theatrical life of the capital until Sarah Bernhardt took over the theatre in 1899. One of the few successes, and surely the most interesting production of the intervening years, was Busnach's adaptation of Zola's Le Ventre de Paris (1887). The work was hailed as a triumph of naturalism, though the clearest manifestation of this was in the physical production, which involved a scrupulous reconstruction of Les Halles with dogs, cats, horses, and piles of real vegetables. Sarcey pronounced the reconstruction intriguing, "though less intriguing, of course, than Les Halles themselves, which are only a few steps from the theatre." He admitted the mounds of sausages and hams were "appetising" but wondered what all this had to do with the play itself:

> What is the point of all these heaps of cauliflower and carrots, these porters bearing their sacks, these vagabonds rising from the benches where they have been sleeping, if they create only a meaningless milieu? Everything I learn in this

> act could just as easily have been expressed at the horse market of La Villette. It is a setting for the setting's sake, and there is nothing we could give up more easily.[21]

Marie Laurent, the leading lady, was praised by most critics less for her interpretation than for her ability in bringing a touch of art to all this display.

Paul Clèves became the director of the Porte-Saint-Martin in 1879, shifting its emphasis only slightly from spectacular melodrama to spectacular fairy plays. Now came huge works of magic and enchantment, the thirty-scene *Cendrillon* (1879) of Clairville, Mennier and Blum, and a revival in 1881 of *La Biche au bois* by the Cogniard brothers, which boasted eight lions "*en liberté*." Nor were d'Ennery and Verne forgotten; *Le Voyage à travers l'impossible* (1882) was their most elaborate work to date, with twenty-eight scenes depicting the Nautilus, Vesuvius, and the inhabitants of the center of the earth. The next decade at the Porte-Saint-Martin was that of Bernhardt, Sardou, and Duquesnel, with such productions as *Théodora*, *La Tosca*, and *Cléopatra*. Clearly those spectators who had come to love the Porte-Saint-Martin for its spectacle were not disappointed by this new management. When Duquesnel retired and Sarah took over the Renaissance in 1893, Rochard, former director of the Ambigu, came to the Porte-Saint-Martin. Rochard found considerable success in mounting historical pageants--Michel Laya's *Napoléon* (1893) and Pierre Decourcelle's *Le Collier de la reine* (1895)--but his major contribution was surely bringing Coquelin to the Porte-Saint-Martin for Paul Déroulède's *Messire Duguesclin* (1895).

One of the great scandals of the French stage in the early 1890s was the departure of Coquelin *aîné* from the Comédie. Napoleonic legislation provided mechanisms for a *sociétaire* to leave the theatre, of course, but it strictly forbade any such departed actors from thereafter appearing in other theatres in Paris. Sarah Bernhardt had successfully defied this legislation, since no Comédie administration was inclined to try to force the erratic actress to return, but Coquelin's attempt to follow her example aroused strong opposition. Aside from the loss of another major talent, and this time a more tractable one, the Comédie administration was deeply concerned over the establishment of a precedent which might seriously erode the uniqueness of the national theatre. As we have seen, Claretie kept Coquelin at the

Comédie for a time with the 1891 production of Sardou's *Thermidor*, but the problem arose again in 1894 when Bernhardt announced that Coquelin would be joining her for a series of classics at the Renaissance, which she had purchased the year before. In defiance of legal proceedings begun against him by the Comédie, Coquelin did appear later that year at the Renaissance in *Le Médecin malgré lui* and in *Amphitryon* with Bernhardt. He was then invited to the Porte-Saint-Martin by Clèves to appear in *Messire Duquesclin*. The play was a minor one, but it proved crucial in Coquelin's career since it was attended by several high government officials and even by the President of the Republic. Doubtless these dignitaries were attracted more by the play's reputation as a stirring patriotic piece than by an interest in Coquelin, but this official manifestation of support for a renegade actor totally undermined the Comédie's legal proceedings against him. The charges were dropped shortly after, and Coquelin was left free to continue at the Porte-Saint-Martin, or wherever else he chose.

When Coquelin's brother Ernest appeared in Rostand's *La Princesse Lointaine* at the Renaissance in 1895, the older actor was sufficiently impressed by the work to ask for a Rostand play for himself. The result, *Cyrano de Bergerac*, delighted Coquelin but aroused scepticism in almost everyone else who read it. The play was long and costly, its leading character historical but virtually unknown, and worst of all, it was written in verse at a time when the triumph of realism seemed to have destroyed such artifice forever. There seemed no potential audience for such a play. The general public's taste clearly ran to operetta, *vaudeville*, melodrama, and spectacle. The various elitist groups of the 1890s--the naturalists, the symbolists, the enthusiasts of foreign drama --were even less promising. Finally Coquelin was able to present the play only by purchasing a half interest in the Porte-Saint-Martin and assuming most of the expenses himself. His faith was rewarded from the very opening night of the play, when he, his brother, Marie Legault, Volny, and Desjardins were given one of the most enthusiastic receptions of the century, and the play went on to a continuous run of a year and a half, a record for the French stage. Typical was the enthusiasm of Emile Faguet, who called *Cyrano* "the most beautiful dramatic poem that has appeared in half a century" and went on to describe Rostand as a great poet:

> who at twenty-five has inaugurated the twentieth century in a brilliant and triumphant manner... the

> herald for us of a new era upon which the eyes of Europe will be fixed with envy and those of France with an ecstasy of pride and hope... there shall be again in France a great poetic literature worthy of 1550, worthy of 1630, worthy of 1660, worthy of 1830! It is here--it is at hand! I shall have lived long enough to see it! In my yearning to see it in its fullness, I shall begin to dread death![22]

Little wonder that with the appearance of this great success the feeling was widespread in the French theatre that realism had run its course.

The Gaîté's fortunes had fallen so low in 1880 that it was used during that year by three different ventures, all unsuccessful. The director Debruyère brought the theatre a certain financial stability after 1882 by adjusting the repertoire to whatever seemed most likely to attract public interest, though this put an understandable strain on the physical resources of his company. He thus began with spectacular dramas such as _Pirates de la Savane_ (1882) which featured guest artist Ada Menken tied to the back of a horse and riding up a series of ramps into the flies. When such attractions seemed to be declining in interest, he turned to the operetta, presenting revivals and a few successful new works by Audran and Planquette. These significantly based their appeal almost as much on spectacle as on music or book, and in the 1890s Debruyère had the profitable idea of focusing his repertoire on revivals of such classic operettas as _Les Cloches de Corneville_ with far more elaborate settings than in the original productions.

Clairville, Gabet, and Planquette's _Les Cloches de Corneville_, first presented in 1877 at the Folies, was unquestionably the most frequently revived work in Paris for the remainder of the century. It was a strange work, described by one critic as "a curious mixture of operetta and melodrama,"[23] a tale of suspense and violent turns told with folk tunes, waltzes, polkas and comic opera situations. Yet this old blend proved so popular that _Les Cloches_ had received an unprecedented 800 performances at its home theatre by 1883 with no waning in public interest. Little wonder that with a repertoire which contained works such as this and _La Fille de Madame Angot_, the Folies director Blandin was satisfied for several years to live almost entirely on revivals. A series of successful new works appeared between 1883 and 1886, one of them, Meilhac and Gille's _Rip_ (1884), becoming one of the standard revival pieces in later years. The Folies suffered from increased competition from the Gaîté and other houses in the late 1880s but regained its popularity in the next decade with such operettas as Victor Roger's *Les Vingt-huit jours de Clairette* (1892) and Louis Varney's *La Falote* (1896).

Several other houses devoted a significant part of their efforts to operetta during this period--the Nouveautés and the Renaissance in the early 1880s, the Variétés and the Menus-Plaisirs in the 1890s--but none really challenged the Folies' leadership in this genre except the Bouffés, which as a larger house tended to place more emphasis on production. After the great success of Ferrier, Prével and Varney's *Les Mousquetaires au couvent* (1880), the Bouffés relied almost entirely for a number of years on revivals. The single notable new work was a burlesque up-dating of the Joseph story, *Joséphine vendue par ses soeurs* (1886) by Ferrier, Carré, and Roger, its major role winning a great following for Mlle Mily-Meyer. New works were more frequent after 1890, most of them the productions of Victor Roger and Edmond Audran. Maxime Boucheron and Audran's *Miss Héylett* (1890) was the first play to enjoy an uninterrupted year-long run in Paris.

Although operettas had occasionally been presented at the Variétés during the 1870s, few major works in this genre were seen here until the end of the decade, just when they were disappearing from the Renaissance. The theatre's leading actors, Céline Chaumont, Anna Judic, and José Dupuis were as comfortable in operetta as in the theatre's traditional genre, the *vaudeville*, and Mme Judic in particular was generally considered the only real rival in Paris to Jeanne Granier, the operetta star of the Renaissance. The Variétés relied on her so heavily for both *vaudeville* and operetta between 1878 and 1884 that her departure for two years to the Palais-Royal was a serious blow to the theatre. Her greatest *vaudeville* successes were a series of works by Maurice Hennequin and Albert Millaud beginning with *Niniche* (1878). The popularity of this first collaboration was in part due to a notorious bathing costume worn by Mme Judic (causing the banning of the play in England), but even fully clothed the actress repeated her success in *La Femme à papa* (1879) and *Lili* (1882). In operetta, Hervé, Offenbach's old rival, created two popular works for her, *La Roussote* (1881) and *Mam'zelle Nitouche* (1883).

The Palais-Royal in 1880 gained a dynamic new director, Briet, who completely redecorated the house and offered works by the most popular comic authors of the period. The very first year of the new administration saw Sardou's great success *Divorçons*. In 1883 came Meilhac and Gilles' *Ma Camarade*, and in 1884 Briet succeeded in attracting to the Palais-Royal not only Mme Judic but also the dramatist Hennequin, who created with Arnold Mortier and Albert de Saint-Albin *Le Train de plaisir*, a popular *vaudeville* imitated from the classic *Chapeau de paille d'Italie*. In the midst of the prosperity from these works, the theatre celebrated in 1884 a most happy centenary.

In the latter part of the decade, however, the Palais-Royal enjoyed no comparable successes. Briet came to rely more and more on revivals, and the lead in comedy returned to the Variétés and the Vaudeville, though neither committed itself exclusively to this genre. Social drama and even early naturalist works were mixed in with farces and *vaudevilles*, and many actors and authors moved frequently from theatre to theatre to offer their talents. A striking and not unusual example was Réjane, one of the period's outstanding actresses in social drama and comedy, who appeared at the Palais-Royal in *Ma Camarade* in 1883, then at the Vaudeville in Gondinet and Pierre Civac's *Clara Soleil* (1885), at the Variétés in Meilhac's *Mademoiselle Clochard* (1886), at the Vaudeville in Meilhac's *Monsieur de Murat* (1887), and at the Variétés again in Halévy's *Décoré* (1888).

Georges Feydeau, the major comic dramatist of the next decade, made his debut at the Renaissance with *Tailleur pour dames* (1886). Though he subsequently provided works for most of the comedy-*vaudeville* theatres of Paris, he was most closely associated during the 1890s with the Palais-Royal. *Monsieur Chasse!* (1892), *Un Fil à la patte* (1894), and *Le Dindon* (1896) continued to rework traditional *vaudeville* situations--wives and husbands engaged in mutual deception, wilful and chance misunderstandings, unexpected encounters in unlikely places--but the wit and exuberance of Feydeau gave them new life. Lesser successes were achieved by Gandillot with *Sous-Préfect de Château-Buzard* (1893) and by Hennequin and various collaborators with *Le Paradis* (1896) and *Coralie et Compagnie* (1899).

The 1890s were for the Variétés a period of experiment. Bertrand, the director until 1892, was sufficiently influenced by Antoine to introduce two odd naturalistic pieces to this traditional home of comedy and operetta, Alexis and Méténier's Monsieur Betsy (1890) and Méténier and de Laforest's La Bonne à tout faire (1892), but public interest was slight and Bertrand's successor, Fernand Samuel, turned to other possible attractions. He produced a few comedies, most notably Valabrègue's Le Premier Mari de France (1893), then began emphasizing operetta. When he rehired both Jeanne Granier and Mme Judic, lovers of the operetta hoped a new productive period was beginning, but Samuel chose to rely almost entirely on popular but undistinguished revivals of proven successes by Hervé and Offenbach. The only significant original musical offering of the decade was Blum, Ferrier, and Serpette's fantasy, Carnet du diable (1895). In staging, too, Samuel promised much more than he produced. His only real innovation was the installation of the first revolving stage in Paris in 1898, and this was removed almost immediately when the machinists of the theatre protested that it was too complicated to run. Toward the end of the decade, Samuel came to rely on Lavedan, a dramatist from the Théâtre-Libre whose comedies for the Variétés lacked the bitter and ironic edge of his other works and therefore exactly suited the tastes of Samuel's audiences. Le Nouveau Jeu (1898) was a new treatment of divorce, and one of the lightest, remembered most for its carefree hero's oft-quoted remark to the judge: "Marriage is like spinach. You don't know you dislike it until you've tasted it."

The Vaudeville reflected even more clearly the influence of Antoine during the 1890s. Its director, Albert Carré, began Thursday matinees in 1890 in obvious imitation of the Théâtre-Libre offerings. One such matinee, in 1891, produced the first Hedda Gabler in France. No theatre, moreover, was so receptive to the young dramatists discovered by Antoine; Lavedan, Curel, Boniface, Guinon, Wolff, and Brieux were all represented here. Carré himself discovered an important new naturalist in Paul Hervieu, whose Les Paroles restent was given in 1892.

Rather surprisingly, the Vaudeville was able to mount along with these works a number of popular comedies, mostly the work of Bisson and his collaborators, such as La Famille Pont-Biquet (1892) and Jalouse (1897). Like Feydeau, Bisson constantly reworked traditional comedy-vaudeville themes--mistaken identity, and the elaborate plots of husbands to elude their wives' surveillance, or that of meddling in-laws. On these themes, however, Bisson worked variations of staggering complexity. In Les Surprises du *divorce* (1888), for example, Duval divorces his wife to get rid of her irascible mother, but when he remarries, finds that his new father-in-law has wed his ex-wife. The complex *ménage* is completed by the lover of Duval's first wife, who has shifted his attentions to the second, supposing her the unwed sister of the first.

The last theatre to make an important contribution to the comedy-*vaudeville* tradition of the nineteenth century was the Nouveautés, a minor house opened in 1876 and until 1890 a moderately popular but not outstanding producer of operettas by Lecocq, Serpette, and Varney. In 1891 a new director, Henri Micheau, turned the theatre toward *vaudeville* and was rewarded by an immediate success--Mars, Maurice Desvallières, and Serpette's *La Demoiselle du téléphone.* Desvallières then began collaborating with Feydeau to produce two of that dramatist's most popular works--*Le Champignol malgré lui* (1893) and *Hôtel du Libre Échange* (1894). The success of these productions attracted other major comic writers to the Nouveautés. *Hôtel du Libre Échange* filled the theatre through 1895, and was followed by works of Gandillot and Gascogne, and by Bisson's popular *Le Contrôleur des wagons-lits.* Feydeau returned in 1899 with another great success, *La Dame de chez Maxim's.* The *Annales du théâtre* for 1900 called particular attention to Micheau's remarkable record at the Nouveautés; in nine years he had mounted nine full-length plays which had achieved more than one hundred performances (the test of a major success in the period) with the average run of these nine being nearly three hundred performances![24] Théâtre-Libre realism entered the Nouveautés in the work of Alfred Capus, whose most successful offering was *Les Maris de Léontine* (1899). In its themes and its reliance on comic coincidence the play was quite traditional: the divorced and remarried heroine, disloyal to her new husband and threatened with legal action, finds that her first husband is now the commissioner of police with whom she must deal. The characters are treated, however, with a seriousness and concern far removed from the manipulations of Feydeau or Bisson.

Few theatres in Paris during the 1890s escaped the influence of the new generation of playwrights, many of them, though by no means all, the protégés of Antoine. Not surprisingly, the most consistent promoter of the young remained Antoine himself, who opened his own major theatre in 1897. His rich and varied program revived all the most memorable plays from the Théâtre-Libre and offered new works by Théâtre-Libre authors, such as Curel's Répas du lion (1897) and Coolus' Coeurblette (1899), as well as premieres of authors yet unknown, such as Gabriel Travieux' Sur la foi des étoiles (1900). Antoine's success also inspired a host of other experimental theatres during the 1890s, many of them committed to developing new talent. The 1894 Annales du Théâtre considered twenty-five of these sufficiently important to include in its survey. Of course, the majority of discoveries by these little theatres proved as ephemeral as the theatres themselves, but several authors went on from them to make distinct contributions to the turn-of-the-century theatre: Paul Adam of the Théâtre X, Octave Mirabeau of the Théâtre d'Application, Jules Renard of the Cercle des Escholiers. One such theatre not only contributed several new dramatists to the French stage--Maurice Beaubourg, Henry Bataille, Henri de Regnier, Pierre Quillard, Romain Rolland--but also brought a new concern with foreign dramatic traditions, and ultimately rivalled in influence the Théâtre-Libre itself. This was Lugné-Poe's Théâtre de l'Oeuvre, a venture which merits separate consideration.

4. Lugné-Poe and the Théâtre de l'Oeuvre, 1886-1899

Lugné-Poe, who came eventually to lead the movement most directly opposed to naturalism, began his career closely related to Antoine. He too was involved at first in an amateur group, the Cercle des Escholiers, which he founded with Georges Bourdon but which, unlike the Cercle Gaulois, was founded specifically to produce new or unfamiliar works. Its offerings were generally undistinguished, and after a year Lugné-Poe left to gain other experience. In 1888 he was accepted by the Conservatoire and began appearing at the Théâtre-Libre, thus profiting from the teaching of Worms from the Comédie on the one hand and Antoine on the other.

In 1890 he left Antoine and the following spring joined Paul Fort at the recently-formed Théâtre d'Art. None of the 1890 Théâtre d'Art productions--mediocre Parnassian or romantic verse plays--were of great importance, but The Cenci in January, 1891, established the theatre as a significant one, and the following month Fort gained new attention by announcing in the Echo de Paris:

> The Théâtre d'Art after this presentation will be-

> come totally symbolist. It will be henceforth at the service of the masters of the new school--Stéphane Mallarmé, Paul Verlaine, Jean Moréas, Henri de Régnier, Charles Morice. At the end of March it will give the first symbolist presentation, for the benefit of Verlaine and the admirable symbolist painter Paul Gaugin.[25]

The symbolists had emerged between 1885 and 1890 in Paris as the major new rival of the naturalists. They had no single manifesto, but most aspects of the movement were developed by Mallarmé in his dramatic criticism for the *Revue Indépendante* in 1886 and 1887. His disciples, Charles Morice, Camille Mauclair, and particularly Albert Mocket, further elaborated these ideas in the late 1880s. Mocket summarized the main characteristics of symbolism in two important articles in *La Wallonie* in 1889 and 1890: its suggestiveness and evocativeness, its emphasis on the vague and universal over the particular and specific, its mixture of real and unreal elements, its attempt to harmonize the impressions of movement, color, and sound.

The new movement was, of course, in large part a reaction to naturalism, and in the theatre it is significant that the first tentative steps toward symbolism in the late 1880s came through revival of interest in two distinctly non-realistic dramatic forms, pantomime and marionettes. The year 1888 saw not only the pantomime *Pierrot assassin de sa femme* by Paul Margueritte at the Théâtre-Libre, but the founding of a pantomime theatre, the Cercle Funambulesque, by Félix Larcher, and a marionette theatre by Henri Signoret. His Petit Théâtre des Marionettes lasted until 1894 and had much to do with the development of the symbolist theory of drama. The slow, primitive movements of these figures seemed to many the ideal way to interpret symbolist plays; indeed, Saint-Vel in the *Revue d'Art dramatique* in 1888 reviewed the marionette *Tempest* under the title "*le théâtre symboliste.*" Exotic and antique works, by such authors as Marlowe, Ford, and Kalidasa, were the theatre's speciality, though after 1889 a new director, Maurice Boucher, wrote original works which similarly dealt with the vague and evocative, such as *Le Songe de Kheyam* (1892) and *Les Mystères d'Eleusis* (1894).

The dramatist most closely associated with this movement was the Belgian Maurice Maeterlinck, who not surprisingly considered marionettes the ideal performers for his works. He nevertheless allowed Paul Fort to present *L'Intreuse* in May of 1891, an important success which was also the first appearance of Lugné-Poe at the Théâtre d'Art. Reassessments were now quite common in the world of letters. The influential critic Bauer of the *Echo de Paris* announced that he was shifting his support from Antoine to Fort. Jules Huret conducted an "*Enquête sur l'évolution littéraire*" which found a widespread feeling that naturalism had run its course. Typical was the response of Goncourt, who said naturalism was "in its death throes."[26] Fort, however, lacked the power either as director or actor to sustain the momentum of a new movement. He mounted only three programs in the 1891-1892 season (including Marlowe's *Doctor Faustus* and another Maeterlinck, *Les Aveugles*), while Antoine at the Théâtre-Libre offered eight. Yet Fort had taken an important first step, and the far more influential Théâtre de l'Oeuvre was soon raised by Lugné-Poe on the foundations Fort had laid.

Lugné-Poe returned in 1891 to the Escholiers, presenting five programs in six months there and elevating that venture briefly to rival the Théâtre-Libre among private theatres. In 1892, Lugné-Poe accepted an invitation from Porel to perform at the Eden, with the proviso that he need not break his ties with the Escholiers. After a brilliant decade at the Odéon, Porel was now interested in trying his fortunes in a large boulevard house, and had therefore purchased the Eden, a huge structure built in 1876 in the style of a Hindu pagoda and which had run itself into bankruptcy by the production of spectacular ballet. Daudet's *Sapho*, with Réjane and Lugné-Poe, and a contemporary reworking of *Lysistrata* (1892) by Maurice Donnay, were modest successes, but they were the only ones Porel enjoyed. Early the next spring he closed the Eden and joined Carré as co-director of the Vaudeville. Lugné-Poe's professional engagement was over almost as soon as it had begun.

Ironically, then, the actor added more to his reputation during this season in his work at the presumably amateur Escholiers. There he gave *The Lady from the Sea* in December, 1892, the fourth Ibsen production in Paris (after *Ghosts* and *The Wild Duck* at the Théâtre-Libre and the matinee performance of *Hedda Gabler* at the Vaudeville), and the first really successful one. This greatest triumph of the Escholiers was also its last offering with Lugné-Poe, who left when he was unable to convince his fellows to present Maeterlinck's *Pelleas et Mélisande*. Finally, he leased the

Bouffés to present the play on his own, designing and directing the production in which he was also the leading actor. Criticism was mixed, but the event attracted sufficient interest to encourage him to form an organization to continue his experiments, which he called the Théâtre de l'Oeuvre.

In its early years, the new theatre distinctly favored the Scandinavians. The first season, 1893-94, opened with Ibsen's *Rosmersholm* and included *Enemy of the People* and *The Master Builder*, Björnson's first part of *Beyond Human Power*, and Strindberg's *Creditors.* The only other foreign dramatist represented was Hauptmann, with *Lonely Lives.* Lugné-Poe sought also to introduce young symbolist writers to rival the naturalists discovered by Antoine--Maurice Beaubourg with *L'Image* (1893), Henry Bataille with *La Belle au bois dormant* (1894), and Henri de Régnier with *La Guardienne* (1894)--but their achievements were slight. Only Bataille went on to become a dramatist of real importance, and he soon deserted the light fancy of his first work for psychological studies of love, more like Porto-Riche or Donnay than the symbolists.

Much more memorable were Lugné-Poe's interpretations of these works. The house, as in the realist theatre, was darkened, but the stage also was dim, and some plays, such as *La Guardienne,* were even presented behind a gauze curtain to add to their vagueness. Settings were sparse, movements mysterious and "evocative," costumes odd and unrealistic--Lugné-Poe favored a long frockcoat with a high, stiff collar buttoned under the chin, no matter what the production. Guest actors would not always follow their director's style, so interpretations were mixed, and so, naturally, were reviews of the productions. Henry Bauer and Jean Jullien, two former supporters of Antoine, became the strongest partisans of Lugné-Poe. Anatole Cleaveau of *Le Soleil* and Henry Fouquier of *Le Figaro* were his most determined enemies. Most of Paris' other influential critics, such as Sarcey, Lemaître, Céard, and Mendès, maintained what might best be described as a suspicious neutrality.

This middle group expressed general approbation when in his 1894-95 season Lugné-Poe drew back somewhat from the symbolist extremes of the previous year. Tristan Bernard's *Les Pieds nickelés* suggested Feydeau, and Paul Vérola's *L'Ecole de l'idéal* seemed actually to be returning to the style of Augier! The symbolist movement contributed only Beaubourg's *La Vie muette* and Maeterlinck's *Intérieur.*

From the foreign theatre came Strindberg's The Father, Ibsen's Brand and Little Eyolf, Ford's 'Tis Pity She's a Whore (translated by Maeterlinck as Annabella), and the Sanskrit drama, The Little Clay Cart. Though Lugné-Poe was praised by some critics for bringing these unusual classics to the stage, purists viewed his work with some consternation. He had warm praise for William Poel's experiments with simplified staging and the search for an authentic Shakespeare in England, but his own settings became steadily more heavy, ornate, and elaborately painted, while his disregard for texts was notorious. The Little Clay Cart drew strong criticism for flying in the face of scenic unity by displaying motley crowds in costumes of all nations and periods (a few extras even appearing nude).

Whatever the reservations of the critics, however, Antoine's departure from the Théâtre-Libre in 1894 unquestionably elevated the Théâtre de l'Oeuvre to first place among Paris' experimental theatres, with its nearest rival ironically the Escholiers, directed since Lugné-Poe's departure by Georges Bourdon. The success of Antoine and Lugné-Poe had inspired a whole series of similar ventures--the Théâtre de l'Avenir dramatique (1891), the Théâtre d'Art social (1893), the Théâtre des Poètes (1893), and the Théâtre des lettres (1894) were the best known--but no other significant rivals.

For his third season, 1895-96, Lugné-Poe issued a manifesto expanding his offerings to eight plays representing "a history of dramatic art." Only two works from this ambitious program were actually presented, however: Otway's Venice Preserved and Kalidasa's Shakuntala, one of the theatre's few undisputed successes. A Chinese play, La Fleur Palan enlevée, provided another exotic note in a season composed mostly of works by minor young French dramatists. Late in 1896 came the theatre's most famous, or notorious work, Alfred Jarry's Ubu Roi. Even those accustomed to being mystified by Lugné-Poe were startled by this free-wheeling and grotesque parable. The action and characters were crude, cartoon-like and the presentation was designed to emphasize this quality. Scenery was mostly pantomimed, with one actor, for example, representing a door. It was a stormy evening, awakening inevitably memories of Hernani--catcalls, hisses, shouted jokes often drowned the dialogue. The dramatist Courteline stood on his seat to shout his protests. Jules Renard wrote that night in his journal "Ubu Roi. The day of enthusiasm ended in the grotesque."[27] The controversy over the play continued as the reviews appeared.

The majority of Paris' major critics dismissed the evening as a hoax or a tasteless joke but a few sensed something more. Catulle Mendès recognized that Ubu was consciously anti-literary and iconoclastic and its leading character, as a personification of anarchy, made a "perhaps reprehensible but undeniable contribution to the theatre." Before the opening Henry Bauer in the Echo de Paris called Ubu in the tradition of Gargantua and Pantagruel: "from this enormous and powerfully evocative figure blows the wind of destruction, the inspiration of modern youth which will break down traditional respect and secular prejudice. And the type will endure."[28] Time has proven Bauer right, for the general spirit of hearty, exuberant iconoclasm in Ubu has made it a reference point and a rallying cry for the avant-garde French theatre through much of our own century. Unhappily for Bauer, the scandal of the opening made him regret his favorable words. He attempted to qualify his position, but the damage was done, and his championship of Ubu cost him his position with the influential Echo de Paris.

The rest of the 1896-97 season was of minor importance, and at its completion, Lugné-Poe startled the theatre world of Paris by issuing a statement breaking with the symbolists, on the grounds that they had been unable to provide him with a single important young dramatist. He promised henceforth to present only works of "life and humanity"--all foreign if necessary.

As the nineteenth century drew toward its close, literary schools succeeded one another with ever-greater rapidity. Less than four years after launching symbolism in the theatre, Lugné-Poe was able to desert that movement and find another one already well established. He now threw in his lot with the naturists, whose manifesto, written by Saint-Georges de Bouhélier, had appeared in the Figaro in January of 1897. The naturists were to the symbolists what the école de bon sens was to the romantics, a reaction toward simplicity and realism, but not to the opposite extreme of a Zola. There was a certain influence from Rousseau in naturism and its authors replaced the lilies, pale medieval lovers, and tapestries of the symbolists with rough and simple peasants eating bread and fruit in humble cottages. Unfortunately, the naturists produced no more remarkable works for Lugné-Poe than the symbolists, and the decisive failure of Bouhélier's La Victoire (1898) convinced almost everyone that the new school had little future in the theatre. Some success, however, was gained by the less extreme anti-symbolist works of Romain Rolland: Les Loups (1898) and Le Triomphe de la raison (1899).

In the closing years of the century Lugné-Poe evolved a style between realism and symbolism which interested his support among the critics. His emphasis remained on foreign works. Ibsen's John Gabriel Borkman was a great success in 1897, so great that the poet Laurent Tailhade predicted gloomily that it marked the end of verse drama in the French theatre (an amusingly ill-timed remark, since it preceded by only a month the revolutionary success of Cyrano de Bergerac). The new translations of 1898--Gunnar Heiburg's The Balcony, Gogol's Revizor, and Measure for Measure--were far less fortunate, and marked the beginning of the Oeuvre's decline. Only by means of revivals was Lugné-Poe able to keep the theatre going during 1898 and 1899. Rosmersholm and The Master Builder continued to attract the public, but most popular of all was An Enemy of the People, whose success was due to the non-artistic stimulus of the Dreyfus affair. Zola's solitary stand against all the established authorities on behalf of the exiled captain seemed to audiences of 1898 strikingly paralleled by Dr. Stockman in Ibsen's play. Intellectuals of the day begged for a chance to be included among the extras and the text could frequently hardly be heard over cries of Vive Zola! The enthusiasm, however misplaced, brought Ibsen's name to a wider public than ever, and the memory of this popular revival largely determined the selection of An Enemy of the People as the first Ibsen work to be presented, twenty years later, by the Comédie. By the spring of 1899, however, Lugné-Poe had seemingly exhausted his resources. He had renounced the symbolists and the naturalists had failed him. A trip to Scandinavia in 1897 to obtain new manuscripts had produced nothing for the theatre but John Gabriel Borkman, another work by its already most often-produced dramatist. Even revivals were wearing out. New competition was appearing, too, most notably with the opening of Antoine's major new theatre in 1897. In June of 1899 Lugné-Poe considered his work, or this phase of it, completed, and after Rolland's Triomphe de la raison, he announced the closing of the Théâtre de l'Oeuvre.

5. Lyric Theatre, 1877-1900

During the last quarter of the nineteenth century there

were several attempts to increase the number of lyric theatres in Paris, but even with subsidies from the city such experiments as the conversion of the minor Château-d'Eau into a second home for French opera or the revival of Italian opera at the Nations did not long survive. The most successful of these attempts was the installation of Italian ballet in 1883 at the luxurious Eden, built near the Opéra and second only to it in size and magnificence. Such offerings as Manzoni's *Excelsior* (1883) and *Sieba* (1883) featured noted Italian ballerinas, Mmes Cornalba and Zucchi, but the real interest of the productions was in their spectacle, and horses, cannon, and drill corps were at least as important there as the dancers. Such offerings were popular, but their expense was ruinous. In 1888 the director Bertrand attempted to reduce the burden of the spectacular ballets by alternating them with operettas, but even though he hired the popular Jeanne Granier and Mme Judic, he was unable to make the theatre turn a profit. By 1891 he was forced to close.

For most of this period, therefore, lyric drama in Paris was largely the product of two theatres, the Opéra and the Opéra-Comique. Carvalho, who assumed direction of the Opéra-Comique in 1877, brought new prosperity to that theatre, as he had done earlier to the Lyrique. He added important new talents to an already excellent company: Marguerite Ugalde, the baritone Morlet, the outstanding tenor Talzac. His impressive repertoire was steadily enriched by important new works: Gounod's *Cinq Mars* and Poise's *La Surprise de l'amour* in 1877; Léo Delibes' *Jean de Nivelle* in 1880 and *Lakmé* in 1883; Massenet's *Manon Lescaut*, which with Talzac and a new singer, Marie Heilbron, became the greatest success of the Opéra-Comique, in 1884; Saint-Saëns' *Proserpine* in 1887.

One of Carvalho's rare disappointments was Marie van Zandt, whose triumph in *Lakmé* promised to make her one of the theatre's greatest attractions. Soon after, in a revival of *Le Barbier de Séville*, she was unable to complete the second act; rumor accused her of being drunk, and the scandal drove her from Paris. Another theatre might have suffered severely from this loss, but within a month Carvalho had compensated for the departure of Mme van Zandt by hiring two popular singers from the unsuccessful experiment in Italian opera at the Nations--Marie Heilbron and Philippe Gille. Then disaster struck. On May 25, 1887, fire broke out on the stage. The iron curtain could not be lowered, all lights were extinguished for fear of an explosion, the fire escape doors were inexplicably locked. Patrons in the orchestra escaped with relative ease, but over one hundred persons lost their lives on the upper floors in one of the greatest theatre catastrophes of the century. Carvalho was brought to trail, found guilty of negligence and sentenced to prison.

The Opéra-Comique was many years recovering from this blow. Carvalho's successor, Paravey, moved the theatre to a temporary home in the Châtelet and brought it almost to bankruptcy before returning it to Carvalho, who was acquitted and released in 1891. The old director's spirit was gone, however, and his final administration, until his death in 1897, was little more distinguished than Paravey's.

Productions at the Opéra improved somewhat under the administration of Vaucorbeil, who replaced Halanzier in 1879. The company was becoming accustomed to working in the new theatre and their new director gave them every encouragement. He brought the popular Faure back to the theatre, who became with Mme Krauss the keystone of the company. Even the ballet revived somewhat, thanks largely to the talent of Rosita Mauri. Only in the presentation of original works was Vaucorbeil as undistinguished as his predecessor. Verdi's _Aïda_ with Mme Krauss was an important contribution to the season of 1880, but it had already proven its popularity at the Italien. Aside from a few of Mlle Mauri's ballets, Vaucorbeil's only other new success was Gounod's _Le Tribut de Zamora_ (1881). The bulk of the program until his death in 1884 consisted of revivals of proven works by such composers as Rossini, Halévy, and Meyerbeer.

Vaucorbeil's followers Ritt and Gailhard were warmly welcomed by press and public; as a successful director and an Opéra artist they seemed an ideal combination to restore the theatre's spirit and its finances. Yet by the end of the decade, there was an almost universal cry for their dismissal. Their company grew steadily weaker as such singers as Mme Krauss retired, to be replaced by less popular figures. No replacement at all appeared when the great Faure left the theatre. Moreover, both new works and revivals were undistinguished and conservative. In Magnet and Salvayre's _La Dame de Monsoreau_ (1888) even the settings were hissed. The few successes--Sardou and Paladilhe's _Patrie_ (1886), Saint-Saëns' _Ascanio_ (1890), and Massenet's _Le Mage_ (1891)--could not save the administration, which was dissolved in 1891.

The new director, Bertrand of the Variétés, promised sweeping reforms--to bring back forgotten classics and discover new ones, to "democratize" the Opéra by introducing low-cost evenings and matinee concerts, and most important, to introduce the controversial Wagner, ignored by the two previous administrations. Astonishingly, thirty years after the tempestuous production of Tannhäuser, Wagner still awaited a second major production in Paris. His music had been most steadily supported in these intervening years by Pasdeloup, director of the Concerts populaires de musique classique, which after Tannhäuser continued to expose the Parisian public to Wagner's music at least in concert form. In 1868 Pasdeloup briefly replaced Carvalho at the Lyrique before its closing. His vision of presenting all of the German composer's works there was destroyed at the outset by a badly adapted and interpreted Rienzi.

Then came a new setback, the Franco-Prussian War. The blatantly teutonic Wagner would have aroused the antipathy of French nationalists after 1870 in any case, but he exacerbated the difficulty by openly gloating over French defeats. An even more violent antagonism than that directed against English writers in pre-romantic years was now directed against the Germans, and particularly against Wagner. For some years after the war, "Wagnerism" became a general term of opprobrium that could be and was applied to any work which its critics wished to suggest was iconoclastic and even potentially subversive. Few original composers therefore escaped this epithet, no matter what their relation to Wagner; Lalo, Massenet, Saint-Saëns, Bizet, even the conservative Paladilhe were all at one time or another called Wagnerians. Under such circumstances, it is a tribute to the vitality of Wagner's music and to the determination of directors like Pasdeloup that selections were again appearing in public concerts as early as 1873, though anti-German outcries forced Pasdeloup for a time in 1876 to suspend such presentations. Two years later Lohengrin was produced with much acclaim in Brussels, and shortly after, a group of Italian singers headed by Albini presented Wagner's work in their native language in Paris at the Ventadour. The interest stimulated by this production encouraged Wagner's supporters in Paris, but production of a complete Wagnerian opera in French still lay some years in the future. Pasdeloup in 1879 ventured to present the first act of Lohengrin at the Cirque d'Hiver, with gratifying success. Other concert directors now followed his lead in including Wagner on their programs. A pro-Wagner movement took shape, its mouthpiece the Revue Wagnérienne founded in 1885 by Edmond Dujardin.

Lohengrin, now the Wagnerian work most familiar to the Parisians, formed the center of the controversy. An 1881 project to present it in German aroused such wrath among French patriots that it was hastily abandoned. Carvalho then promised to offer it in French at the Opéra-Comique with his best artists, Talzac and Mme Heilbron, in the leading roles. Again committees of protest were formed, and such influential critics as Albert Wolff of the Figaro begged Carvalho to reconsider "in the interest of patriotism and public tranquillity."[29] The production, first planned for 1885, was postponed several times, and had still not been mounted when the fire of 1887 ended all Carvalho's projects. In the meantime Lamoureux, who had taken the lead from Pasdeloup as the champion of Wagner, rented the Eden theatre specifically to produce Lohengrin, bringing it at last before the public in 1887. Friends and enemies of Wagner came more to express their opinions than to listen to the opera, which was presented only for one tumultuous and inconclusive evening. Paris' real introduction to the German composer still lay ahead.

The administration of Bertrand, who led the Opéra from 1892 until his death in 1900, at last provided this introduction, but the honor of the first extended and clearly successful Paris presentation of Wagner was denied him by the retiring Ritt and Gailhard, who at last, after notification by the state that their contract would not be renewed, mounted the long-suppressed Lohengrin in 1891. With Van Dyck and Rose Caron in the leading roles, it was a great success for singers, composer, administration, and particularly for Lamoureux, who presided over the evening from the conductor's stand. Bertrand subsequently opened the Opéra to Die Walküre (1893), Tannhäuser (1895) and Die Meistersinger (1897). These productions, however, were only the most obvious manifestations of a whole new orientation Bertrand brought to the theatre. The old repertoire, based on Meyerbeer, Rossini, Donizetti, and Auber, disappeared, to be replaced by the works of Wagner, Gounod, Verdi, and the contemporaries Saint-Saëns with Samson et Dalila (1892) and Massenet with Thaïs (1894).

This new trend was already clear when in 1894 a catastrophic fire destroyed the Opéra warehouse and all the settings stored there, representing the great achievements of such artists as Cambon, Despléchin, and Ciceri. Robert le diable, La Muette de Portici, La Juive, Aïda, and twenty-four other massive settings were lost; only the eleven in active repertoire at the Opéra and three others stored elsewhere remained. This effectively ensured, at the moment of Wagner's triumph, that those very authors whose works had kept him from the Opéra stage fifty years before were now consigned in turn to darkness.

With government support, the repertoire was gradually rebuilt, but the fire gave Bertrand an excellent excuse for restoring works quite selectively, and he eventually revived only eleven of the thirty burned works. Thus chance and the times fitted in well with the new director's desire for innovation, and his influence on the national theatre was great. Less spectacular than his changes in the repertoire were his programs to democratize the Opéra, but the special concerts and Sunday performances he inaugurated to this end were extremely popular, and his death in 1900 was a source of much sorrow in the theatre world of Paris.

6. Odéon and Comédie, 1880-1900

Émile Perrin, the director of the Comédie, had many reasons to be relieved at the departure of Sarah Bernhardt in 1880, but even so he would surely not have finally consented to accept her resignation if he had not had in reserve Sophie Croizette to step into Bernhardt's roles. L'Aventurière, Bernhardt's recent failure, was revived immediately after her departure, and both Perrin and Croizette were surely gratified at its considerable success. But in 1881, Croizette accepted an offer of marriage and retired from the theatre, so that Perrin in the space of little more than a year was deprived of both his most popular actresses. This gave the director great problems of balance, for though Madeleine Brohan, Mlles Reichenberg, Favart, and seven other female sociétaires remained, among the male sociétaires were three of the most popular actors of the century: Mounet-Sully in tragedy, Got in comedy, and Delaunay in young romantic leads. Behind these, of course, were quite respectable lesser talents, such as Febvre, Worms, Coquelin, Thiron, and Maubant. Julia Bartet, whose Comédie debut in Sardou's Daniel Rochat (1880) had been so successful, was promoted to sociétaire soon after Bernhardt's departure, but other major actresses were badly needed, and the next few years saw an unusual number of important debuts as Perrin sought to fill this need.

The year 1881 was the year of Pailleron at the Comédie. Le Monde où l'on s'ennuie proved his masterpiece, a gently ironic study of contemporary blue-stockings which amassed the huge run of 123 performances. Pailleron's Le Dernier Quartier, written eighteen years before, was then revived for a run of 113 performances. Far less spectacular, but worthy of note, was Mounet-Sully's interpretation of Lacroix' Oedipe Roi, played with such violence that he was accused by some of bringing melodrama to the Comédie. Antoine reported hearing speculation during the intermission that the original play had not been written by a Greek at all, but by Dennery or Bouchardy.[30] Some reviews of the production expressed a desire to see Mounet-Sully turn his talents next to Hamlet.

The Annales du Théâtre of 1881 stated that the Comédie at that time possessed four major living authors: Hugo, Dumas fils, Augier, and Sardou, and two minor ones: Pailleron and Erckmann-Chatrian.[31] The year after Pailleron's success came the turn of the other minor Comédie "author," though the popularity of Les Rantzau (1882) never rivalled that of Le Monde où l'on s'ennuie. In this Alsacian version of the Romeo and Juliet legend Got and Coquelin portrayed the feuding fathers, Worms and Mlle Bartet the young lovers. The Comédie's major authors were represented this year by important revivals of Le Demi-Monde and Ruy Blas (this the first performance of Hugo's play since its banning after opening night in 1832).

Sarah Bernhardt offered to return to the Comédie in 1882. Since he now could rely on Mlle Reichenberg and Mlle Bartet, Perrin could afford to refuse, but he was still willing to strengthen the female side of his company if he could do so with less difficult performers. Céline Montaland, who had achieved some fame on the boulevards, made an impressive debut in an 1884 revival of Scribe's Bataille des dames. The same year, on the advice of Dumas fils, Perrin invited Blanche Pierson from the Vaudeville to play opposite Julia Bartet in L'Etrangère. The success of this combination led to the two actresses assuming the leading roles in the next Dumas realistic drama, Denise (1885), which proved the most popular Comédie offering since Le Monde où l'on s'ennuie. Denise Brissot, one of Mlle Bartet's greatest roles, is a girl betrayed in love who vows never to love again or to reveal her reason, who lives in mysterious silence until her betrayer's plan to wed another innocent victim forces her to speak. The sentimentality of the piece has not worn well--a 1936 revival at the Comédie inspired general hilarity--but audiences of 1885 found it moving, and even Francisque Sarcey, who was no unqualified champion of Dumas, joined in its praise.

The success of this production was soon dimmed by two great losses for the Comédie. Victor Hugo died in May, 1885, and though he had long since ceased writing for the theatre, his contribution to it had been such that it seemed a pillar of the art had fallen. Hugo revivals, often presided over by the master himself, had been an important part of the repertoire since 1870, and the Comédie was one of the centers of the Hugo celebrations which dominated all activity in Paris this spring and summer. On the day of Hugo's funeral the theatre gave a free presentation of Hernani, and the apotheosis in June was celebrated by a special program including a crowning of Hugo's bust.

In October came the second great loss, the death of Perrin, after an illness of almost a year. His fourteen-year administration had been conservative but one of the most successful of the century, noted for its outstanding and unusually well-rehearsed revivals (his seventy rehearsals for Le Mariage de Figaro were considered quite extraordinary). "Especially and above all," complained Sarcey, "he sought successes that could be measured by large attendance, by high receipts" which, the critic charged, led Perrin to elevate decor, costume, and spectacle over the intrinsic worth of the plays.[32] There was truth in the charge, for Perrin's concern with the popular attraction affected his company as well as his staging and repertoire. He continued to rely on the same stars until deprived of their services by retirement or resignation, not even permitting doubling (in defiance of the decree of Moscow), so that the illness of an actor automatically removed certain plays from the stage and the loss of a leading player could mean the temporary paralysis of much of the repertoire and the eventual sudden appearance of a virtually unknown replacement. Perrin's successor, Jules Claretie, therefore inherited a brilliant, popular, but aging company, and one of the major tasks facing the new administrator was the discovery and development of new talents.

Though Duquesnel, director of the Odéon before 1879,

was much criticized for his lack of interest in new playwrights, his successor, La Rounat, who remained until 1884, was more conservative still. The only outstanding new works he offered were by established dramatists: Vacquerie's _La Formosa_ (1883) and Coppée's _Severo Torelli_ (1883), and his most successful productions were revivals: Ponsard's _Charlotte Corday_ in 1880, Dumas' _Antony_ and Labiche's _Les Petits Mains_ in 1884. New actors fortunately fared better than new playwrights during this administration. Paul Mounet, brother of the great Mounet-Sully, was warmly welcomed by the public in his 1880 debut as _Horace_, and in the subsequent production of _Severo Torelli_ Mounet shared the honors of the production with two promising new actors, Raphaël Duflos and Albert Lambert _fils_.

Porel, director of the Odéon from 1885 until 1894, was one of that theatre's most memorable leaders--active, experimental, interested in scenic reform and the encouragement of new talent. He greatly increased the popularity of the theatre, so that its receipts more than doubled during his administration, but the increased resources did not lie idle, for they allowed him to take more risks with both new works and old, and to indulge his interest in spectacular but expensive productions. Noteworthy among the latter were his presentations of Shakespeare, which created a distinct vogue for the English dramatist in Paris during the late 1880s. The most outstanding of these productions were Paul Meurice's _Songe d'une nuit d'été_ (1886) with music by Mendelssohn, and Louis Legendre's _Beaucoup de bruit pour rien_ (1887), starring Paul Mounet, with music by Godard and settings by Rubé and Chaperon. Other adaptations included _Le Conte d'avril (Twelfth Night)_ by August Dorchain, _Shylock_ by Edmond Haraucourt (with Réjane and Albert Lambert), _Roméo et Juliette_ by Georges Lefebvre and _Macbeth_ by Georges Clerc. In 1886 the Comédie made its major contribution to this series, a revival of the melodramatic Hamlet of Dumas _père_ and Paul Meurice. Mounet-Sully's interpretation of this part was considered, with his Oedipus, the greatest of his career. As his public anticipated, he played a passionate and emotional Hamlet, but the trait most critics praised in his interpretation was its intellectual clarity. At last, the French thought, here was a Hamlet they could understand:

> In his interpretation, we can see what he wants to do; we understand Hamlet, as clearly explained as possible, and it is no small achievement for an actor to put across to us so admirably the thought

> of a Shakespearian hero. In his encounter with the ghost on the platform of Elsinor castle his pantomime expressed admirably the terror of the supernatural overcome by his courage. He spoke the famous monologue marvelously, and played most artistically the scene where Hamlet, during the representation of the Murder of Gonzago rages across the stage, Ophelia's fan in his hand, and leaps up to confront the blanching Claudius. He was applauded _con furore_, and called back from act to act as he deserved to be applauded and called back.[33]

Hamlet was the first production mounted by Claretie, an inheritance from his predecessor, and for the next several years the new director relied generally on the dramatists Perrin had favored: Gondinet, Feuillet, Dumas _fils_, Pailleron, and Richepin. Among the younger dramatists only Becque received any attention, since the success of _La Parisienne_ at the Renaissance in 1885 assured public interest in him. But Claretie was gradually forced to seek new resources. Augier had written nothing since _Les Fourchambault_ in 1878, and was to write no more. _Francillon_ (1887) was the last play from Dumas, _Chamillac_ (1886) the last from Feuillet. Pailleron's _Le Souris_ (1887) was his penultimate work. Perrin's famous company was also beginning to disappear. The theatre lost one of its most popular artists when Delaunay, after toying for some years with the idea of retiring, finally left in 1887 at the age of 60. Coquelin withdrew from the Comédie in 1889, Maubant retired in 1888. To help offset these losses, Claretie called to the Comédie some of the outstanding actors of the Odéon--Eugénie Weber in 1887, Aimée Tessandier in 1889, Paul Mounet and Albert Lambert in 1891.

This meant, of course, that Porel in his turn had to seek new actors. His first important hiring, Réjane, was one of his most fortunate. She gained an immediate personal triumph in the stage version of the Goncourts' _Germinie Lacerteux_, a production otherwise distinguished only by its last act setting, a snow scene in a Montmartre cemetery by Rubé and Chaperon which was much praised for its realism. Réjane had been performing with some distinction at various boulevard theatres since her debut in 1875, but it had been her misfortune always to be subordinated to a more popular rival--Julia Bartet at first, and later, Marie Legault and Sarah Bernhardt. She suffered no such restriction at the

Odéon and by 1890 was generally recognized as an equal of the highly praised Bartet, now at the Comédie. When Porel left the Odéon in 1892 for his ill-fated administration of the Eden, Réjane accompanied him. The other new actors whom he introduced to the Odéon were less important; both Lucien Guitry and Edouard de Max made significant contributions to the French stage, but these contributions began later, after they had left the Odéon to work with Sarah Bernhardt.

Not surprisingly, when both Porel and Claretie found themselves at the end of the 1880s seeking new playwrights, they turned to the generation introduced by the Théâtre-Libre. At the Odéon, Ancey's Grand'mère (1890) and Hennique's Amour (1890) were unfortunately among their authors' weakest works, but Porto-Riche's L'Amoureuse (1891) quite made up for these disappointments. This sympathetic depiction of a busy physician and his sexually frustrated wife brought to the stage a psychological realism unknown in Augier or Dumas, and its interpretation by Réjane and Lucien Guitry won over even such moderately conservative critics as Sarcey. Particular praise went to Réjane, who demonstrated in the two roles of Germinie Lacerteux and Germaine in L'Amoureuse, widely apart in social class but each a rich character study, that she had a far greater range as an actress than the light comedies of the Vaudeville had utilized.

> We saw Réjane in that rather stormy evening of Germinie Lacerteux at the Odéon; she portrayed the distress of that humble creature with the most poignant simplicity... the play was thin and ill-balanced, but Réjane had all the misery, all the fatality of a tragic heroine. And by contrast, L'Amoureuse, where Réjane was so vibrant, so empassioned, so tormented, so desolate in Germaine's regret for her lost happiness, that happiness which she destroyed herself! On opening night a curious, almost exceptional thing happened: she expressed such intense emotion that the audience could not wait until she had completed a fairly lengthy speech before bursting into applause.[34]

The Comédie revived from the Théâtre-Libre Mendès' La Femme de Tabarin in 1894, Porto-Riche's La Chance de Françoise in 1895, and Curel's Les Fossiles in 1897, while premiering Lavedan's Une Famille (1890), Curel's L'Amour brode (1893), and Brieux' L'Evasion (1896). Henri de Bornier had proved prophetic indeed when he asserted in 1892: "The authors of the Théâtre-Libre will before long be the masters of the stage. Tomorrow perhaps some audacious soldier of M. Antoine will demolish with melenite shells even the fortifications of the Comédie-Française."[35] The influence of the new realism did not stop, moreover, with the production of Théâtre-Libre dramatists. Charles Edmond's La Bûcheronne (1890), though essentially a satire on the beau monde, featured a realistic blood transfusion on stage. In Louis Legendre's Jean Dariot (1892) Worms appeared as a mechanic and Mlle Bartet as a shopkeeper, a particularly significant success for the actress, who demonstrated her versatility by achieving even greater triumphs the following year in the classic roles of Antigone and Bérénice.

Aside from the authors associated with Antoine, the most significant new dramatists to appear in the national theatres during the 1890s represented three very different approaches. They were Jules Lemaître, Edmond Rostand, and Paul Hervieu. Lemaître, now less remembered as a dramatist than as the influential critic for the Débats between 1887 and 1896, produced a number of plays of qualified realism, somewhere between Antoine's authors and Augier: Révoltée (1889) at the Odéon and Le Mariage blanc (1891) and Le Pardon (1895) at the Comédie. Le Mariage blanc, probably the best of these, seems a weak echo of a Curel situation--a rather morbid study of a rich libertine who is attracted to a dying consumptive. As a critic, Lemaître was a leader of the "impressionists," critics who, while not eschewing distinct standards, still championed a measure of subjective judgement which was condemned by the "objectivists," led by Brunetière. Like Sarcey and Faguet, whose writings on the theatre were similarly collected, Lemaître was essentially conservative but willing to recognize the value of the contributions of the young dramatists. The refined eclecticism of his critical writings also permeates his plays, and is probably one reason why no one of them is particularly outstanding.

Paul Hervieu was well established as a novelist before turning to the stage. His second work, Les Paroles restent, given at the Vaudeville in 1892, established him as a dramatist of importance and set the style for his later plays. It might be described as the purest sort of thesis play, illustrating by the most direct and simple means the lesson that gossip can kill. Later plays at the Comédie,

Les Tenailles (1895) and *La Loi de l'homme* (1897), presented somewhat more complex messages, but each shared the conscious arrangement and didactic tone which separated Hervieu, despite his dealing with contemporary concerns, from the indirect approach of the naturalists.

Rostand was further removed still. A disciple of Hugo and Banville, he brought surprising new life to the genre of lyric romanticism at a time when the influence of realism still dominated the theatre. The year before his classic *Cyrano de Bergerac* at the Porte-Saint-Martin, the Comédie presented his charming fantasy on young love, *Les Romanesques* (1894). In a modern reworking as *The Fantasticks* (1960), this became the most popular of the off-Broadway musical comedies.

Porel's departure from the Odéon in 1894 left that theatre in the hands of his subordinates Marck and Deslaux, who kept it only until 1896. Their administration produced only one offering of importance: Coppée's *Pour la couronne* (1895), a Hugoesque fantasy of intrigue in the Balkans. When illness forced Marck to retire, many felt that a strong personality such as Porel's was necessary to restore the Odéon to its former reputation and prosperity. Antoine's success with the Théâtre-Libre made him a leading candidate, but his lack of experience in a major theatre and his radical reputation frightened the ministry, and as a compromise Antoine was asked to serve as co-director with the more experienced and stable Paul Ginisty. Though Ginisty had been represented by two plays at the Théâtre-Libre, he by no means shared Antoine's aims, and serious differences developed as soon as the co-directors began preparing a program. Such writers as Curel and Brieux were distasteful to Ginisty, and Antoine's schemes often seem to him foolhardy and extravagant. As the disputes continued, Antoine seemed to become more radical and Ginisty more conservative than either would have been without the other. Antoine grudgingly acceded to the presentation of occasional lucrative offerings such as Bergerat's *Capitaine Fracasse*, but insisted that the majority of the programs be dedicated to efforts that Ginisty feared would bankrupt the theatre; at least once a month he wished to present a classic revival (his first selection was *The Persians*), a foreign masterpiece (beginning with *Don Carlos*), and a new author (beginning with Lugné-Poe's most produced young symbolist, Maurice Beaubourg).

The ill-advised union lasted only five months, and

only the last seventeen days of it was actually part of the season. On October 27, 1896, Ginisty submitted his resignation; the Minister dissolved the administration, then reappointed Ginisty almost at once as sole director, a bit of administrative sleight-of-hand which was carried out apparently without the complicity of Ginisty. Antoine was offered the lesser position of stage director, which he refused. The following fall he opened his own Théâtre-Antoine, where he gained experience in managing a large public stage. In 1906 he returned to the Odéon as Ginisty's successor, and launched that theatre on one of its most brilliant periods.

Though the later years of his administration showed some falling-off, Ginisty's decade at the Odéon proved him quite capable of carrying on the momentum established by Porel. The receipts rose again as new plays such as Richepin's Le Chemineau (1897) and Porto-Riche's Le Passé were offered. Les Corbeaux, revived in 1897, was not a great success but was a further proof of Ginisty's willingness to fulfill his obligation to the new generation. On the other hand, he instituted classic matinees for the introduction of little-known works by Marivaux, Alfred de Vigny, Rotrou, and Tristan l'Ermite.

All the theatres of Paris looked forward to 1900 when a new great Exposition could be expected to provide them with a much larger public, but for the Comédie and Odéon a disaster early in the year destroyed these hopes. On March 8, the very eve of the opening of the Exposition, the Comédie was destroyed by fire. Fortunately, the blaze broke out in the morning and not during a performance, but even so it cost the life of one pensionnaire, Jane Henriot. The troupe moved to the Odéon while a new home was being constructed, and the Odéon company was in turn forced to move to the Gymnase, where Ginisty began to lose the momentum of his earlier years. Yet, all things considered, the disruption was not a lengthy one, for the new Comédie, designed by Guadet, was completed before the new year. Richepin composed a prologue for the opening ceremony of December 29, and a special program featured almost all the members of the company. As the new century began, the historian Joannidès totalled the productions to date of the national theatre, to find that it had produced over 3000 plays by over 1, 500 authors. The figures on individual dramatists showed how aptly the Comédie styled itself the "maison de Molière," for his works had been presented 20, 290 times, more than the next four most popular dramatists added together! After him, the order ran Racine, Regnard, Corneille, Voltaire, Augier, Marivaux, Musset, Beaumarchais, Dumas, and Hugo.[36] The first regular offering in the new theatre was on January 1, 1901, and the Comédie began the new century appropriately with works from the cornerstones of its tradition, Molière and Corneille.

CONCLUSION

The theatre world of Paris in 1900 bore little resemblance to the carefully circumscribed and controlled system with which Napoleon had opened the century. The most significant remains of his effort were the state-subsidized theatres, the Comédie, Odéon, Opéra, and Opéra-Comique, the first still operating under essentially the same regulations established for it by the First Emperor. Outside these houses, such forces as commercial competition, the development of the star and touring system, the long run, and the new bourgeois audiences brought into the theatre during the century had altered Napoleon's plans beyond all recognition. The combination of these forces had created by 1900 a theatre system in Paris not essentially different from what we find there still.

In addition to the national and commercial stages, a third form had arisen and established itself late in the century, to become increasingly important in more modern times. This was the avant-garde, experimental, or art stage, an alternative unknown in Napoleon's period. By 1900 the separation between the general public and the artistic vanguard, so typical of our own century, was already well established, and the experimental theatre was already the coterie stage which it has remained since.

The major movements of romanticism and realism, with many lesser movements, had waxed and waned during the century, but all had broadened the range of potential theatre fare and traces of almost all could be found in the eclectic French stage which ended the century--romantic operas, realistic slices of life, melodramas still echoing Pixérécourt, vaudevilles, operettas, farces, classic tragedies and symbolist poetic dramas. This eclecticism was by 1900 being further expanded by a growing awareness of other national theatrical traditions as well, an important change for the traditionally introspective French stage.

In 1800 the French stage found itself, like most of French society, cut off by the Revolution from the traditions and practice of generations. During the nineteenth century it rediscovered some of these traditions and built others, developing by 1900 most of the features it still possesses today.

Notes to Part IV

1. Preface to Soirées Parisiennes, quoted in A. Arnaouvitch, Henry Becque (Paris, 1927), I, 31n.

2. Arnaouvitch, Henry Becque, III, 43.

3. M. Descotes, Henry Becque et son théâtre (Paris, 1962), pp. 141-46.

4. J. Jullien, Le Théâtre vivant (Paris, 1892), p. 11.

5. F. Sarcey, Quarante Ans de théâtre (Paris, 1902), VII, 249.

6. E. Noël and E. Stoullig, Annales du Théâtre et de la musique, XIII (Paris, 1888), 321.

7. A. Antoine, Memories of the Théâtre-Libre (trans. M. Carlson, Coral Gables, 1964), pp. 108-9.

8. Noël and Stoullig, Annales, XIII (1888), 343.

9. Antoine, Memories, p. 139.

10. Noël and Stoullig, Annales, XVI (1891), p. 354.

11. Sarcey, Quarante Ans, VII, 302-3.

12. Antoine, Memories, p. 233.

13. S. M. Waxman, Antoine and the Théâtre-Libre (Cambridge, 1926), p. 145.

14. Waxman, Antoine, p. 73.

15. J. A. Hart, Sardou and the Sardou Plays (Philadelphia, 1913), pp. 84-85.

16. G. G. Geller, *Sarah Bernhardt* (Paris, 1931), p. 217.

17. G. B. Shaw, *Dramatic Opinions and Essays* (New York, 1906), I, 115.

18. H. Lyonnet, *Les Premieres de Alfred de Musset* (Paris, 1927), p. 178.

19. Quoted in Eva Le Gallienne, *Eleonora Duse* (New York, 1966), p. 50.

20. Sarcey, *Quarante Ans,* VII, 214.

21. Sarcey, *Quarante Ans,* VII, 49.

22. Quoted in Jules Haraszti, *Edmond Rostand* (Paris, 1913), pp. 123-24.

23. Noël and Stoullig, *Annales*, II (1877), 530.

24. Noël and Stoullig, *Annales*, XXV (1900), 284.

25. J. Robichez, *Le Symbolisme au théâtre* (Paris, 1957), p. 113.

26. J. Huret, *Enquête sur l'évolution littéraire* (Paris, 1891), p. 166.

27. Quoted in J. H. Levesque, *Alfred Jarry* (Paris, 1967), p. 46.

28. Quoted in P. Chaveau, *Alfred Jarry* (Paris, 1932), p. 84.

29. Servières, *Richard Wagner,* p. 290.

30. A. Antoine, *Le Théâtre* (Paris, 1932), II, 132.

31. Noël and Stoullig, *Annales,* VII (1882), viii-ix.

32. Sarcey, *Quarante Ans,* I, 258.

33. Noël and Stoullig, *Annales,* XII (1887), 88.

34. Ginisty in *l'Opinion,* quoted in C. Antona-Traversi, *Réjane* (Paris, 1930), p. 339.

35. Antoine, Memories, p. 204.

36. J. Valmy-Baisse, Naissance et Vie de la Comédie-Française (Paris, 1945), p. 313. Joannidès' complete analysis of the Comédie repertoire appears in his La Comédie-Française de 1680 à 1920 (Paris, 1921).

BIBLIOGRAPHY

General

Abraham, P. La Physique au théâtre. Paris, 1923.

Albert, M. A. Les Théâtres des boulevards. Paris, 1902.

Artus, M. Le Théâtre Montmarte. Paris, 1905.

Avril, A. d' Le Théâtre en France depuis le moyen-age jusqu'à nos jours. Paris, 1877.

Bapst, G. Essai sur l'histoire du théâtre. Paris, 1893.

Beaulieu, H. Les Théâtres du Boulevard du Crime. Paris, 1904.

Beaumount, C. W. Three French Dancers of the Nineteenth Century. London, 1934.

Bellaigue, C. Un Siècle de musique française. Paris, 1887.

Bequet, C. M. E. Encyclopédie de l'art dramatique. Paris, 1886.

Bertant, Jules. Le Boulevard. Paris, 1924.

Boll, A. Du Décor du théâtre. Paris, 1926.

__________. L'Opéra, spectacle intégral. Paris, 1963.

Bonnassies, J. Les Spectacles forains et la Comédie Française. Paris, 1875.

Bonnefort, G. La Comédie-Française. Paris, 1884.

Boski, J. L'Evolution de l'éclairage au théâtre. Paris, n.d.

Bossuet, P. Histoire administrative des rapports des théâtres et de l'état. Paris, 1909.

________. Histoire des théâtres nationaux. Paris, 1909.

Boucheron, M. La Divine Comédie--Française. Paris, 1889.

Bouffe, H. M. D. Mes Souvenirs. Paris, 1880.

Brunetière, J. Les Epoques du théâtre français. Paris, 1892.

Buguet, H. Foyers et coulisses: Bouffés-Parisiens, Folies-Dramatiques, Variétés. Paris, 1873.

________. Foyers et coulisses: Gymnase, Gaîté. Paris, 1875.

________. Foyers et coulisses: Renaissance. Paris, 1882.

________. Foyers et coulisses: Vaudeville. Paris, 1874.

Campardon, E. Les Comédiens du roi. Paris, 1870.

________. Les Spectacles de la foire. 2 vols. Paris, 1877.

Champfleury. Comédie-Française: décrets et ordonnances. Lille, 1911.

Champion, E. La Comédie Française. 5 vols. Paris, 1927-1937.

Chancerel, L. Le Théâtre et les comédiens. Paris, n. d.

Chouquet, G. Histoire de la musique dramatique en France depuis ses origines jusqu'à nos jours. Paris, 1893.

Claretie, J. Profils de théâtre. Paris, 1902.

Cohen, G. L'Evolution de la mise-en-scène dans le théâtre français. Lille, 1916.

Coursaget, R. and M. Gauthier. Cent ans de théâtre par la photographie. Paris, n. d.

Dandelot, A. L'Evolution de la musique de théâtre depuis Meyerbeer jusqu'à nos jours. Paris, 1927.

Daniels, May. The French Drama of the Unspoken. Edinburgh, 1953.

Decugis, N. and S. Reymond. Le Décor de théâtre en France du moyen age à 1925. Paris, 1953.

Delattie, André. Le Théâtre de l'Ambigu-Comique. Paris, 1895.

Deligny, E. Histoire de l'Ambigu-Comique. Paris, 1841.

Delvigne, F. Le Théâtre de l'Opéra. Paris, n. d.

Desarbres, N. Deux siècles à l'Opéra. Paris, 1868.

Descotes, M. Le Public de théâtre. Paris, 1864.

Deux habitués. Histoire des Délassements-Comiques. Paris, 1862.

Doumic, René. De Scribe à Ibsen. Paris, 1913.

Du Fayl, E. Académie Nationale de Musique 1671-1877. Paris, 1878.

Dubech, L. Histoire général du théâtre. 5 vols. Paris, 1931-1934.

Dumesnil, R. L'Opéra et l'Opéra-Comique. Paris, 1961.

Dureau, A. Notes pour servir à l'histoire du théâtre et de la musique en France. Paris, 1860.

Dussane, B. La Comédie-Française. Paris, 1960.

Fabre, E. La Comédie Française. Paris, 1942.

________. De Thalie à Melpomène. Paris, 1947.

________. Notes sur la mise en scène. Abbeville, 1933.

Faucher, T. Histoire du boulevard du temple. Paris, 1863.

Febvre, F. Au bord de la scène. Paris, 1889.

Filon, Augustin. De Dumas à Rostand. Paris, 1898.

Fischer, C. Les Costumes de l'Opéra. Paris, 1931.

Forentino, P. A. Comédies et comédiens. 2 vols. Paris, 1856.

Foucher, P. Les coulisses du passé. Paris, 1873.

__________. Entre cour et jardin. Paris, 1867.

Fouque, O. Histoire du Théâtre Ventadour. Paris, 1881.

Fournel, V. Curiosités théâtrales. Paris, 1859.

Franchetti, E. Essais de critique dramatique. Paris, n. d.

Gaiffe, F. Le Rire et la scène française. Paris, 1931.

Gautier, Théophile. Comédies et ballets. Paris, 1872.

__________. Souvenirs de théâtre. Paris, 1883.

Genest, E. L'Opéra-Comique: Connu et inconnu. Paris, 1925.

__________ and E. Duberry. La Maison de Molière connu et inconnu. Paris, 1922.

Grandval, Charles. De la Comédie Française aux boulevards. Paris, 1906.

Gueulette, C. Répertoire de la Comédie Française. 8 vols. Paris 1885-1892.

Gueulette, T. S. Théâtre des boulevards. Paris, 1881.

Guex, J. Le Théâtre et la société française de 1815 à 1848. Vevey, 1900.

Guillemot, G. L'Evolution de l'idée dramatique... de Corneille à Dumas fils. Paris, 1910.

Haines, C. M. Shakespeare in France. London, 1928.

Hallays-Dabot, V. Histoire de la censure théâtrale en France. Paris, 1862.

Héros, Eugène. Notice sur le théâtre du Palais-Royal. Paris, 1901.

Hervey, Charles. The Theatres of Paris. London, 1846.

Heylli, G. d'. La Comédie Française. Paris, 1877.

__________. Foyers et coulisses. L'Opéra. Paris, 1875.

__________. Léon Guillard, archiviste de la Comédie Française. Paris, 1878.

Histoire du Théâtre Lyrique en France depuis les origines jusqu'à nos jours. 3 vols. Paris, 1938.

Horn-Monval, M. Traductions et adaptations françaises du théâtre étranger. 2 vols. Paris, 1858-1859.

Horowicz, E. Le Théâtre d'Opéra. Paris, 1946.

Houssaye, A. La Comédienne. Paris, 1885.

Hugot, E. Histoire littéraire... du théâtre du Palais-Royal. Paris, 1886.

Hugounet, P. Mimes et Pierrots. Paris, 1889.

Janin, Jules. Critique dramatique. 4 vols. Paris, 1877.

__________. Histoire de la littérature dramatique. 6 vols. Paris, 1853-1858.

Joannidès, A. La Comédie Française de 1680 à 1900. Paris, 1901.

Jullien, A. Histoire du costume au théâtre. Paris, 1880.

__________. L'Opéra connu et inconnu. Paris, 1870.

Jusserand, J. Shakespeare en France. Paris, 1898.

Kindermann, H. Theatergeschichte Europas. Vols. 6 and 7. Salzburg, 1964-65.

Kochno, B. Le Ballet en France. Paris, 1954.

La Laurencie. Les Créateurs de l'opéra français. Paris, 1921.

La Rounat, C. de. Le Théâtre Francais. Paris, 1879.

Lacroix, A. Histoire de l'influence de Shakespeare sur le théâtre français. Brussels, 1856.

Laine, E. Le Costume au théâtre. Paris, 1886.

Lajarte, T. de. _Bibliothèque musicale du Théâtre de l'Opéra._ London, 1943.

Lambert, A. _Le Théâtre classique, romantique, naturaliste._ Rouen, 1889.

Lanson, G. _Les Origines du drame contemporain._ Paris, 1903.

Lasalle, A. de. _Histoire des Bouffes-Parisiens._ Paris, Paris, 1908.

__________. _Trieze salles de l'Opéra._ Paris, 1875.

Laumann, E. M. _La Machinerie au théâtre._ Paris, 1898.

Lecomte, L. H. _Le Théâtre Historique._ Paris, 1906.

__________. _Théâtres de Paris: Le Renaissance._ Paris, 1905.

__________. _Les Jeux Gymniques._ _Le Panorama Dramatique._ Paris, 1908.

__________. _Les Nouveautés._ Paris, 1907.

Legouvé, E. _Soixante ans de souvenirs._ 2 vols. Paris, 1886-1887.

Lejeune, A. and S. Wolf. _Les Quinze Salles de l'Opéra à Paris._ Paris, 1955.

Lelievre, R. _Le Théâtre dramatique Italien en France._ Paris, 1959.

Lenient, C. _La Comédie en France au dix-neuvième siècle._ 2 vols. Paris, 1898.

Levrault, L. _Le Théâtre des origines à nos jours._ Paris, 1932.

Linthilhac, E. _Histoire générale du théâtre en France._ Paris, 1906.

Lioure, Michel. _Le Drame._ Paris, 1963.

Loliée, F. _La Comédie Française._ Paris, 1907.

Lorsay, E. Les Théâtres de Paris, Paris. 1855.

Loukomski, G. K. Les Théâtres anciens et modernes. Paris, 1934.

Lucas, H. Histoire philosophique et littéraire du Théâtre Français. Paris, 1882.

Mahé, Y. Théâtre. Paris, 1961.

Malherbe, C. and A. Soubies. Histoire de l'Opéra-Comique. Paris, 1893.

Malliot, A. L. La Musique au théâtre. Paris, 1863.

Marsan, Jules. Théâtre d'hier et d'aujourd'hui. Paris, 1926.

Martine, J. Examen des tragiques anciens et modernes. Paris, 1834.

Matthews, J. Brander. French Dramatists of the Nineteenth Century. New York, 1881.

__________. The Theatres of Paris. London, 1880.

Maurice, Charles. Epaves. Paris, 1865.

__________. Feu le boulevard du Temple. Paris, 1863.

__________. Histoire anecdotique du théâtre. Paris, 1865.

__________. Le Théâtre-Français: monument et dépendances. Paris, 1860.

Melcher, E. Stage Realism in France between Diderot and Antoine. Bryn Mawr, 1928.

Michause, L. Histoire et description du théâtre de la Gaîté. Paris, 1883.

__________. Histoire et description du théâtre du Châtelet. Paris, 1883.

__________. Histoire et description du théâtre Lyrique. Paris, 1883.

__________ Histoire et description du théâtre du Vaudeville. Paris, 1883.

Mirecourt, Eugène de. *Les Contemporaines.* 34 vols. Includes Auber, Barrière, Beauvallet, Berlioz, Bocage, Bourgeois, Brohan, Champfleury, Cheri, Dumas *fils*, Dumas *père*, Feuillet, George, de Girardin, Gozlan, Hugo, Houssaye, Janin, Labiche, Lemaître, Mélingue, Meyerbeer, Monnier, Musset, Offenbach, Ponsard, Rachel, Rossini, Sand, Sardou, Scribe, Taylor, Véron, de Vigny. Paris, 1854-1865.

Monselet, C. *Les Premières représentations célebrés.* Paris, 1867.

Montagne, E. *Le Manteau d'Arlequin.* Paris, 1866.

Montchamp, L. de and C. Mosout. *Les Reines de la rampe.* Paris, 1863.

Monval, G. *Les Collections de la Comédie Française.* Paris, 1897.

Monval, J. *La Comédie Française.* Paris, 1931.

Nostrand, H. L. *Le Théâtre antique et à l'antiquité en France de 1840 à 1900.* Paris, 1934.

Ollone, M. d'. *Le Théâtre lyrique et le public.* Paris, 1955.

Ortigue, J. d'. *Du Théâtre Italien et de son influence sur le gout musical français.* Paris, 1840.

Pélissier, P. *Histoire administrative de l'Académie de Musique.* Paris, 1906.

Pellet, A. *Essai sur l'opéra en France depuis Lulli.* Nimes, 1874.

Péricaud, L. *Le Panthéon des comédiens.* Paris, 1922.

Perrin, M. *Biographie historique de tous les théâtres de Paris.* Paris, 1850.

Petit de Julleville, L. *Histoire de la langue et de la littérature française.* 8 vols. Paris, 1896-1899.

__________. *Le Théâtre en France.* Paris, 1889.

Pierrefitte, P. L. *Histoire du théâtre des Folies-Marigny.* Paris, 1893.

Plunkett, J. Fantômes et souvenirs de la Porte-Saint-Martin. Paris, 1946.

Poizat, A. Les Maîtres du théâtre. Paris, n. d.

Poniatowski, J. M. Le Progrès de la musique dramatique. Paris, 1958.

Porel, P. and G. Monval. L'Odéon. 2 vols. Paris, 1876-1882.

Pougin, A. Acteurs et actrices d'autrefois. Paris, 1896.

__________. Dictionnaire historique et pittoresque du théâtre. Paris, 1885.

__________. Figures d'Opéra-Comique. Paris, 1875.

__________. Traité de la construction des théâtres. Paris, 1886.

__________. Les Vrais Créateurs de l'Opéra français. Paris, 1886.

Proud'homme, J. G. L'Opéra. Paris, 1925.

Pyat, F. Le Théâtre-Français. Paris, 1833.

Rahill, F. The World of Melodrama. London, 1967.

Raphanel, J. and C. Legrand. Histoire anecdotique des théâtres de Paris. Paris, 1896.

__________. Histoire anecdotique de l'Opéra-Comique. Paris, 1891.

Reyna, F. Histoire du ballet. Paris, 1864.

Reyval, A. L'Eglise, la Comédie, et les comédiens. Paris, n. d.

Royer, A. Histoire de l'Opéra. Paris, 1875.

__________. Histoire universelle du théâtre. 6 vols. Paris, 1878.

Schuré, E. Le Drame musical. 2 vols. Paris, 1875.

Siaud, S. *La Comédie Française.* Paris, 1936.

Sigaux, G. *Un Siècle d'humor théâtral et d'histoire de théâtre.* Paris, 1964.

Solie, E. *Histoire du Théâtre Royal de l'Opéra-Comique.* Paris, 1847.

Sonrel, P. *Traité de scénographie.* Paris, 1943.

Soubies, A. *La Comédie-Française depuis l'époque romantique.* Paris, 1895.

__________. *Histoire de l'Opéra-Comique.* 2 vols. Paris, 1892-1893.

__________. *Soixante-neuf ans à l'Opéra-Comique en deux pages.* Paris, 1894.

__________. *Soixante-sept ans à l'Opéra en une page.* Paris, 1893.

__________. *Le Théâtre Italien de 1801 à 1913.* Paris, 1913.

__________. *Une Première par jour.* Paris, n. d.

Soulié, F. *Les Théâtres de Paris.* Paris, n. d.

Thelmier, Dr. *Histoire du théâtre Montparnasse.* Paris, 1886.

Thurner, A. *Les Transformations de l'Opéra-Comique.* Paris, 1865.

Touchard, P. A. *Histoire sentimentale de la Comédie Française.* Paris, 1955.

__________ and Crepineau. *Grandes Heures de théâtre à Paris.* Paris, 1965.

Vaillat, L. *Ballets de l'Opéra de Paris.* Paris, 1947.

__________. *La Danse à l'Opéra de Paris.* Paris, 1951.

Valmy-Baisse, J. *Naissance et vie de la Comédie Française.* Paris, 1945.

Vanel, E. Histoire populaire de tous les théâtres de Paris. Paris, 1841.

Veinstein, A. La Mise en scène théâtrale et sa condition esthétique. Paris, 1955.

Véron, M. L. Les Gens de théâtre. Paris, 1862.

__________. Les Théâtres de Paris depuis 1806. Paris, 1860.

Voltz, P. La Comédie. Paris, 1963.

Warnod, A. L'Ancien Théâtre Montparnasse. Paris, 1930.

Weiss, J. J. Le Drame historique et le drame passionnel. Paris, 1888.

__________. Le Théâtre et les moeurs. Paris, 1889.

__________. Les Théâtres parisiens. Paris, 1896.

Wild, R. L'Art du ballet des origines à nos jours. Paris, n. d.

Winter, M. H. Le Théâtre du merveilleux. Paris, 1962.

1800-1827 (see also General Biblography)

Abrantès, Duchesse d'. Mémoires. Paris, 1831-1835.

Aglaé, Mlle. Mémoires. Paris, n. d.

Albert, M. La Littérature française sous la Révolution, l'Empire, et la Restauration. Paris, 1898.

Alhoy, P. Dictionnaire théâtrale. Paris, 1825.

Allard, L. La Comédie de moeurs en France au dix-neuvième siècle. 2 vols. Cambridge, 1923.

__________. Les Auteurs, la vie, les théâtres. Paris, 1933.

Allevy, M. A. La Mise en scène en France dans la première moitié du dix-neuvième siècle. Paris, 1938.

Almanach des spectacles de Paris pour l'an 1809. Paris, 1810.

Almanach des spectacles depuis le commencement du dix-neuvième siècle. Paris, 1824.

Alméras. La Vie Parisienne sous la Restauration. Paris, 1910.

Annuaire dramatique. 4 vols. Paris, 1805-1822.

Antoine, A. La Vie amoureuse de Talma. Paris, 1924.

Aristippe, A. Théorie de l'art du comédien. Paris, 1826.

Arnault, A. V. Souvenirs d'un sexagénaire. Paris, 1833.

Audibert. Histoire du roman: Talma. Paris, 1834.

Auger, H. Physiologie du théâtre. 3 vols. Paris, 1840.

Augustin-Thierry, A. Mademoiselle George. Paris, 1936.

__________. La Tragédien de Napoléon: F. J. Talma. Paris, 1942.

Aulard, A. Paris sous le Consulat. Paris, 1903-1909.

B.......... Le Cirque Olympique. Paris, 1817.

B.........., J. D. Essai sur l'état actuel du théâtre français. Paris, 1839.

Babault et al. Annales dramatiques. 9 vols. Paris, 1808.

Le Baisser du rideau. Paris, 1827.

Bapst, G. Essai sur l'histoire des panoramas et des dioramas. Paris, 1892.

Barbier-Vemars, E. Talma. Paris, 1822.

Beauvoir, R. de. Confidences de Mlle Mars. Paris, 1855.

__________. Mémoires de Mlle Mars. 2 vols. Paris, 1845.

Bellen, E. C. van. Les Origines du mélodrame. Utrecht, 1927.

Bellier-Dumaine, C. *Alexandre Duval.* Paris, 1905.

Bergman, G. "Les Agences théâtrales et l'impression des mises en scène au XIXe siècle," *Revue d'Histoire du Théâtre,* VIII (1956).

Bernilly, F. *Mademoiselle Mars.* Paris, 1823.

Biffault, E. *Mademoiselle Mars.* Paris, 1847.

Biographie des acteurs de Paris. Paris, 1837.

Biré, E. *Victor Hugo avant 1830.* Paris, 1883.

Borgnis, M. J. A. *Traité complet de méchanique appliquée aux arts.* Paris, 1820.

Bossuet, J. B. *Réflexions sur la comédie.* Paris, 1881.

Bouillaut, J. *La Conspiration de Mlle Duchesnois contre Mlle George Weymer.* Paris, 1803.

Bouilly, J. *Soixante ans du théâtre-français.* Paris, 1842.

Boullet, F. *Essai sur l'art de construire les théâtres.* Paris, 1801.

Bourgeois, A. *Les Débuts de Mlle Georges et la critique de son temps.* Paris, 1910.

Brazier, N. *Le Boulevard du Temple.* Paris, 1832.

__________. *Histoire des petits théâtres de Paris.* 2 vols. Paris, 1838.

Brockett, O. G. "Pixérécourt and Unified Production," *Educational Theatre Journal,* XI, 3 (Oct., 1959).

Cain, G. *Anciens théâtres de Paris.* Paris, 1906.

Castel, L. *Mémoire d'un claqueur.* Paris, 1829.

Castil-Blaze, F. J. *La Danse et le ballet depuis Bacchus jusqu'à Taglioni.* Paris, 1832.

__________. *De l'Opéra en France.* Paris, 1820.

__________. *Mémorial du grand Opéra.* Paris, 1847.

_________. L'Opéra-Italien de 1548 à 1856. Paris, 1856.

Chaalons d'Argé, A. P. Histoire...des théâtres de Paris. 2 vols. Paris, 1822, 1825.

Chapus, E. Essai critique sur le théâtre français. Paris, 1827.

Charlemagne, A. Le Mélodrame aux boulevards. Paris, 1809.

Chéramy, P. A. Mémoires inédits de Mlle George. Paris, 1912.

Cherru, H. Mademoiselle George. Fontency-le-Comte, 1829.

Chevalley, S. "Talma, Comédien français," Revue d'Histoire du Théâtre, XIV (1962).

Collins, H. F. Talma. New York, 1964.

Copin, A. Talma et l'Empire. Paris, 1887.

Courtois, C. L'Opinion du parterre. 10 vols. Paris, 1803-1813.

Cuchet and Lagarencière. Almanach des plaisirs de Paris. Paris, 1815.

Cuisin, P. Le Peintre des coulisses. Paris, 1822.

Daguerre, L. J. M. Esquisse historique et déscription des procédés du Daguerréotype et du Diorama. Paris, 1839.

Delaforest, A. Cours de littérature dramatique. 2 vols. Paris, 1836.

_________. Théâtre moderne. 2 vols. Paris, 1836.

DeManne, E. D. Galerie historique de la Comédie-Française. Lyon, 1876.

_________. Galerie historique des comédiens de la troupe de Talma. Paris, 1866.

_________. Galerie historique des comédiens de Nicolet. Paris, 1867.

_________. Parallèle de Talma et de Joanny. Paris, 1822.

Descotes, M. L'Acteur Joanny et son journal inédit. Mayence, n. d.

Des Granges, C. M. La Comédie et les moeurs sous la Restauration. Paris, 1902.

_________. Geoffroy et la critique dramatique. Paris, 1897.

_________. Le Romantisme et la critique. Paris, 1902.

Deshayes, A. J. J. Idées générales sur l'Académie de Musique. Paris, 1822.

Doumic, R. "Le Mélodrame et la théâtre romantique," Histoire de la langue et de la littérature de la France, Vol. VIII. Paris, 1889.

Dumas, A. Mémoires de Talma. 4 vols. Paris, 1849-1850.

Dumersan, T. Manuel des coulisses. Paris, 1826.

Duperier, R. La Franconiade. Bordeaux, n. d.

Duronceray, P. A qui le fauteuil. Paris, 1817.

Duval, E. Talma. Paris, 1826.

Edmond, F. Les Etrennes. Paris, 1813.

Eggli, E. and P. Martino. Le Débat romantique en France. Paris, 1933.

Etrennes dramatiques. Paris, 1821.

Etrennes dramatiques pour l'année 1801. Paris, 1802.

Evans, O. L'Evolution du théâtre social en France de 1750 à 1850. Paris, n. d.

Favart, C. S. Mémoire et correspondance. 3 vols. Paris, 1808.

Favre, G. Boieldieu. 2 vols. Paris, 1944-1945.

Fay, E. Plan d'une organization générale de tous les théâtres de l'Empire. Paris, 1813.

Fleischmann, H. Une maîtresse de Napoléon. Paris, 1908.

Foucard, E. Les Comédiens français depuis Molière jusqu'à nos jours. Paris, 1839.

Gavoty, A. La Grassini. Paris, 1947.

Geoffroy, J. L. Cours de littérature dramatique. Paris, 1836.

George, Mlle. Mémoires. Paris, 1908.

Ginisty, P. Chronique parisienne des six derniers mois d'Empire. Paris, 1912.

__________. La Féerie. Paris, 1910.

__________. Le Mélodrame. Paris, n. d.

Grille, J. F. Les Théâtres. Paris, 1817.

Grobert, J. De l'Exécution dramatique considérée dans ses rapports avec le matériel de la salle et de la scène. Paris, 1809.

Hapdé, A. De l'Anarchie théâtrale. Paris, 1814.

Haquette, M. and H. Buffenoir. Le Décret de Moscou et la Comédie Française. Paris, 1902.

Harel, F. A. Dictionnaire théâtrale. Paris, 1824.

Hartog, W. G. Guilbert de Pixérécourt. Paris, 1913.

Heinnin, M. Des Théâtres et de leur organization légale. Paris, 1819.

Héquet, G. Boieldieu, sa vie et ses oeuvres. Paris, 1864.

Hermite du Luxembourg. Grande biographie dramatique. Paris, 1825.

Jerrmann, E. Fragments aus seinem Theater-leben. Munich, 1833.

Joanny. Biographie véridique. Paris, 1845.

__________. Ma Confession. Paris, 1846.

Joliment, T. de. La Nouvelle Salle de l'Opéra. Paris, 1821.

Jouy, E. Essai sur l'opéra français. Paris. 1823.

Jullien, A. Paris dilettante au commencement du siècle. Paris, 1884.

Kotzebue, A. Souvenirs de Paris en 1804. Paris, 1805.

La Borderie, A. de. Alexandre Duval. Rennes, 1893.

Lablée, J. De la Théâtre de la Porte Saint-Martin. Paris, 1812.

Laboullaye, F. de. Le Théâtre-Français, Mlle George Weimar et l'Odéon. Paris, 1822.

Lacy, A. Pixérécourt and the French Romantic Drama. Toronto, 1928.

Lanzac de Labordie, L. de. Paris sous Napoléon: Spectacles et Musées. Paris, 1913.

__________. Paris sous Napoléon: Le Théâtre-Français. Paris, 1911.

__________. Les Petits Théâtres de Paris sous le Consulat et l'Empire. Paris, 1912.

Laugier, E. Documents historiques sur le Comédie...pendant le regne de...Napoléon. Paris, 1853.

__________ and Mottet. Galerie biographique des artistes des théâtres royaux. Paris, 1826.

Le Roy, A. L'Aube du théâtre romantique. Paris, 1904.

Le Senne, C. M. Etienne et le théâtre sous l'Empire. Paris, 1913.

Lecomte, L. H. Napoléon et l'Empire racontés par le théâtre. Paris, 1900.

__________. Napoléon et le monde dramatique. Paris, 1912.

__________. Le Théâtre de la Cité. Paris, 1910.

__________. Les Variétés Amusantes. Paris, 1908.

Legouvé, E. Un conseilleur dramatique: M. J. F. Mahérault. Paris, 1879.

Lejeune, L. F. Souvenirs d'un officier de l'Empire. Paris, 1895.

Lelièvre, R. "Le Théâtre des Variétés-Etrangères," Revue d'Histoire du Théâtre, XII (1960).

__________. "Les Acteurs du Théâtre des Variétés-Etrangeres," Revue d'Histoire du Théâtre, XIII (1961).

Lemazurier, P. D. Galerie historique des acteurs du théâtre français. Paris, 1810.

Lerebours, P. S. Lettre... sur l'état actuel de la scène française. Paris, 1822.

Lyonnet, H. Mlle Georges. Paris, 1907.

Malherbe, H. Auber, biographie critique. Leipzig, 1911.

Marsan, J. "Le Mélodrame et Guilbert de Pixérécourt," Revue d'histoire littéraire de France (July, 1911).

Maudit-Larive. Cours de déclamation. 3 vols. Paris, 1804-1810.

__________. Moyen de régénérer les théâtres. Paris, 1806.

__________. Réflexions sur l'art théâtrale. Paris, 1801.

Milton, H. Letters on the Fine Arts, written from Paris in the year 1815. London, 1816.

Moreau, M. Mémoires historiques et littéraires sur F. J. Talma. Paris, 1826.

Muret, T. L'Histoire par le théâtre. Vols. 1 and 2. Paris, 1865.

Ortigue, J. d'. De la Guerre des dilettanti. Paris, 1829.

__________. Le Balcon de l'Opéra. Paris, 1833.

Paccard, J. E. Mémoires et confessions d'un comédien.

Paris, 1839.

Petite biographie des acteurs et actrices des théâtres de Paris. Paris, 1826.

Pitou, A. "Les Origines du mélodrame français à la fin du XVIII siècle," Revue d'histoire littéraire (June, 1911).

Pixérécourt, G. de. Le Mélodrame. Paris, 1832.

__________. Oeuvres completes. Paris, 1796-1836.

__________. Théâtre choisi. 4 vols. Paris, 1841-1843.

Pougin, A. Auber. Paris, 1873.

__________. Boieldieu. Paris, 1875.

__________. Figures d'opéra-Comique. Paris, 1875.

__________. Monsigny et son temps. Paris, 1868.

Quicherat, L. Adolphe Nourrit. 3 vols. Paris, 1867.

Ragueneau de la Chainaye, A. H. Chronique. 2 vols. Paris, 1818.

Regnault-Warin. Mémoires historiques et critiques sur F. J. Talma. Paris, 1827.

Rémusat, A. La Révolution du théâtre. Paris, 1820.

Ricord aîné. Journal général des théâtres. Paris, 1816.

__________. Quelques réflexions sur l'art théâtrale. Paris, 1818.

Robillon, C. Considérations sur l'art dramatique. Versailles, 1828.

Ruggieri, C. Précis historique sur les fêtes, les spectacles, et les réjouissances publiques. Paris, 1830.

Sarrut, G. Etudes rétrospectives sur l'état de la scène tragique. Paris, 1842.

Saunders, E. Napoléon and Mlle George. London, 1918.

Sevelinges, C. de. *Le Rideau levé*. Paris, 1818.

Soubies, A. *Le Théâtre Italien sous Napoléon et la Restauration.* Paris, 1910.

Soyé, F. H. *Ces Messieurs et ces dames.* Paris, 1823.

Staël-Holstein, Mme de. *De l'Allemagne*. Paris, 1814.

Talma, F. J. *Correspondance avec Mme de Staël.* Paris, 1928.

__________. *Etudes sur l'art théâtrale.* Paris, 1836.

__________. *Lettres à Benjamin Constant.* Paris, 1933.

Thibault, T. *Manuel de souffleur*. Paris, 1830.

Thompson, L. F. *Kotzebue: A Survey of his Progress in France and England.* Paris, 1928.

Tissot, P. F. *Souvenirs historiques sur la vie et la mort de Talma.* Paris, 1826.

Touchard-Lafosse, G. *Chroniques secrètes et galantes de l'Opéra.* Paris, 1846.

Trotain, M. *Les Scènes historiques*. Paris, 1923.

Van-Bellen, E. *Les Origines du mélodrame*. Paris, 1933.

Vauthier, G. *L'Opéra sous la Restauration.* Poitiers, 1910.

Victor, P. *Documents pour servir à l'histoire du Théâtre Français sous la Restauration*. Paris, 1843.

Viollet-le-Duc, E. M. *Précis de l'art dramatique*. Paris, 1830.

Virely, A. *René Charles Guilbert de Pixérécourt.* Paris, 1909.

Welschinger, H. *La Censure sous le Premier Empire.* Paris, 1882.

__________. *Un Chapitre de la censure théâtrale sous la Restauration.* Paris, 1885.

1827-1850 (see also General Bibliography)

Agate, J. Rachel. New York, 1928.

Allais, G. Les Débuts dramatiques de Victor Hugo. Paris, 1903.

Allard, L. La Comédie Française au temps de Mlles Mars et Rachel. Paris, 1925.

Allevy, M. A. Edition critique d'une mise en scène romantique. Paris, 1938.

________. La Mise en scène en France dans la première moitié du dix-neuvième siècle. Paris, 1938.

Alméras. La Vie parisienne sous le régime de Louis-Philippe. Paris, 1911.

Arago, J. Foyers et coulisses. Paris, 1852.

________. Mémoires d'un petit banc de l'Opéra. Paris, 1844.

________. Physiologie des foyers de tous les théâtres de Paris. Paris, 1841.

Ariste, Paul d'. La Vie et le monde du boulevard. Paris, 1930.

Arnyvelde, A. La Question de l'Opéra en 1831. Paris, 1914.

Arvin, N. C. Eugene Scribe and the French Theatre. New York, 1924.

Auger, H. Physiologie du théâtre. 3 vols. Paris, 1840.

B......., A. Mlle Rachel et l'avenir du théâtre Français. Paris, 1839.

Badin, E. Charles Séchan. Paris, 1883.

Baldick, R. The Life and Times of Frederick Lemaitre. London, 1959.

Banville, Théodore de. Les Pauvres Saltimbanques. Paris, 1853.

Barba, J. N. *Souvenirs.* Paris, 1846.

Barbou, A. *Victor Hugo et son siècle.* Paris, 1889.

Barine, A. *Alfred de Musset.* Paris, 1873.

Barrere, J. B. *La Fantaisie de Victor Hugo.* 2 vols. Paris, 1950.

__________. *Hugo, l'homme et l'oeuvre.* Paris, 1952.

Barthou, Louis. *Rachel.* Paris, 1926.

Beauvallet, A. *Rachel et le nouveau monde.* Paris, 1856.

Befort, A. *Alexandre Soumet.* Luxembourg, 1908.

Bergerat, Emile. *Théophile Gautier.* Paris, 1879.

Berret, P. *Victor Hugo.* Paris, 1827.

Biographie des acteurs de Paris. Paris, 1837.

Blanchet, E. *Victor Hugo et la renaissance théâtrale.* Meaux, 1879.

Boigne, C. de. *Petits Mémoires de l'Opéra.* Paris, 1857.

Bolot, A. *Mlle Rachel et l'avenir du théâtre.* Paris, 1839.

Bonjour, C. *Coup d'oeil sur le théâtre.* Paris, 1838.

Borgerhoff, J. L. *Le Théâtre Anglais à Paris sous la Restauration.* Paris, 1912.

Boschot, A. *Un Romantique sous Louis-Philippe.* Paris, 1908.

__________. *Théophile Gautier.* Paris, 1933.

Bouchet, H. *Souvenirs d'un Parisien pendant la Second République.* Paris, 1908.

Bouilly. *Soixante ans du théâtre-Français.* Paris, 1842.

Bray, A. *Chronologie du romantisme.* Paris, 1932.

Briffaut, E. *Galerie biographique des artistes dramatiques* de Paris. Paris, 1846.

Broglie, A. L. C. V. Sur l'Othello d'Alfred de Vigny et sur l'état de l'art dramatique en France. Paris, 1852.

Brun, A. Deux proses de théâtre. Gap, 1954.

Burnand, R. La Vie quotidienne en France en 1830. Paris, 1843.

Cain, G. Anciens théâtres de Paris. Paris, 1906.

Capon, G. Les Vestris. Paris, 1908.

Casteux, P. G. Vigny. Paris, 1952.

Castil-Blaze, F. J. Mémorial du grand Opéra. Paris, 1847.

__________. L'Opéra-Italien de 1548 à 1856. Paris, 1856.

Cesena, G. de. Le Baron Taylor. Paris, 1841.

Challamel, A. Souvenirs d'un hugolâtre. Paris, 1885.

Chambrun, C. Quelques réflexions sur...Mlle Rachel. Paris, 1853.

Champfleury, H. M. Les Vignettes romantiques. Paris, 1883.

Champfleury, J. F. F. Souvenirs des funambules. Paris, 1859.

Chancerney, L. Les Illustrations de notre époque. Paris, 1855.

Charlier, G. "Hernani jugé par le Figaro," Revue d'histoire du théâtre, II (1950).

Chasles, P. Les Beautés de l'Opéra. Paris, 1845.

Chaulin, N. P. Biographie dramatique... précédée de souvenirs historiques du théâtre anglais à Paris en 1827 et 1828. Paris, 1828.

Chennevières, P. de. Notice sur le baron Taylor. Paris, 1881.

Cherpin, J. "Daumier et le théâtre," Revue d'histoire du

théâtre, III (1953).

Clément-Janin. *Drames et comédies romantiques.* Paris, 1928.

Clovard, H. *Alexandre Dumas.* Paris, 1955.

Constant, C. *Parallèle des principaux théâtres modernes de l'Europe et des machines théâtrales françaises.* Paris, 1842.

Couailhac, L. *Physiologie du théâtre à Paris et en province.* Paris, 1842.

Coupy, E. *Marie Dorval.* Paris, 1868.

Cresp, J. *Essai sur la déclamation oratoire et dramatique.* Paris, 1937.

Darcie, J. *The Biography of Mlle Rachel.* New York, 1855.

Dauriac, L. *Meyerbeer.* Paris, 1930.

De la Salle, J. *Souvenirs sur le Théâtre Français.* Paris, 1900.

Dechanel, E. *Le Romantisme des classiques.* 2 vols. Paris, 1883.

Delaborde, H. *Notice sur... M. le baron Taylor.* Paris, 1880.

Delacroix, E. *Lettres.* Paris, 1880.

Delaforest, A. *Théâtre moderne.* 2 vols. Paris, 1836.

Delalande, J. *Victor Hugo, dessinateur génial et halluciné.* Paris, 1964.

Delecluze, E. J. *Souvenirs de soixante années.* Paris, 1862.

Deschamps, E. *Un Manifeste du romantisme.* Paris, 1924.

Descotes, M. *Le Drame romantique et ses grands créateurs.* Paris, 1955.

Deshayes. *Observations sur les salles de spectacle.* Paris, n. d.

Deslandes, R. Les Jolies Actrices de Paris. Paris, 1849.

Desnoyers, L. L'Opéra en 1847. Paris, 1847.

Deutsch, L. Déjazet. Paris, 1928.

Deveria, A. Réorganization des théâtres. Lyon, 1848.

Doazan, G. Lettre sur le Théâtre Français en 1839 et 1840. Paris, 1841.

Dollingen, Z. Bocage. Paris, 1860.

Donnet, A. and J. A. Kaufmann. Achitectonographie des théâtres. 2 vols. Paris, 1837-1840.

Donville, F. de. Frédérick Lemaître. Paris, 1876.

Dorval, M. Lettres à Alfred de Vigny. Paris, 1942.

Draper, E. W. M. The Rise and Fall of the French Romantic Drama. London, 1923.

Dubois, A. Julia Bartet. Paris, 1920.

Dumas, A. Aventures et tribulations d'un comédien. Paris, 1854.

__________. La Dernière Année de Marie Dorval. Paris, 1855.

__________. Mes Mémoires. Paris, 1854.

__________. Souvenirs dramatiques. 2 vols. Paris, 1868.

Dupuy, E. Alfred de Vigny. Paris, 1913.

__________. La Jeunesse des romantiques. Paris, 1928.

Duval, G. F. Lemaître et son temps. Paris, 1876.

Eggli, E. Schiller et le romantisme français. 2 vols. Paris, 1927.

Escholier, R. La Vie glorieuse de Victor Hugo. Paris, 1928.

Escudier, M. Vie et aventures des cantatrices célèbres.

Paris, 1856.

Etrennes dramatiques. Paris, 1829.

Evans, D. O. Le Drame moderne à l'époque romantique. Paris, 1937.

__________. Les Problèmes d'actualité au théâtre à l'époque romantique. Paris, 1923.

__________. Le Théâtre pendant la période romantique. Paris, 1925.

Evans, O. L'Evolution du théâtre social en France de 1750 à 1850. Paris, n. d.

Falk, B. Rachel the Immortal. London, 1935.

Faucigny-Lucinge, Mme A. de. Rachel et son temps. Paris, 1910.

Faure, F. Déjazet. Paris, 1859.

Fleischmann, H. Rachel intime. Paris, 1910.

__________. Une Maîtresse de Victor Hugo. Paris, 1912.

Flutre, F. Victor Hugo. Paris, 1927.

Foucard, E. Les Comédiens français depuis Molière jusqu'à nos jours. Paris, 1839.

François, C. Le Baron Taylor. Paris, 1879.

Gallet, Théâtre Historique. Paris, 1847.

Gautier, T. Galerie des artistes dramatiques. Paris, 1841.

__________. Histoire de l'art dramatique depuis vingt-cinq ans. 6 vols. Paris, 1858-1859.

__________. Histoire du romantisme. Paris, 1874.

Ginisty, P. Bocage. Paris, 1926.

__________. Mémoires d'une danseuse de corde: Mme Saqui. Paris, 1907.

__________. Le Théâtre romantique. Paris, 1922.

Giraud, J. L'Ecole romantique française. Paris, 1927.

Glanchart, P. and V. Un Laboratoire dramatique: essai critique sur le théâtre de Victor Hugo. Paris, 1903.

Glinel, C. Alexandre Dumas père. Reims, 1884.

Gochberg, H. S. Stage of Dreams. Geneva, 1967.

Gosse, E. De l'abolition des privilèges et de l'émancipation des théâtres. Paris, 1830.

Gribble, F. H. Dumas, Father and Son. London, 1930.

__________. Rachel. New York, 1911.

Griffith, D. "Les Caprices de Rachel," Revue d'histoire du théâtre, II (1959).

Guest, I. Fanny Cerito. London, 1956.

__________. Romantic Ballet in Paris. London, 1966.

Guimbaud, L. Victor Hugo et Juliette Drouet. Paris, 1914.

Hagenauer, P. Rachel, princesse de théâtre. Paris, 1957.

Halévy, L. Fromental Halévy, sa vie et ses oeuvres. Paris, 1862.

Hennin, M. Lettres à un journaliste sur les théâtres. Paris, 1849.

Hervey, C. Theatres of Paris. Paris, 1846.

Heylli, G. d'. Rachel d'après sa correspondance. Paris, 1882.

Hostein, H. La Réforme théâtrale. Paris, 1848.

Hugo, A. Victor Hugo raconté par un témoin de sa vie. Paris, 1893.

Ihrig, G. P. Heroines in French Drama of the Romantic Period. New York, 1950.

Indiscret des coulisses, L'. Paris, 1841.

Initiation théâtrale de l'à propos du romantisme. Paris, 1856.

Jallais, A. de. *Sur la scène et dans la salle.* Paris, 1854.

Janin, J. *Alexandre Dumas.* Paris, 1871.

__________. *Dubureau.* Paris, 1832.

__________. *François Ponsard.* Paris, 1872.

__________. *Rachel et la tragédie.* Paris, 1859.

Jay, A. *La Conversation d'un romantique.* Paris, 1830.

Jouin, H. *Le Baron Taylor.* Paris, 1892.

Jouvin, B. *Auber.* Paris, 1864.

Kennard, N. H. *Rachel.* London, 1885.

Labussière, P. *Louis Véron.* Paris, 1930.

Lafoscade, L. *Le Théâtre d'Alfred de Musset.* Paris, 1901.

Lami, P. *Obsérvations sur la tragédie romantique.* Paris, 1824.

Larcher, L. *Emile de Girardin.* Paris, 1849.

Larousse, F. *Annales du théâtre.* Paris, 1833.

Lasalle, A. de. *Meyerbeer.* Paris, 1864.

Lasserre, P. *Le Romantisme français.* Paris, 1907.

Latreille, C. *La Fin du théâtre romantique et François Ponsard.* Paris, 1899.

Laugier, E. *De la Comédie Française depuis 1830.* Paris, 1844.

Lauviere, E. *Alfred de Vigny.* Paris, 1945.

Launay, R. *La Vraie Rachel.* Paris, 1921.

Leathers, V. *British Entertainers in France.* Toronto, 1959.

Lebreton, A. _Le Théâtre romantique._ Paris, 1923.

Lecomte, L. H. _Marie Dorval au Gymnase._ Paris, 1900.

________. _Un Comédien au XIXe siècle: Frédérick Lemaître._ Paris, 1888.

________. _Virginie Déjazet._ Paris, 1892.

Lefebvre, H. _Alfred de Musset._ Paris, 1886.

Legouvé, E. _Eugène Scribe._ Paris, 1874.

Lemaître, F. _Souvenirs._ Paris, 1880.

Léotard, P. _Mémoires._ Paris, 1860.

Levaillant, M. _L'Oeuvre de Victor Hugo._ Paris, 1931.

Levinson, A. _Le Ballet romantique._ Paris, 1919.

________. _Marie Taglioni._ Paris, 1929.

Lifar, S. _Carlotta Grisi._ Paris, 1941.

________. _Giselle._ Paris, 1942.

Lireux, A. _Mlle Mars._ Paris, 1847.

Lote, G. _En Préface à Hernani--cent ans après._ Paris, 1930.

Loydreau, E. _Les Jolies actrices de Paris._ Paris, 1843.

Lucas, H. _Mlle Mars._ Paris, n. d.

Lucas-Dubreton, J. _Rachel._ Paris, 1936.

Lyonnet, H. _Les Premières d'Alfred de Musset._ Paris, 1927.

________. _Les Premières de Victor Hugo._ Paris, 1930.

Maigron, L. _Le Romantisme et la mode._ Paris, 1911.

________. _Le Romantisme et les moeurs._ Paris, 1910.

Mailly, H. _Charges d'acteurs, d'auteurs, compositeurs, et peinteurs._ Paris, n. d.

Maingot, E. Le Baron Taylor. Paris, 1963.

Mantel, A. P. Rachel, détails inédits. Paris, 1858.

March, H. Frédéric Soulié. New Haven, 1931.

Marolles, M. Mémoires. Paris, 1857.

Mars, Mlle. Biographie anonyme. Paris, 1847.

Marsan, J. La Bataille romantique. Paris, 1912.

Marteau, E. De la Décadence de l'art dramatique. Paris, 1849.

Maurice, C. La Vérité Rachel. Paris, 1850.

Maurois, A. Olympio. Paris, 1954.

__________. Les Trois Dumas. Paris, 1957.

Milliet, P. Notes romantiques sur Marion de Lorme. Paris, 1873.

Mogador, C. Adieux au monde. 3 vols. Paris, 1854.

Montifaud, M. de. Les Romantiques. Paris, 1878.

Moreau, F. J. Souvenirs du théâtre anglais à Paris. Paris, 1827.

Moreau, P. Le Classicisme des romantiques. Paris, 1932.

__________. Le Romantisme. Paris, 1932.

__________. Le Théâtre romantique. Paris, 1949.

Moreau d'Orgelaine. Réflexions sur la pièce de Henri III et sa cour. Auxerre, 1829.

Mornet, D. Le Romantisme en France. Paris, 1907.

Moser, F. Marie Dorval. Paris, 1947.

Muret, T. L'Histoire par le théâtre. Vol. 3. Paris, 1865.

Nallier, J. P. Recherches sur les causes de la decadence

des théâtres et de l'art dramatique. Paris, 1841.

Nebout, P. Le Drame romantique. Paris, 1899.

Nerval, G. de. "Les derniers romains," Revue d'histoire du théâtre I (1948).

Nisard, D. Essais sur l'école romantique. Paris, 1891.

Notice descriptive du théâtre historique. Paris, 1847.

Nozière, F. Madame Dorval. Paris, 1926.

Oliver, A. R. Charles Nodier. Syracuse, 1964.

P.........., L. Quelques observations sur...Mlle Rachel. Paris, 1842.

Pailleron, M. L. François Buloz et ses amis. Paris, 1920.

Palmarola, E. Un Mot sur le théâtre de nos jours. Marseilles, 1842.

Parigot, H. Alexandre Dumas père. Paris, 1902.

__________. Le Drame d'Alexandre Dumas. Paris, 1899.

Pavie, A. Médallions romantiques. Paris, 1909.

__________. La Tradition classique dans le théâtre de Victor Hugo. Angers, 1899.

Pellissier, G. Le Réalisme du romantisme. Paris, 1912.

Pendell, W. Victor Hugo's Acted Drama and the Contemporary Press. Baltimore, 1947.

Pericaud, L. Le Théâtre des Funambules. Paris, 1897.

Piéchard, M. La Vie privée de Rachel. Paris, 1954.

Pierron, E. Virginie Déjazet. Paris, 1856.

Planche, G. Marie Dorval. Paris, 1839.

Pollitzer, M. Trois reines de théâtre. Paris, 1958.

Pougin, A. Figures d'Opéra-Comique. Paris, 1875.

________. Fromental Halévy. Paris, 1865.

________. Meyerbeer. Paris, 1864.

Quentin, E. Etude sur la mise en scène. Paris, 1833.

Rachel (Elisa Rachel Félix). Lettres inédites. Paris, 1947.

Rault, A. and B. Hyck. Scribe, auteur dramatique. Paris, 1935.

Reclus, M. Emile de Girardin. Paris, 1934.

Rémy, T. Débureau. Paris, 1954.

Rhéal, S. Mémoire pour la réorganisation du Théâtre-Français. Paris, 1847.

________. Les Deux Phèdre: Mme Ristori et Mlle Rachel. Paris, 1858.

Richard, J. Rachel. London, 1956.

Richardson, J. Théophile Gautier. London, 1959.

Ristori, A. Memoirs and Artistic Studies. New York, 1907.

Robert, P. L. La Bataille romantique. Rouen, 1931.

Rolland, J. Les Comédies politiques d'Eugène Scribe. Paris, 1912.

Rollé, H. Marie Dorval. Paris, 1841.

Romain, J. Le Baron Taylor. Paris, 1844.

Saint-Romain, A. L. Coup d'oeil sur les théâtres du royaume. Paris, 1831.

Sakellarides, E. Alfred de Vigny, auteur dramatique. Paris, 1902.

Salomon, M. Charles Nodier et la groupe romantique. Paris, 1908.

Samson, J. I. Mémoires. Paris, 1882.

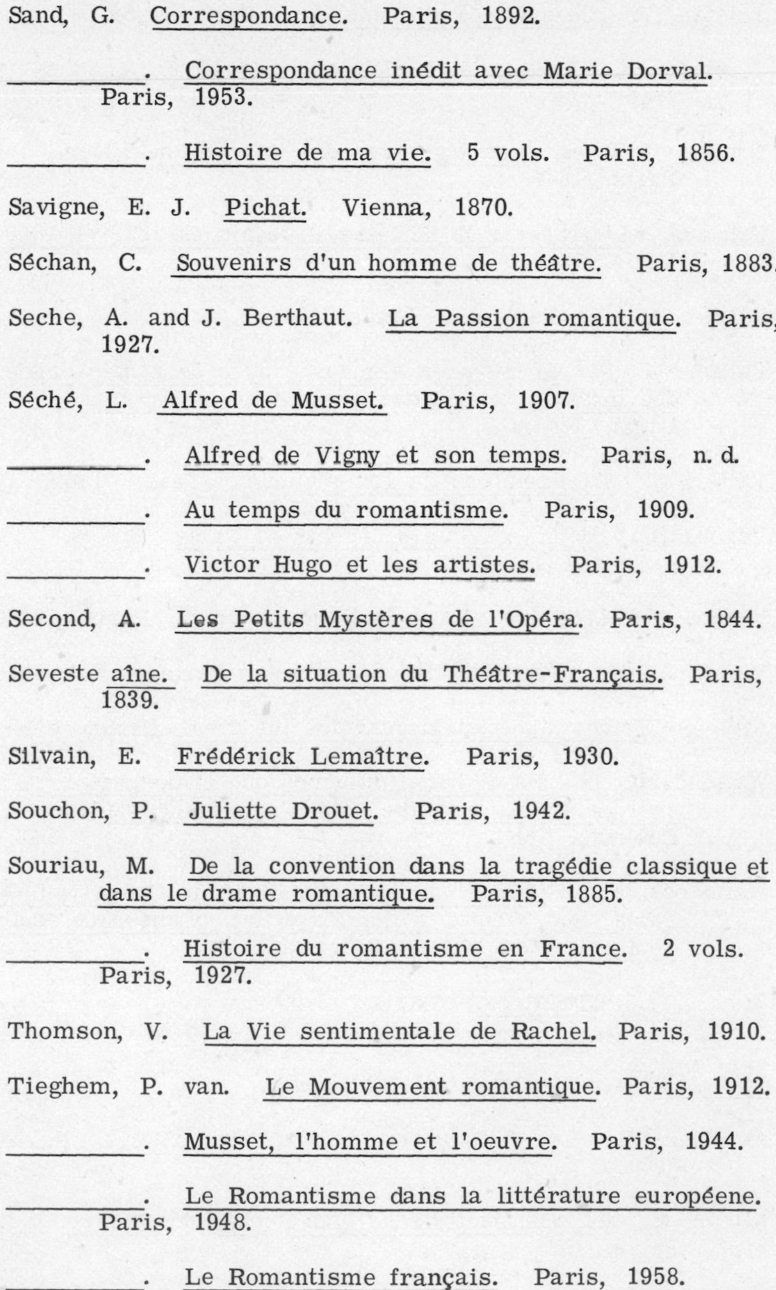

Sand, G. *Correspondance.* Paris, 1892.

__________. *Correspondance inédit avec Marie Dorval.* Paris, 1953.

__________. *Histoire de ma vie.* 5 vols. Paris, 1856.

Savigne, E. J. *Pichat.* Vienna, 1870.

Séchan, C. *Souvenirs d'un homme de théâtre.* Paris, 1883.

Seche, A. and J. Berthaut. *La Passion romantique.* Paris, 1927.

Séché, L. *Alfred de Musset.* Paris, 1907.

__________. *Alfred de Vigny et son temps.* Paris, n. d.

__________. *Au temps du romantisme.* Paris, 1909.

__________. *Victor Hugo et les artistes.* Paris, 1912.

Second, A. *Les Petits Mystères de l'Opéra.* Paris, 1844.

Seveste *aîne.* *De la situation du Théâtre-Français.* Paris, 1839.

Silvain, E. *Frédérick Lemaître.* Paris, 1930.

Souchon, P. *Juliette Drouet.* Paris, 1942.

Souriau, M. *De la convention dans la tragédie classique et dans le drame romantique.* Paris, 1885.

__________. *Histoire du romantisme en France.* 2 vols. Paris, 1927.

Thomson, V. *La Vie sentimentale de Rachel.* Paris, 1910.

Tieghem, P. van. *Le Mouvement romantique.* Paris, 1912.

__________. *Musset, l'homme et l'oeuvre.* Paris, 1944.

__________. *Le Romantisme dans la littérature européene.* Paris, 1948.

__________. *Le Romantisme français.* Paris, 1958.

Tristan, R. Jean-Gaspard Débureau. Paris, 1954.

Trollope, F. Paris and the Parisians in 1835. London, 1836.

Truffet, J. B. S. Les Mystères des théâtres de Paris. Paris, 1844.

Urbanus. Lettres sur le Théâtre Français en 1839 et 1840. Paris, 1841.

Vaillat, L. La Taglioni. Paris, 1942.

Vallier, J. P. Recherches sur les causes de la décadence des théâtres et de l'art dramatique en France. Paris, 1841.

Valter, J. La Première du Roi s'amuse. Paris, 1882.

Véron, Dr. Mémoires d'un bourgeois de Paris. 6 vols. Paris, 1854-1855.

Victor, P. Mémoire contre le Baron Taylor. Paris, 1827.

Vigny, A. de. Correspondance. 2 vols. Paris, n. d.

Vivien. Etudes administratives: les théâtres. Paris, 1844.

Wattendorff, L. Essai sur l'influence que Shakespeare a exercée sur la tragédie romantique française. Coblentz, 1888.

Weinstock, H. Donizetti and the World of the Opera in Italy, Paris, and Vienna in the First Half of the Nineteenth Century. New York, 1963.

Z.......... Théâtres. Paris, 1849.

1850-1880 (see also General Bibliography)

Abraham, E. Les Acteurs et les actrices de Paris. Paris, 1861.

Allem, M. La Vie Quotidienne sous le Second Empire. Paris, 1948.

Alméras, H. d'. La Vie parisienne sous la république de

1848. Paris, 1921.

__________. La Vie parisienne sous le règne de Louis-Philippe. Paris, 1911.

__________. La Vie parisienne sous le second Empire. Paris, 1933.

Arbelli, H. P. Les Trois Nouveaux Théâtres. Paris, 1863.

Argus. Jacques Offenbach. Paris, 1872.

__________. Victorien Sardou. Paris. 1872.

Ariste, P. d'. La Vie et le monde du boulevard. Paris, 1930.

Arvin, N. C. Alexandre Dumas fils. Paris, 1939.

Aubry, J. E. Passe-temps de l'Entr'acte. Paris, 1863.

Bac, F. Intimités du Second Empire. Paris, 1931.

Baldick, R. The Life and Times of Frederick Lemaitre. London, 1959.

Banville, T. de. La Comédie-Française. Paris, 1863.

__________. Critiques. Paris, 1917.

Bellanger, J. Entre deux spectacles. Paris, 1879.

Benoist, A. Essais de critique dramatique. Paris, 1898.

Billy, A. La Vie de Balzac. Paris, 1897.

Biré, E. Honoré de Balzac. Paris, 1897.

Bonnassies, J. Le Théâtre et le peuple. Paris, 1872.

Bonney, M. Les Idées morales dans le théâtre de Dumas fils. Quimper, 1921.

Bord, G. Rosina Stoltz. Paris, 1909.

Borrensen, A. Le Théâtre d'Octave Feuillet. Paris, 1929.

Bouchard, A. La Langue théâtrale. Paris, 1878.

Boutet de Monvel, R. *Les Variétés, 1850-1870.* Paris, n. d.

Brancour, R. *Offenbach.* Paris, 1929.

Brunetière, J. *Honoré de Balzac.* Paris, 1905.

Burgess, F. *Carmen.* London, 1905.

Busser, H. *Charles Gounod.* Paris, 1961.

Cartier, L. A. *Zola and the Theatre.* New Haven, 1963.

Cavalier, G. *Ce que je pense d' "Henriette Maréchal."* Paris, 1866.

Champfleury, H. M. *Foyers et coulisses.* 2 vols. Paris, 1873-1874.

Claretie, J. *Eugène Labiche.* Paris, 1883.

__________. *Octave Feuillet.* Paris, 1883.

__________. *Profils de théâtre.* Paris, 1902.

Claudin, G. *Mes Souvenirs.* Paris, 1884.

Coppée, F. *Souvenirs d'un Parisien.* Paris, 1910.

Curtiss, M. *Bizet et son temps.* Paris, 1961.

Dabland, H. *Le Troisième Théâtre Français.* Paris, 1879.

Daly, C. and G. Davioud. *Les Théâtres de la place du Châtelet.* Paris, n. d.

Decaux, A. *Offenbach, roi du Second Empire.* Paris, 1966.

Delécluze, E. J. *Journal.* Paris, 1948.

__________. *Souvenirs de soixante années.* Paris, 1862.

Deries, L. *Octave Feuillet.* Paris, 1901.

Dumas *fils*, A. *Entr'actes.* Paris, 1878.

Epine, L'. *Une Danseuse française du XIXe siècle: Emma Livry.* Paris, 1909.

Ernest-Charles, J. Le Théâtre des poètes, 1850-1910. Paris, 1910.

Ernst, A. L'Oeuvre dramatique d'Hector Berlioz. Paris, 1884.

Fahmy, D. George Sand: auteur dramatique. Paris, 1934.

Failly. Sur l'art du comédien. Paris, 1852.

Faucon, T. Le Nouvel Opéra. Paris, 1875.

Fisher, D. Emile Augier. Columbus, 1899.

Gaillard de Champris, H. Emile Augier et la comédie sociale. Paris, 1910.

Gallois, N. Biographie contemporaire des artistes du théâtre français. Paris, 1867.

__________. Théâtres et artistes dramatiques. Paris, 1855.

Garnier, C. Le Nouvel Opéra de Paris. 2 vols. Paris, 1880.

__________. Le Théâtre. Paris, 1871.

Gaulot, P. Les Trois Brohan. Paris, 1930.

Gauthier-Villars, H. Berlioz. Paris, 1911.

Gautier, L. and Odell. Nouvelle Galerie des artistes dramatiques vivants. Paris, 1855.

Gautier, T. Portraits contemporains. Paris, 1874.

Geoffrey, H. Une Soirée au Gymnase Dramatique. Paris, 1857.

Gheorghiu, M. O. Le Théâtre de Dumas fils. Nancy, 1932.

Giozet, J. Dictionnaire universel du théâtre en France. Paris, 1867.

Goncourt, E. and J. de. Journal. 4 vols. Paris, 1959.

Gordon, Z. Labiche et son oeuvre. Toulouse, 1932.

Gottschall, R. von. Paris unter dem zweiten Kaiserreich. Leipzig. 1871.

Gribble, F. H. Dumas, Father and Son. London, 1930.

Guest, I. The Ballet of the Second Empire. 2 vols. London, 1953, 1955.

__________. Fanny Cerito. London, 1956.

Halévy, L. Carnets. Paris, 1935.

__________. Notice sur la vie et les ouvrages d'Adam. Paris, 1859.

Heylli, G. d'. Bressant. Paris, 1877.

__________. Brindeau. Paris, 1882.

__________. Journal intime de la Comédie Française. Paris, 1879.

__________. Madeleine Brohan. Paris, 1886.

Hillemacher, P. L. Gounod. Paris, 1906.

Hippeau, E. Berlioz et son temps. Paris, 1890.

Hörner, R. La Dame aux camélias et Diane de Lys. Tübingen, 1910.

Hostein, H. Souvenirs d'un homme de théâtre. Paris, 1878.

Houssaye, A. La Comédie-Française. Paris, 1879.

__________. Confessions. 6 vols. Paris, 1885-1891.

Janin, J. Portraits et caractères contemporains. Paris, n.d.

Kracauer, W. Orpheus in Paris (trans. David and Mosbacher). New York, 1938.

Labarthe, G. Le Théâtre pendant les jours du siège et de la commune. Paris, 1910.

Labiche, G. Eugène Labiche. Paris, 1938.

Lacour, L. Gaulois et Parisiens. Paris, 1883.

__________. Trois théâtres. Paris, 1883.

Lagarde, A. and C. Desoine. Les Nouveaux Théâtres. Paris, 1864.

Lalia-Paternostro, A. Edouard Pailleron. Paris, 1931.

Lamy, P. Le Théâtre d'Alexandre Dumas fils. Paris, 1928.

Landormy, P. Gounod. Paris, 1942.

Larouche-Joyce, Mlle P. de. Mémoires artistiques. Paris, 1861.

Lavergne, J. Biographie complète des artistes de l'Ambigu-Comique. Paris, 1856.

Lecigne, C. Octave Feuillet et son théâtre. Paris, n. d.

Lecomte, H. Bouffé. Paris, 1867.

Lecomte, L. H. Les Folies-Nouvelles. Paris, 1909.

__________. Odry et ses oeuvres. Paris, 1900.

Lelien-Damiens. Le Bréviaire des comédiens. Paris, 1858.

Liesville, A. R. De la décadence de l'art dramatique. Paris, 1858.

Loliée, F. Les Femmes du Second Empire. Paris, n. d.

Lyon, R. and L. Sauger. Les Contes d'Hoffmann. Paris, 1948.

Lyonnet, H. "La Dame aux camélias" de Dumas fils. Paris, 1930.

Mahalin, P. Les Jolies Actrices de Paris. Paris, 1866.

Malherbe, H. Georges Bizet. Paris, 1921.

Marie, A. Henry Monnier. Paris, 1931.

Martinet, A. Offenbach. Paris, 1887.

Masson, P. M. Berlioz. Paris, 1930.

Mauclair, A. *Le Théâtre aujourd'hui.* Paris, 1855.

Maurois, A. *Les Trois Dumas.* Paris, 1957.

Mémoires d'un jeune premier. Paris, 1858.

Merlant, J. *Le Théâtre de Labiche.* Nantes, 1893.

Miltzchitch, D. *Le Théâtre de Balzac.* Paris, 1930.

Molénes, E. de. *Desclée.* Paris, 1874.

Monnier, H. *Galerie d'originaux.* Paris, 1858.

__________. *Les Mémoires de Joseph Prudhomme.* Paris, 1892.

Morillot, P. *Emile Augier.* Grenoble, 1901.

Moss, A. *Cancan and Barcarolle.* New York, 1954.

Moynet, M. J. *L'Envers du théâtre.* Paris, 1873.

Noël, C. M. *Les Idées sociales dans le théâtre de Dumas fils.* Paris, 1912.

Noufflard, G. *Hector Berlioz et le mouvement de l'art contemporain.* Florence, 1883.

Pailleron, E. *Emile Augier.* Paris, 1889.

Palianti. *Almanach des spectacles.* Paris, 1852, 1853.

__________. *Souvenirs de dix ans.* Paris, 1865.

Parigot, H. *Le Théâtre d'hier.* Paris, 1893.

Pinkney, D. H. *Napoleon III and the Rebuilding of Paris.* Princeton, 1958.

Plouvier, E. *Nouvelle galerie des artistes dramatiques vivants.* Paris, 1855.

Pollock, J. *The Modern French Theatre.* Paris, 1878.

Pontmartin, A. *Mes Mémoires.* Paris, 1885-1886.

Pougin, A. *A. Adam.* Paris, 1876.

Ratiere, A. L'Art de l'acteur selon Doret et Samson. Geneva, 1969.

Rayer, A. Théâtre contemporain en France et à l'étranger. Paris, 1870.

Roqueplan, N. Les Coulisses de l'Opéra. Paris, 1855.

Rouff, M. and T. Casewitz. Hortense Schneider. Paris, 1930.

Roujon, F. Ludovic Halévy. Paris, 1912.

Sainte-Beuve, C. A. Portraits contemporains. 3 vols. Paris, 1869-1871.

Saint-Léon, A. Sténochoréographie. Paris, 1852.

Saint-Victor, P. de. Le Théâtre contemporain: Augier, Dumas fils. Paris, 1889.

Samson, J. I. L'Art théâtrale. 2 vols. Paris, 1863-1865.

Sarcey, F. Le Bilan de l'année 1868. Paris, 1869.

__________. Comédiens et comédiennes. Paris, 1876.

Schneider, L. Hervé. Charles Lecocq. Paris, 1924.

__________. Offenbach. Paris, 1923.

Schwartz, H. S. Alexandre Dumas fils, dramatist. New York, 1927.

Scillière, E. L'Evolution passionelle dans le théâtre contemporain. Paris, 1921.

Sitwell, S. La Vie Parisienne: A Tribute to Offenbach. London, 1937.

Sonrel, P. Traité de scénographie. Paris, 1943.

Sonolet, L. La Vie Parisienne sous le Second Empire. Paris, 1929.

Soreau, G. La Vie de la "Dame aux camélias." Paris, 1898.

Soubies, A. Documents inédits sur le Faust de Gounod. Paris, 1912.

________. Histoire du Théâtre Lyrique 1851-1870. Paris, 1899.

________. Le Théâtre à Paris du ler octobre, 1870, au 31 décembre, 1871. Paris, 1892.

________. Le Théâtre en France de 1871 à 1892. Paris, 1893.

Soucault, P. Eugène Labiche. Paris, 1945.

Spoll, E. A. Mme Carvalho, notes et souvenirs. Paris, 1885.

Taylor, F. A. The Theatre of Alexandre Dumas fils. Oxford, 1937.

Tessier, H. and L. Maral. Almanach théâtral. Paris, 1874.

Tiersot, J. Hector Berlioz et la société de son temps. Paris, 1955.

Trélat, E. Le Théâtre et l'architecte. Paris, 1860.

Tsao, Hsi-Wen. La Question d'argent dans le théâtre français sous le Second Empire. Paris, 1934.

Vacquerie, A. Profils et grimaces. Paris, 1857.

Vapereau, G. L'Année littéraire et dramatique. Paris, 1859-1867.

Vauzat, G. Blanche d'Antigny, actrice et demi-mondaire. Paris, 1933.

Vizotty, E. A. Emile Zola. London, 1904.

Williams, R. C. The World of Napoleon III. New York, 1957.

Zola, E. Le Naturalisme au théâtre. Paris, 1903.

________. Nos auteurs dramatiques. Paris, 1881.

1880-1900 (see also General Bibliography)

Aderer, A. Le Théâtre à côté. Paris, 1894.

Alexandre, A. Suzanne Reichenberg. Paris, 1898.

Allotte de la Füye, M. Jules Verne: sa vie, son oeuvre. Paris, 1927.

Alméras, H. d'. Ludovic Halévy. Paris, 1902.

Ama, L. de. Francisque Sarcey. Florence, 1919.

Andrieu, P. Souvenirs des frères Isola. Paris, 1943.

Antoine, A. Mes Souvenirs sur le Théâtre Antoine et l'Odéon. Paris, 1928.

__________. Mes Souvenirs sur le Théâtre Libre. Paris, 1921.

__________. Le Théâtre. Paris, 1932.

Arnaoutovitch, A. Henry Becque. Paris, 1927.

Audebrand, P. Petits mémoires d'une stalle d'orchestre. Paris, 1885.

Badin, A. Couloirs et coulisses. Paris, 1884.

Banville, T. de. Mes Souvenirs. Paris, 1888.

Barbey d'Aurevilly, J. Le Théâtre contemporaine. 5 vols. Paris, 1861.

Baudelaire, C. Richard Wagner et Tannhäuser à Paris. Paris, 1861.

Becq de Fouquières, L. L'Art de la mise en scène. Paris, 1884.

Becque, H. Querelles littéraires. Paris, 1890.

__________. Souvenirs d'un auteur dramatique. Paris, 1895.

Bellaigue, C. Gounod. Paris, 1910.

Bellier de la Chavignerie. Dictionnaire général des artistes de l'école française. 3 vols. Paris, 1882-1885.

Bernhardt, S. Ma Double Vie. Paris, 1907.

Bernheim, A. and L. Leymarie. L'Enseignement dramatique au Conservatoire. Paris, 1883.

Bertal, G. August Vacquerie. Paris, 1889.

Berteaux, E. En ce temps-là. Paris, 1946.

Berton, Mme P. Sarah Bernhardt as I Knew Her. London, 1923.

Berton, P. F. S. Souvenirs de la vie de théâtre. Paris, 1914.

Binet-Valmer, G. Sarah Bernhardt. Paris, 1936.

Bissel, H. C. Les Conventions du théâtre bourgeois contemporain en France 1887-1914. Paris, 1930.

Blanchart, P. Henry Becque, son oeuvre. Paris, 1930.

Block, H. M. Mallarmé and the Symbolist Drama. Detroit, 1963.

Bovet, M. A. Charles Gounod. London, 1891.

Braunstein, E. François de Curel. Paris, 1962.

Brémont, L. Le Théâtre et la vie. Paris, 1930.

Broech, T. van den. La Mise en scène. Brussels, 1889.

Cahuet, A. La Liberté du théâtre. Paris, 1902.

Carlson, M. "Meiningen Crowd Scenes and the Théâtre-Libre," Educational Theatre Journal, XIII, 4 (Dec., 1961).

Carré, A. Souvenirs de théâtre. Paris, 1950.

Castelot, A. Sarah Bernhardt. Paris, 1961.

Charles, E. Le Théâtre des poètes, 1850-1910. Paris, 1910.

Claretie, J. François Coppée. Paris, 1883.

__________. Profils de théâtre. Paris, 1902.

Coppée, F. Souvenirs d'un Parisien. Paris, 1910.

Coquelin, C. L'Art et le comédien. Paris, 1880.

Curzon, H. Croquis d'artistes. Paris, 1898.

Damianov, H. L'Oeuvre de Becque au théâtre. Grenoble, 1927.

Daudet, A. Entre les frises et la rampe. Paris, 1894.

__________. Souvenirs d'un homme de lettres. Paris, 1888.

__________. Trente Ans de Paris. Paris, 1888.

Dauriac, L. La Psychologie dans l'opéra français. Paris, 1890.

Dawson, E. A. Henry Becque, sa vie et son théâtre. Paris, 1923.

Descotes, M. Henry Becque et son théâtre. Paris, 1962.

Dupierreux, R. Lugné-Poe: homme de théâtre. Paris, 1949.

Durrière, G. Jules Lemaître et le théâtre. Paris, 1934.

Faguet, E. Etudes littéraires. Paris, n. d.

__________. Notes sur le théâtre contemporain. 3 vols. Paris, 1889.

__________. Propos de théâtre. Paris, 1905.

Febvre, F. Journal d'un comédien. Paris, 1896.

Filon, Mlle. Mémoires. Paris, 1903.

Fleury, M. Souvenirs de M. Delaunay. Paris, 1901.

Fuchs, M. Théâtre de Banville. Paris, 1912.

Garcia, M. La Confession d'Antonine. Paris, 1864.

Gauthier-Villars, H. Soirées perdues. Paris, 1894.

Geller, G. G. Sarah Bernhardt. Paris, 1931.

Giffard, P. La Vie au théâtre. Paris, 1888.

Ginisty, P. Choses et gens de théâtre. Paris, 1892.

________. La Vie d'un théâtre. Paris, 1898.

Girard, R. Cri d'alarme sur la situation d'art dramatique. Paris, 1876.

Glachant, P. and V. Papiers d'autrefois. Paris, 1899.

Goncourt, E. and J. de. Journal. 4 vols. Paris, 1959.

Got, A. Henry Becque. Paris, 1920.

Got, E. Journal. Paris, 1910.

Gounod, C. Mémoires d'un artiste. Paris, 1895.

Grappe, G. Jules Claretie. Paris, 1906.

Guest, I. Adeline Genée. London, n. d.

Halhade, C. Daughter of Paris. London, 1961.

Haraszti, J. Edmond Rostand. Paris, 1913.

Hart, J. A. Sardou and the Sardou Plays. Philadelphia, 1913.

Heylli, G. d'. Brindeau. Paris, 1882.

________. Delaunay. Paris, 1883.

________. Dix mois à la Comédie Française. Paris, 1885.

Hoffman, E. Singulières tribulations d'un directeur de théâtre. Paris, 1908.

Holtzem, L. A. Une Vie d'artiste. Paris, 1885.

Huret, J. Sarah Bernhardt. Paris, 1899.

Indy, V. d'. *Richard Wagner et son influence sur l'art musical français.* Paris, 1930.

James, H. *The Scenic Art.* New York, 1957.

Jasper, G. R. *Adventure in the Theatre.* New Brunswick, 1947.

Jullien, J. *Le Théâtre vivant.* Paris, 1892.

Kahn, A. *Le Théâtre social en France de 1870 à nos jours.* Lausanne, 1907.

Kahn, G. *Sarah Bernhardt.* Paris, 1901.

Knowles, D. *La Réaction idéaliste au théâtre depuis 1890.* Paris, 1934.

Kovatchevitch, M. *La vie, l'oeuvre... de André Antoine.* Clermont-Ferrand, 1941.

Lacour, L. *Gaulois et Parisiens.* Paris, 1881.

Laferrière, A. *Souvenirs d'un jeune premier.* Paris, 1884.

Lambert, A. *Sur les planches.* Paris, 1894.

Larcher, F. and E. *Pantomimes de Paul Legrand.* Paris, 1887.

Laroque, A. *Acteurs et actrices de Paris.* Paris, 1895.

Larroumet, G. *Etudes de critique dramatique.* 2 vols. Paris, 1906.

__________. *Etudes d'histoire et de critique dramatique.* Paris, 1892.

__________. *Nouvelles études.* Paris, 1899.

Laumann, E. M. *La Machinerie au théâtre.* Paris, 1897.

Le Meur, L. *La Vie et l'oeuvre de François Coppée.* Paris, 1932.

Le Senne, C. *Le Théâtre à Paris 1883-1889.* Paris, 1888-1890.

Lecomte, L. H. Les Fantasies-Parisiennes. Paris, 1911.

________. Les Folies-Nouvelles. Paris, 1909.

Lefranc, F. Etudes sur le théâtre contemporain. Paris, 1887.

Lemaître, J. Impressions de théâtre. Paris, 1886.

Lençon, H. Le Théâtre nouveau. Paris, 1896.

Lescure, A. de. François Coppée. Paris, 1889.

Levesque, J. H. Alfred Jarry. Paris, 1967.

Lugné-Poe, A. F. Acrobaties. Paris, 1931.

________. Le Sot du tremplin. Paris, 1931.

Lyonnet, H. Dictionnaire des comédiens français. Geneva, 1912.

________. Les Premières de Alfred de Musset. Paris, 1927.

Macchetta, B. R. Victorien Sardou. London, 1892.

Mahalin, P. Les Demoiselles de l'Opéra. Paris, 1887.

Mapes, V. Duse and the French. New York, 1898.

Maret-Leriche, J. Les Matinées littéraires... fondées par M. H. Ballande. Paris, 1874.

Martin, J. Nos Artistes. Paris, 1895.

Miller, A. I. The Independent Theatre in Europe. New York, 1931.

Montorgueil, G. Les Déshabillés au théâtre. Paris, 1896.

Monval, G. Les Collections de la Comédie Française. Paris, 1897.

Mortier, A. Les Soirées parisiennes de 1874-1884. Paris, 1875-1885.

Mouly, G. La Vie prodigieuse de Victorien Sardou. Paris, 1931.

Mounet-Sully. Souvenirs d'un tragedien. Paris, 1917.

Moynet, M. J. La Machinerie théâtrale. Paris, 1893.

__________. Trucs et décors. Paris, n. d.

Nansouty, M. de. Les Trucs du théâtre, du cirque, et de la foire. Paris, 1909.

Noël, E. and Stoullig. Les Annales du théâtre et de la musique. Paris, 1876-1901.

O'Monroy, R. La Soirée parisienne. Paris, 1890.

Perrin, E. Etude sur la mise en scène. Paris, 1883.

Peter, R. Le Théâtre et la vie sous la troisième république. 2 vols. Paris, 1945.

Les Premières illustrés. 7 vols. Paris, 1881-1888.

Pruner, F. Les Luttes d'Antoine au Théâtre-Libre. Paris, 1964.

__________. Le Théâtre-Libre: le répertoire étranger. Paris, 1958.

Quéant, G. Encyclopédie du théâtre contemporain. Paris, n. d.

Rebell, H. Victorien Sardou. Paris, 1903.

Richardson, J. Sarah Bernhardt. London, 1959.

Ripert, E. Edmond Rostand. Paris, 1968.

Robichez, J. Lugné-Poe. Paris, 1955.

__________. Le Symbolisme au Théâtre. Paris, 1957.

Saint-Môr, G. de. Paris sur scène. 2 vols. Paris, 1887, 1888.

Saint-Saëns, C. de. Portraits et souvenirs. Paris, 1899.

Sarcey, F. Quarante ans de théâtre. 4 vols. Paris, 1901.

Sardou, V. Mes Plagiats. Paris, 1882.

Sasse, M. Souvenirs d'une artiste. Paris, 1902.

Schneider, L. Sous la lance. Paris, 1896.

Schuré, E. Le Drame musical. 2 vols. Paris, 1875.

Sée, E. Henry Becque. Paris, 1936.

Servières, G. Richard Wagner jugé en France. Paris, 1887.

Shattuck, R. The Banquet Years. New York, 1955.

Soubies, A. Costumes et mise en scène. Paris, 1910.

__________. Le Théâtre en France de 1871 à 1892. Paris, 1893.

Souvenir à M. Jules Claretie. Paris, 1905.

Strakosch, M. Souvenirs d'un impresario. Paris, 1887.

Thalasso, A. Le Théâtre-Libre. Paris, 1909.

Thénard, M. Ma Vie au théâtre. Paris, 1902.

Thierry, E. La Comédie-Française pendant les deux sièges. Paris, 1887.

Treich, L. L'Esprit de Georges Feydeau. Paris, 1927.

__________. L'Esprit d'Henry Becque. Paris, 1927.

Vaucaire, M. Effets de théâtre. Paris, 1886.

Veinstein, A. Du Théâtre Libre au Théâtre Louis Jouvet. Paris, 1955.

Vernet, N. Dix Ans de coulisses. Paris, 1908.

Waxman, S. M. Antoine and the Théâtre-Libre. Cambridge, 1926.

Weiss, J. J. _A propos de théâtre._ Paris, 1893.

__________. _Le Drame historique et le drame passionel._ Paris, 1894.

__________. _Les Théâtres parisiens._ Paris, 1896.

__________. _Le Théâtre et les moeurs._ Paris, 1889.

__________. _Trois Années de théâtre 1883-1885._ Paris, 1893.

INDEX